The New
Machiavelli

ALSO BY JONATHAN POWELL

Great Hatred, Little Room: Making Peace in Northern Ireland

The New Machiavelli

How to Wield Power

in the Modern World

JONATHAN POWELL

THE BODLEY HEAD
LONDON

THE BODLEY HEAD
LONDON

Published by The Bodley Head 2010

2 4 6 8 10 9 7 5 3 1

Copyright © Jonathan Powell 2010

First published in Great Britain in 2010 by
The Bodley Head
Random House, 20 Vauxhall Bridge Road,
London SW1V 2SA

www.bodleyhead.co.uk
www.rbooks.co.uk

Addresses for companies within The Random House Group Limited can be found at:
www.randomhouse.co.uk/offices.htm

The Random House Group Limited Reg. No. 954009

A CIP catalogue record for this book is available from the British Library

ISBN 9781847921222

The Random House Group Limited supports the Forest Stewardship
Council (FSC), the leading international forest certification organisation. All our titles that
are printed on Greenpeace approved FSC certified paper carry the FSC logo. Our paper
procurement policy can be found at www.rbooks.co.uk/environment

Mixed Sources
Product group from well-managed
forests and other controlled sources
www.fsc.org Cert no. TT-COC-2139
© 1996 Forest Stewardship Council

Typeset in Walbaum MT by Palimpsest Book Production Limited,
Falkirk, Stirlingshire

Printed and bound in Great Britain by
Clays Ltd, St Ives PLC

To Sarah

Contents

Preface

Let me first be clear what this book is not. It is not another memoir of the Blair years; there are enough of those already. It is not an academic treatise on Machiavelli; there aren't enough of those but I am not the person to write one. And it is not a considered history of the Blair era; sufficient time has not yet passed for such a work to be written.

Instead it is designed to be three things. Firstly, it is an attempt to test whether Machiavelli's maxims still hold in the world of modern politics as well as they did when they were written. Secondly, it tries to draw some lessons on leadership and the exercise of power for future practitioners, based on my experience in Number 10. And lastly, it illustrates a series of generalisations by means of anecdotes from my time in government with Tony Blair and my knowledge of other British governments and US administrations, in the same way that Machiavelli illustrated his works with personal anecdotes from his time in the Florentine government. These anecdotes form the raw material for the use of future historians, not an attempt at writing history itself.

I am conscious that it is foolhardy to compare myself to Machiavelli. He was a genius and I am not. His works have lasted centuries and mine will not. It is also rash to try to rehabilitate the thinking of Machiavelli given how deeply rooted his caricature is in our culture. The fact that I am writing about him will be held by opponents to prove that the Blair government was unprincipled all along and it will certainly lead to my being described as 'Machiavellian', which will raise a smile on the lips of my former colleagues at Number 10. If anything I was at the 'Candide' end of the spectrum rather than calculating, and like Voltaire's hero I was an innocent unable to stop asking gauche questions and blurting out the truth, however inconvenient. But I am not too worried by any such criticisms because they will just illustrate the ignorance of those who make them about Machiavelli himself, about his thinking and about the way in which the Blair government really operated. And it is worth risking the opprobrium because I hate to see myths remain unchallenged when British politics desperately needs a dose of realism and honesty.

I would worry, however, if anyone read this book and thought politics was just about cynical manoeuvring and manipulation. It is not. After thirty years in government I am, if anything, more optimistic than I was when I started about the ability of government to change things. Politics is above all about idealism, values and ideas. This book is of limited scope, though, and does not address those important aspects. It is confined to looking at the art of government and at the mechanics of power, not why a leader might want to get hold of power or what they would want to do with it once they got it. It is worth writing because it is important that idealistic and optimistic people who come to office understand the reality of how power can be wielded effectively so they can make the country a better place.

The book is based on Machiavelli's *The Prince* and *The Discourses*. The bibliography sets out the editions I have used and lists his other works and wider reading about Machiavelli. For raw material I have drawn on my diaries from 1997 to 2007. I have kept a diary on and off since I was fourteen years old and it was never intended for publication but rather as a means of letting off steam and recording what I thought at particular moments. It has, however, provided an extraordinary quarry of anecdotes with which to illustrate this book. In 1995, I stumbled across the first few pages of a handwritten diary that Tony Blair had started to keep as Leader of the Opposition in the study of the family home in Islington. It is a great pity he did not continue or we would have had a remarkable, vivid, first-hand account of a prime minister's life, but there simply isn't time for a prime minister to set out detailed reflections and lead a country at the same time.

The problem with a diary is that it gives one person's view, not an overall and well-rounded appreciation of events, and so it is skewed. No one could describe this book as objective; it is entirely written from my viewpoint. And furthermore, diaries are not holy writ – they contain errors. When I made a TV programme about the Northern Ireland peace negotiations I discovered that even on obvious things you can be just plain wrong. In my diaries, I had described a green space outside the Clonard monastery in West Belfast (where Gerry Adams and I had met for some of our most interesting conversations) as a graveyard for the monks. I was amazed when I went back to the monastery to film to discover there were no graves at all. It was just a garden.

But even if they are not always right, diaries have one big advantage over other recollections: they are completely free of the sin of retrospection. They give an accurate account of how I saw things at the time. Most political books are written to justify what you did or didn't do. You can't do that with honest diaries. They uncompromisingly illustrate your idiocies and your mistakes.

Because I am not publishing the diaries, there is no point in referring to the particular entries that are drawn upon, so there are no footnotes in this book. Passages in quotation marks are taken from the diaries, for example things that Tony Blair told me Gordon Brown had said to him immediately after they had met, rather than verbatim accounts of their conversations.

This book is the second of three about the Blair years. The first was *Great Hatred, Little Room: Making Peace in Northern Ireland.* The third will be a defence of liberal interventionism and an account of foreign and defence policy under Tony Blair. For that reason this volume has little on Northern Ireland or on foreign and defence policy. I know I will be criticised for not writing in detail about Iraq, but the critics will just have to wait for the next book for that.

I would like to thank Will Sulkin of Bodley Head and Natasha Fairweather, my agent, without whom this book would never have seen the light of day, and my editor David Milner, without whom it would have been an indigestible lump of words rather than a book.

I am enormously grateful to Tony Blair for allowing me the privilege of being part of his Number 10 and putting up with me for so long when I must have been deeply irritating for much of the time, and I would like to pay tribute to all of my colleagues in Downing Street and more widely in government, civil servants and politicians and supporting staff, most of whom I have spared the embarrassment of being mentioned in these pages despite the central roles they played.

Dr John Adamson, Dr Leslie Mitchell, Professor Anthony King and my son Charles Powell have all kindly looked at parts of the text for me and I am grateful to them for their advice. All the mistakes are of course my own.

I would also like to thank my long-suffering assistant Debbie Ailes for her help with the book and in looking after me more generally, and my colleagues Thomas Kaplan, Ali Erfan and Aamer Sarfraz for their understanding and tolerance.

Above all I would like to thank my wife Sarah and my children John, Charlie, Jecca and Roa for their support and love during my time in government and in writing this book. I am really more grateful than I can say, even if I didn't always show it.

In Defence of Machiavelli

Niccolò Machiavelli is much misunderstood. Even in his own life-time his views were caricatured, and 'Machiavellian' became a term of abuse not long after his death. In fact, Machiavelli wasn't at all Machiavellian. He was the son of a Florentine lawyer born under Medici rule who became secretary to the Second Chancery in 1498 and later secretary to the Ten of War, two of the key bodies governing the republic after the Medici had been thrown out and the radical friar Savonarola, who succeeded them, had been deposed. He served in these posts for fourteen years, playing the role of a civil servant and a diplomat, dabbling in administration, politics and military matters. Machiavelli's Florence was at the centre of the Renaissance and he rubbed shoulders with thinkers and artists like Michelangelo and Leonardo da Vinci, and on his diplomatic missions he met the great leaders of the age including King Louis XII of France, the Holy Roman Emperor Maximilian, and Cesare Borgia, the son of Pope Alexander VI, and observed their triumphs and failings. For most of his time in office he served under the *gonfaloniere* (first minister) for life, Piero Soderini, but it is clear from his later writings that he had little respect for the indecisive Soderini, and most of Machiavelli's diplomatic missions were fail-ures. When the Medici were restored to their former domain by the Pope in 1512, Machiavelli lost his job and was thrown into a sort of internal political exile. He took on occasional negotiating missions for Florentine businessmen to neighbouring states and retired to his farm at San Casciano to write *The Prince*.

I like to amuse myself by identifying the strange parallels between Machiavelli's life and my own, almost exactly five hundred years later.

I served as a civil servant and diplomat for sixteen years around the turn of a century and carried out a series of negotiating missions for the British government, including the return of Hong Kong to the Chinese, the 'two-plus-four' talks on German unification, and negotiations with the Soviet Union on arms control and on human rights. I met many of the great figures of the time from Reagan and Thatcher to Gorbachev and Yeltsin, and closely observed their characters and actions. I was sent to the British Embassy in Washington in 1991 and attached myself to Bill Clinton, a long-shot candidate in the presidential race, because he had been at my college at Oxford. As a diplomat I joined the press pack accompanying him on his first campaigning visit to New Hampshire that same year, where we all travelled around in a little minibus, and I stayed on his campaign until his eventual triumph in November 1992. Having been a voyeur of American politics, I aspired to leave diplomacy and become a practitioner in British politics and had ambitions to become a Labour MP. I watched Neil Kinnock's defeat with despair on television in the large rotunda at the British Embassy in May 1992. It was clear that Gordon Brown and Tony Blair were the two big hopes for dragging the Labour Party back to the centre and making it electable, and I chaperoned Gordon Brown round the Democratic Convention in New York as his Embassy minder in the summer of that year.

Gordon and Tony visited Washington six months later, and I was able to introduce them to the team around Bill Clinton that had helped win him the presidency. I kept in touch with Tony thereafter and was surprised when I got a call from Peter Mandelson after Tony's victory in the Labour Party leadership election in 1994, asking if I would like to come and work for Tony. I said I would, as long as the job was a big one like chief of staff. I was invited to London for an interview, although I had to pay for my own plane ticket, and had a rather desultory conversation with Tony in the bare and soulless office of the Leader of the Opposition in the House of Commons. I was then sent to the grandeur of the House of Lords to see the terrifying figure of Derry Irvine, the Shadow Lord Chancellor, for a rather more rigorous grilling. Derry told me that I spoke too fast for the 'brothers' to understand, but he recommended me and I was chosen over other more obvious candidates even though

I did not know Tony well and had not been brought up in the bosom of the Labour Party. Tony wanted to have someone in the job who was not a traditional political hack but had experience of government in order to demonstrate that he was serious about getting to Number 10, even if that meant he was taking on someone who was naive about Labour Party politics.

Three years later I created the job of chief of staff in 10 Downing Street and filled it from May 1997 until Tony left government in June 2007 and the job was abolished by Gordon Brown. Some half a millennium after Machiavelli, I followed the same trajectory as he had at the centre of government, dealing with administration and politics, diplomacy and war, and when my leader was deposed I too went into a sort of internal political exile and in that exile I wrote this book.

I studied Machiavelli's *The Prince* as a student, and in Number 10 I often felt the need of a modern handbook to power and how to wield it. There are many excellent guides to the principles of the British state, from Anthony Sampson to Vernon Bogdanor and Peter Hennessy, but they tell you how the system is supposed to operate rather than how it operates in practice. What I wanted was something that told me what previous practitioners had discovered by experience, and to learn lessons from their triumphs and failures. No such guide existed.

For a book of less than a hundred pages written in a few months between July 1513 and January 1514, *The Prince* has had a remarkable influence on subsequent political thinking. From then on political philosophers, and rulers who fancied themselves as philosophers, have attacked or praised it, but what they have not been able to do is to ignore it. Francis Bacon wrote in 1605 that 'we are much beholden to Machiavelli and others, that write what men do and not what they ought to do'. The English Republican James Harrington's 1656 work *The Commonwealth of Oceana* was inspired by Machiavelli. Frederick the Great of Prussia wrote a 'Refutation du *Prince* de Machiavel' in 1739, in part to convince his people that he himself was not at all Machiavellian. Rousseau described *The Prince* as a 'book of republicans'. Napoleon reportedly said that '*The Prince* is the only book worth reading' and was reputed to keep a copy under his pillow. For Hegel, he was a man of genius who saw the need to unite a chaotic collection of feeble principalities into a coherent whole. The historian Thomas Macaulay thought he was a liberal pragmatist. Karl Marx tried to appropriate his ideas, and Engels described him as 'free from the petit bourgeois outlook'. The philosopher Bertrand Russell dismissed *The Prince* 'as a handbook for gangsters'. Mussolini called it a 'vade mecum for statesmen', and Antonio Gramsci, the Italian Communist leader whom Mussolini imprisoned, suggested that *The Prince* predicted the coming dictatorship of the proletariat and, rather improbably, described Machiavelli as the pre-incarnation of Lenin. The philosopher Isaiah Berlin has pointed out how extraordinary it is that such a short and clear book should have so many different interpretations. In an essay in 1972, he counted more than twenty, depicting Machiavelli as everything from the Antichrist to a humanist.

Machiavelli was misunderstood exactly because he was so original. He was the first to escape from the straitjacket of the Augustinian universe that had imprisoned writers before him, and the first to consider a world where the natural order was not set down by God but dominated by unchanging human nature. Machiavelli did not contest the rules that had bound those who went before him; he simply ignored them. He was not an atheist; but God and religion were irrelevant to what he was writing about, except as a tool of social control. He was the first writer to consider power and how it should be used and retained in a utilitarian rather than a utopian way.

There is no evidence that Machiavelli knew about Martin Luther and the Reformation, but it is striking that he was writing at the time of the 'the monks' quarrel'. Certainly his works were considered dangerous by the Catholic Church and were banned by the Pope in 1559.

He was particularly misunderstood in Britain, in part because of the way his works were introduced here. It is possible that British thinkers in the sixteenth century first learned of his ideas not from *The Prince* itself but from Innocent Gentillet's 'Anti-Machiavell'. Gentillet was an exiled Huguenot who caricatured *The Prince* as a glorification of amorality. The word 'Machiavellian' first appeared in an English dictionary in 1569, defined as 'practising duplicity in statecraft and general conduct', and there it has been stuck ever since, despite occasional attempts by historians and philosophers to persuade people to take a fresh look at his ideas. 'Machiavell' was a pantomime figure representing calculating evil or hypocrisy in the plays of Christopher Marlowe and William Shakespeare, and Machiavelli's name is still synonymous with scheming, manipulation and a lack of principle. Even today, if the media want to insult politicians or advisers they will describe them as 'Machiavellian'.

In fact, what Machiavelli wanted to do in *The Prince* was to advise a ruler on how to acquire a princedom and hang on to it. He described the different sorts of princedoms and the best ways to govern them. He listed the qualities required of a prince and offered advice on how to exercise power. As Isaiah Berlin put it, Machiavelli believed that there was such a thing as the art of government and that it was indispensable to achieving the goals men seek and to getting things done. *The Prince* is full of useful maxims, precepts, practical hints, historical parallels and general laws for a ruler: you may excite fear but not hatred, for hatred will destroy you in the end; when you confer benefits do it yourself, but leave the dirty work to others so they get the blame; do what you have to do anyway, but try to represent it as a special favour to the people; if you have to do something tough, do not advertise it in advance or your enemies will destroy you before you destroy them; if you have to do something dramatic, do it in one fell swoop, not in agonising stages; a wise leader needs both courage and guile; and so on.

Machiavelli set out his guiding principle very clearly in Chapter 15 of *The Prince*:

It now remains for us to consider what ought to be the conduct and bearing of a Prince in relation to his subjects and friends. And since I know that many have written on this subject, I fear it may be thought presumptuous in me to write of it also; the more so, because in my treatment of it I depart from the views others have taken. But since it is my object to write what shall be useful to whosoever understands it, it seems to me better to follow the real truth of things than an imaginary view of them. For many republics and princedoms have been imagined that were never known to exist in reality. And the manner in which we live, and that in which we ought to live, are things so wide asunder, that he who quits the one to betake himself of the other is more likely to destroy than to save himself.

It is this stark realism that makes Machiavelli so interesting still. Even now we are inclined to live by myths; but, if you try and govern by myths, you will certainly fail in whatever you undertake. In Number 10, I used to be deeply irritated by the myths propagated about Cabinet government versus 'sofa government', about the supposed lack of parliamentary accountability and about the role of 'spin'. If those myths are believed and acted on, future governments will fail. Part of the aim of this book is to impose a dose of realism and honesty on those who describe a system of government that was 'never known to exist in reality'.

Machiavelli was focused on human nature, and his writings capture eternal verities in the same way that Shakespeare's plays do, and he draws general lessons by combining observation of his contemporary world with parallels of similar instances drawn from the past. To quote Isaiah Berlin again, Machiavelli thought 'the best source of information is a shrewd observation of contemporary reality together with whatever wisdom may be gleaned from the best observers of the past, in particular the great minds of antiquity'.

Machiavelli's was an empirical approach and he loved to generalise from his reading and personal experience. He would set out a general rule for some aspect of the exercise of power and endeavoured to prove it by quoting examples from fifteenth- and sixteenth-century Italy or from his reading of classical antiquity. The book is full of anecdotes of contemporary events he had experienced or heard about, and he was prolific in assembling them. In a letter to his friend Francesco Vettori he wrote: 'This study of mine, were it to be read, it would be evident that during the fifteen years I have been studying the art of the state I have neither slept nor fooled around'. He thought his experience gave him an insight into human nature and the way it affected both those wielding power and those on the receiving end. As he wrote to Giovan Battista Soderini, the nephew of the *gonfaloniere*, 'My fate has shown me so many and such varied things that I am forced rarely to be surprised or to admit that I have not savoured – either through reading or through experience – the actions of men and their ways of doing things.' And he was often quite indiscreet in passing on the anecdotes he had learned in his official role. He quotes, for example, Father Luke, the royal confessor in the court of Emperor Maximilian, who had been quite frank in his private criticisms of his own ruler and almost certainly never expected to see those criticisms in print.

Machiavelli was particularly fascinated by the Roman Republic and its historians, the subject of *The Discourses*, and he thought the study of the past held important lessons: 'whoever wishes to foretell the future must consider the past, for human events ever resemble those of preceding times'. In a letter about the writing of *The Prince*, he described himself 'stepping inside the courts of the ancients' to ask them questions about their experiences and then recording their answers. Machiavelli thought that history could provide the key to understanding the present and the future: 'if the present be compared with the remote past, it is easily seen that in all cities and in all people there are the same desires and the same passions as there always were. So that, if one examines with diligence the past, it is easy to foresee the future of any commonwealth, and to apply those remedies which were used of old; or, if one does not find that remedies were used, to devise new ones owing to the similarity between events. But, since such studies are neglected and what is read is not understood, or if it be understood, is not applied in practice by those who rule, the consequence is that similar troubles occur all the time.'

He dedicated his book to Lorenzo de' Medici, the new ruler of Florence and grandson of Lorenzo The Magnificent, in a not very subtle and entirely unsuccessful job application, saying that he had looked for a token to present, and 'I have found among my possessions none that I so much prize and esteem as a knowledge of the actions of great men, acquired in the course of a long experience of modern affairs and a continual study of antiquity, which knowledge most carefully and patiently pondered over and sifted by me, and now reduced into this little book, I send to your Magnificence'.

Machiavelli's realism came with a cost: his disregard for the conventional pieties led to his reputation for amorality. He did not think that the rules of personal morality could be applied to governing a country precisely because men in general are not good. A wise prince should not just focus on being good, 'Since anyone who would act up to a perfect standard of goodness in everything, must be ruined among so many who are not good. It is essential, therefore, for a Prince who desires to maintain his position, to have learned how to be other than good, and to use or not to use his goodness as necessity requires.' He took a Hobbesian view of human nature long before Hobbes and advises princes that since men are naturally weak and evil, they have to learn to manipulate those weaknesses to stay in power: 'men are so simple, and governed by their present needs, that he who wishes to deceive will never fail in finding willing dupes'. It is this attitude that led to his fascination with Cesare Borgia, the bloodthirsty and mercurial ruler of Romagna, exactly because – unlike Machiavelli's old boss Soderini – he was decisive, had no regard for morality, and was clever enough to play on other men's weaknesses to stay in power and extend his territories.

Many commentators take this attitude to mean that Machiavelli himself was immoral. But even his critics concede that Machiavelli never called evil good or good evil, nor did he positively encourage princes to be bad. A wise prince 'ought not to quit good courses if he can help it, but should know how to follow evil courses if he must'. In his view the end justified the means, and the end was stable government because only with stable government can laws be respected and life enjoyed. Public morality was different from private morality. He gives it as 'a sound maxim that, when an action is reprehensible, the result may excuse it, and, when the result is good, always excuses it'. He argues that a few acts of cruelty may be better than weak rule for the majority in a state, and a prince 'should therefore disregard the reproach of being thought cruel where it enables him to keep his subjects united and obedient. For he who quells disorder by a very few signal examples will in the end be more merciful than he who from too great leniency permits things to take their course and so result in rapine and bloodshed; for these hurt the whole State, whereas the severities of the Prince injure individuals only.'

A prince then has to be ruthless when the occasion requires it if his power is to be maintained, but Machiavelli was not a cynical manipulator or a shallow defender of power politics in favour of cruelty for its own sake. He had a clear end in mind. Cruelty might be 'well employed' if 'done once for all under the necessity of self-preservation and ... not afterwards persisted in'. As he says in *The Discourses*, 'when the very safety of the country depends upon the resolution to be taken, no considerations of justice or injustice, humanity or cruelty, not of glory or of infamy, should be allowed to prevail. But putting all other considerations aside the only question should be: "What course will save the life and liberty of the country?"'

Machiavelli's approach shocked his contemporaries and continues to shock later generations. He was not, however, as neutral on the outcomes as *The Prince* would suggest. The saying 'What do you know of Machiavelli, who only *The Prince* have read?' is absolutely right. *The Prince* is short and well known while *The Discourses on the First Ten Books of Titus Livy* is long and less well known, but in the latter Machiavelli makes clear his strong views on what is right and what is wrong. He favoured republics over monarchies; he thought that the intrinsic virtue of the Roman people led to a virtuous state; and he believed in the unification of Italy more than three centuries before it happened.

Machiavelli was not therefore morally neutral. In *The Prince* he was merely trying to be honest about what he saw rather than describe the world he wanted to live in. It was not Machiavelli who corrupted the rulers of Europe or the Church. Machiavelli was just being frank in observing the corruption around him and in advising a prince on how to survive in such a world. Isaiah Berlin summed up his argument :'a man must choose . . . one can save one's soul, or one can found or maintain or serve a great and glorious state; but not always both at once'. As I discovered in government, leaders are repeatedly faced with the choice between the lesser of two evils. Not only is ideal virtue frequently not an option, its naive pursuit will bring disaster to prince and people alike.

Much of *The Prince* is, of course, no longer relevant. The issue of whether a state should use *condottori* (mercenaries) or its own army to defend itself – a particular bugbear of Machiavelli's, given his experience in charge of the Florentine army – is of little practical use to modern leaders, and the way to go about lifting sieges has been overtaken by technology. Society and politics today face very different and more complex challenges. In addition, like all handbooks, *The Prince* is far from perfect. In places Machiavelli contradicts himself in disconcerting ways and, like the Bible, his works can be quoted selectively and taken out of context to prove any point you want.

But there are many reasons why *The Prince* is still read: its capacity to transcend the period in which it was written, its radicalism and starkness make the book seem modern. In the dedication Machiavelli writes: 'I have not adorned or amplified with rotund periods, swelling and high-flown language . . . it is my desire that it should either pass wholly unhonoured, or that the truth of its matter and the importance of its subject should alone recommend it.' *The Prince* is almost all black and white; there are seldom shades of grey. He writes in *The Discourses* of the Romans that 'they always avoided a middle course, and preferred the extremes' – and so does he. He thought that Florence had made a mistake in trying to follow a *via media* in dealing with the revolt in Arezzo in 1502 with leniency; they should have razed the area to the ground to prevent future trouble, but the Florentine leadership didn't want to, because it wouldn't look good. Machiavelli couldn't stand 'such arguments . . . based on appearances, not on the truth'. In his view, 'cities which are powerful and accustomed to a life of freedom, either they should be eliminated or they should be caressed. Any other decision is futile. At all costs should the middle course be avoided.' Francesco Guicciardini's criticism of his friend Machiavelli was as 'the writer who always greatly delights in extraordinary and violent remedies'. But that was the point: Machiavelli was trying to be sweeping and radical.

Although 'Fortuna' plays an important part in his writings, Machiavelli did not believe that free will could be wholly set aside, and he was an anti-determinist, a utilitarian and a pragmatist. In his dedication to *The Discourses*, he argues we 'should admire those who know how to govern a kingdom, not those who, without knowing how, actually govern one'. What interested him was not what was right or wrong, but what worked. That is the real reason why *The Prince* is still interesting and relevant and why it remains for all its bleak view of human nature the best practical guide on how to wield power that has yet been written.

In this book I have sought to establish whether Machiavelli's morality of tough choices still applies in modern politics. I have tested his maxims against my experience of Tony Blair's time in government and my personal knowledge of the Clinton and Bush administrations. The world has changed dramatically in the intervening five hundred years since Machiavelli, but many of the qualities required of leaders and the methods of governing for good or ill are remarkably similar. Above all, Machiavelli is right to point out the dangers of governing on the basis of myths rather than reality, and what a modern practitioner needs is a guide that helps him distinguish between the two and to learn how to wield power on the basis of the experience of his predecessors. As well as attempting to prove Machiavelli's generalisations against a new generation of statecraft, I have also tried to derive some lessons from my own experiences which may be useful for future practitioners. These lessons apply every bit as much to leaders in business, sports, the military and other fields as they do to political leaders.

I have focused entirely on the 'how' rather than the 'what' and 'why' of government. The substance of policy and the ideology of politics are, of course, of greater significance, but there is also an art of government and it deserves to be contemplated more carefully than it has been. I have considered only what Walter Bagehot called the 'efficient parts' of the constitution and not the 'dignified parts' like the monarchy. And I have tried to do it in a light and humorous way, more in the style of *Yes, Prime Minster* or Gerald Kaufman's wonderful book *How to be a Minister* than of a traditional constitutional textbook.

In undertaking this exercise, I have been guided by the words of Machiavelli in his dedication to *The Prince*: 'Nor would I have it thought presumption that a person of very mean and humble station should venture to discourse and lay down rules concerning the government of Princes. For as those who make maps of countries place themselves low down in the plains to study the character of mountains and elevated lands, and place themselves high up on the mountains to get a better view of the plains, so in like manner to understand the People a man should be a Prince, and to have a clear notion of Princes he should belong to the People.' Tony Blair certainly understood the people. I have made it my business to try to understand princes.

CHAPTER ONE

'Of New Princedoms Which a Prince Acquires With His Own Arms and by Merit'

Coming to Power

On 2 May 1997 I walked almost unnoticed through the gates of Downing Street and past cheering crowds enthusiastically waving small Union Jacks. Tony and Cherie Blair were ten yards behind me stopping to shake hands and kiss supporters. Alastair Campbell was lurking nearby to ensure everything was picture-perfect. It was a bright sunny day and everyone else was celebrating our landslide victory, but I knew that when we got inside the famous front door and past the rows of clapping civil servants it would be much harder to identify the levers of power than it had been to campaign. I was to be chief of staff to the prime minister, and I had been working on the first steps we would take for more than a year.

In *The Discourses*, Machiavelli repeats the old saw that 'he is of a different opinion in the market place from which he is in the Palace'. He explains that, once a man has risen to the highest office, when he gets there he looks 'at things more clearly and so has come to recognise the source of the disorders, the dangers which they entail, and the difficulty of putting matters right. Realising that it is circumstances, not men, that have brought the disorders about, he has then quickly changed both his mind and his line of conduct; for acquaintance with things in detail has removed the wrong impression that had been taken for granted when only general considerations were taken into account.' Things would look different to us too once we had got out of the market-place and into the palace.

A victorious prime minister has very little time to adjust. The government has to be appointed within the next forty-eight hours, and the Queen's Speech must to be finalised so that it can be printed on goatskin within ten days. The United Kingdom has the shortest period of transition of any democratic country in the world. Assuming the new prime minister has won a parliamentary majority, they take over power the morning after the election without even the benefit of a full night's sleep, rather than having the luxury of the three-month hiatus enjoyed by the US president-elect in which to choose their Cabinet and plan the initial hundred days.

This was not the first time I had walked into Downing Street. For more than six months I had been meeting secretly with Alex Allan, John Major's Civil Service Principal Private Secretary (PPS), and Robin Butler, the Cabinet Secretary, to agree what would happen if New Labour won the election. Alex had even arranged a private tour of Numbers 10, 11 and 12 for me early one evening when John Major and Ken Clarke, the inhabitant of Number 11, were both away. There was something voyeuristic about entering the dilapidated Number 11 flat, which stretches over both Numbers 11 and 12, and observing the signs of the Clarkes' domestic life. I had to work out where Tony Blair and his family were going to live. The security authorities had advised them that they could not stay in their house in Islington, and anyway Cherie was keen that Tony should be able to see the children in the evening rather than returning home only late at night. The traditional Number 10 flat on the third floor where Margaret Thatcher and John Major had lived was far too small to accommodate a family with three children. The Number 11 flat was much bigger, with three floors of rooms and a huge, balconied hall for piano lessons and toys. Although not exactly homely, with a kitchen that reminded me of my grandmother's, it had room for all the Blairs and even a bedroom in the attic that could be converted into a tiny gym for Tony.

Taking over the Number 11 flat entailed negotiations with Gordon Brown, the new Chancellor, to persuade him that he should live in the Number 10 flat instead. He agreed but boycotted the Number 10 flat for the first few years of government, staying instead in his small private flat near the Palace of Westminster. A year later when we tried to take over a couple of rooms for offices since he was not living in the flat, he absolutely refused. In 2000 we had to annex a bedroom to make space for the arrival of Leo Blair, but he said we could only have it temporarily and must hand it back when the Blairs' eldest son, Euan, left to go to university. He even insisted on putting the agreement in writing.

It wasn't just the living accommodation that I had to decide on, but also which offices people would use. One of the first rules of government is that proximity to power is more important than comfort. In the White House, senior staff will settle for a cupboard in the West Wing rather than a palatial suite in the Old Executive Office Building a hundred yards away because they know that being close to the president is the key to influence. George Stephanopoulos, Bill Clinton's young director of communications and one of his closest aides, opted to perch in a tiny room just outside the president's private dining room, off the Oval Office. Behind his desk was a TV screen indicating which room the president was occupying at any given moment. Clinton could slip into George's office along the little corridor later made famous by Monica Lewinsky.

I knew there would be a fight between the staff for the rooms closest to the prime minister, and I knew I needed to settle it before the election. Later it would become almost impossible to evict people from the most sought-after rooms unless you sacked them. Like the membership of the UN Security Council, decided in 1944 and now unalterable, the only time to decide is when everyone is flat on their backs and unable to resist. The wisdom of this observation was brought home to me in 1998 when I had to move three members of staff around in the most prized offices on the ground floor after a reshuffle of jobs. When I finally reached agreement after weeks of negotiations, I recorded in my diary that 'trying to sort out three offices in Number 10 is much harder than trying to sort out Northern Ireland'.

The first thing was to decide where the prime minister himself should be based. John Major and Jim Callaghan had worked in the Cabinet Room at its huge coffin-shaped table, but I couldn't see Tony doing that. He liked to conduct his meetings in a more intimate setting, usually on a sofa rather than behind a desk, which gave rise later to the absurd criticism of 'sofa government'. Margaret Thatcher and Harold Wilson had worked upstairs on the first floor in a drawing room, with a little private bathroom at one end, in the midst of the grand state rooms used for official receptions, but I didn't want

Tony to be cut off miles away from his staff. In the end I chose for him the tiny office next to the Cabinet Room used by Marcia Falkender when she worked for Harold Wilson and subsequently defended fiercely by her successors as political secretary, whichever party was in power. It was a mistake. It was too small, there was no outer office where we could sit fending off unwelcome visitors, and it was north-facing and depressingly gloomy.

In 1998 we decided we had to move him. At first we thought about basing him in the White Room on the first floor, the Churchills' favourite room in the house: but as one of the state rooms it was needed for receptions and would have been too grand as an office. Instead Tony moved into the room on the other side of the Cabinet Room, inhabited for decades, or possibly centuries, by the PPS and the foreign-policy private secretary. This was bigger, lighter, and had the advantage of an anteroom outside where we could sit, always on call and ready to repel people trying to crowd into meetings un-invited. This was the 'den' in which Tony Blair would spend the rest of his time in government, with a sofa, two easy chairs and a desk with a computer which we installed after he took an IT course in Newcastle for the young unemployed but which he never mastered. It lay unused for five years gathering dust until I had it removed. The hotline phone to the White House was on a small table behind, together with another secure phone for Moscow which never worked. There were high-backed chairs arranged around the room for staff when they attended meetings. The room was smaller than the office of any other minister in the Cabinet, less than a quarter the size of the Foreign Secretary's office, and its modesty used to be remarked on by visiting heads of government.

I sat outside in a similar-sized office crammed with five desks to accommodate the key staff Tony wanted to have right by him at all times only a shout away. It was impossibly crowded and noisy – usually filled with ministers and officials waiting to go into Tony's den, making it hard to think or make confidential phone calls – but I had been advised by a friend from the Clinton administration that it was crucial to sit outside the leader's office and so I spent nine years working in considerable discomfort. We had to exile the more junior private secretaries who had occupied that office to a little suite of rooms up a small half-landing, which they thought of as being in Outer Mongolia. I then had to arrange Tony's closest aides, including Anji Hunter, David Miliband and Sally Morgan, within easy hailing distance. Alastair Campbell took over the offices of the press secretary at the front of Downing Street, only a lace curtain away from the camera crews on the street outside. We had to put the Policy Unit in various poky offices on the first and second floors at the front, and even then had to have one bathroom converted into an office.

Number 10 Downing Street is extraordinarily ill-suited to be the headquarters of a modern government. The first two things visitors always observe is how much bigger it is than it looks from outside – because it is in fact several houses – and how quiet it is. The 'upstairs downstairs' atmosphere, with a doorman and uniformed servants serving tea, is reminiscent of a grand country house rather than the centre of government. I argued for leaving Number 10 and setting up open-plan offices in the government-owned Queen Elizabeth II Conference Centre, a short distance away – which would have been much better suited to running an efficient government – and turning Downing Street into a museum. I returned to the idea in the spring of 1998, but it was never going to fly. Visiting dignitaries and ministers always want to be photographed walking through the famous front door, and for security reasons it would not be possible for the prime minister to keep shuttling back and forth to the QEII Centre. Not for the first time in the British system of government, form triumphed over function.

The main thing a prime minister himself notices on entering Downing Street for the first time is how illusory power really is. When you are in Opposition you are convinced that, if only you can get through the door, you can start making things happen. But power, like the crock of gold at the end of the rainbow, is never there when you arrive. Soon after becoming president, Bill Clinton said that he wished when he died he could be reborn as someone with real power, like a member of a focus group in Macomb County Michigan (a key swing district in the US). Prime ministers, too, become convinced that power lies somewhere else, perhaps with newspaper proprietors or the Civil Service mandarins, and keep enviously trying to see if they can seize it.

The only formal power the prime minister has is the power of patronage. He can appoint and dismiss ministers and certain other office holders, but he has no budget and no army of civil servants behind him, unlike every other Cabinet minister. It was a particular problem for us, faced as we were by a Chancellor who not only controlled the purse strings but was also determined to try to assert control over as much domestic policy as he could, and by an old-school Cabinet Secretary who was anxious to assert control over a new and inexperienced prime minister.

On that first morning, Robin Butler was waiting for us at the end of the corridor with a large pile of briefs. These had been worked on by the Civil Service for months in the dead period at the end of the previous government and during the three-week election campaign. The civil servants had parsed every aspect of the manifesto and prepared plans to implement even the craziest ideas floated in the heat of the campaign. Far from aiming to frustrate the new government's plans, they had to be restrained from taking each component too literally.

Many of the 'first-day briefs' are important, but not urgent. The Cabinet Secretary loves giving the prime minister the nuclear-release provisions and orders for last resort and asking him to agree to two nuclear deputies to take charge if he is killed. The latter decision always leads to arguments with, to my surprise, ministers clamouring to be given the task. The prime minister has to write his instructions to Britain's nuclear submarines for what should happen if he is incapacitated in a nuclear attack, and he then sticks them inside a sealed envelope so that no one else knows what he has written. This kind of decision should not be thrust upon a new prime minister who has not slept properly for a week. The Cabinet Secretary's objective in doing so is to seek to overwhelm the new boy with decisions and put him in awe of his responsibilities so that he comes to depend on the mandarin as his guide. The new prime minister is even asked to agree to the order of precedence for ministers so that they know where to sit around the Cabinet table, and to approve the revised Ministerial Code, the Questions of Procedure and the Rules on Travel for Ministers. The latter documents seem innocuous enough at the time, even dull, but they are worth paying attention to as they will come back to bite a prime minister if they are just nodded through. They contain all sorts of detailed rules that ministers will almost certainly breach in future, leading to demands for their resignation.

Over the decades many political advisers have been seen off at this point in the process. Bernard Donoughue, who was policy adviser to Harold Wilson and then Jim Callaghan, describes the hysterical scenes when the Number 10 civil servants wouldn't allow the political appointees to use Number 10 headed writing paper, and only permitted them to read confidential memos standing beside the desk of the Principal Private Secretary. Later, Mrs Thatcher tried to appoint a businessman, David Wolfson, as her chief of staff in 1979, but the Civil Service had him relegated to a tiny room in the attic and he rarely got to see the prime minister who had been whisked off by the Cabinet Secretary. He gave up after a few months.

Machiavelli advises that a new leader 'must keep his mind ready to shift as the winds and tides of Fortune turn'. This is undoubtedly true, as the circumstances new prime ministers find on coming to office will be different from those they expect and, even if they are not, prime ministers generally make a song and dance about how much worse things are than they expected once they open the books. But leaders also need to have a plan if they want to change things rather than being hijacked by events or by the agendas of others. David Miliband and I had taken the precaution of planning out the first hundred days of the government some time in advance and agreeing the key measures to be included in the Queen's Speech. We had our own first-day briefs to give Robin Butler.

It had not been easy to pull them together in the preceding six months. Politicians are superstitious and do not want to tempt fate by agreeing what they will do in government in advance of an election. They have a good pragmatic reason: they do not want to let people think they are already measuring the curtains before the electorate has spoken. Mickey Kantor, a leading Democrat official, drew up an entire transition plan for Bill Clinton in the run-up to the 1992 presidential election, but Clinton would not focus on it during the campaign and jettisoned the whole thing once he won. Tony was just as superstitious and just as focused on winning, so David and I went ahead and worked on the plan ourselves. In the six months before the election, I had to meet Robin Butler and negotiate with him on what should be included in the government programme without any real authorisation. Robin was clearly suspicious and demanded a meeting with Tony at his house in Islington which we finally held on 23 April, just one week before polling day. Robin gave Tony a questionnaire, but Tony wouldn't engage and gave Robin a vague assurance that he agreed with everything we had proposed. Robin gave him a file of government briefs, but at that stage Tony didn't have time to read them.

One idea we wouldn't share in advance was the decision to make the Bank of England independent. The idea had first registered with Tony when he was a junior Opposition spokesman on Treasury matters, listening to Roy Jenkins making the case for it in a debate in the House of Commons in the 1980s. He persuaded Gordon Brown of its merits and they agreed to put it into practice in government. Tony argued for making the idea public in the run-up to the election, but Gordon wanted to keep it secret and announced it the day after we won. We couldn't tell the civil servants in advance for fear it would leak.

Robin Butler wanted to preside over a successful transition from a Conservative government to a Labour one, and he did so elegantly, but he was concerned about the role that Alastair Campbell and I would play in government. He was convinced that I aspired to be Principal Private Secretary in Number 10, a role reserved for the top civil servant. In fact, I had no designs on the job. I wished to be a political appointee and had indeed long wanted to be a Labour MP. Robin, however, was haunted by the spectre of my brother who had been Margaret Thatcher's foreign policy private secretary for eight years. He and Robin had known each other for decades, and Robin served as Mrs Thatcher's PPS and then as Cabinet Secretary while he was at Number 10. Once Charles's normal allotment of time in Number 10 was up after two years, Robin tried to move him out and replace him with a new Foreign Office appointee, but Mrs Thatcher wouldn't hear of it. As time went on, the system's efforts to tempt Charles with offers of plum ambassadorships or just to evict him got more and more desperate as he became more of a fixture and increasingly influential. Now here was another Powell coming into Downing Street. It must have been Robin's worst nightmare.

Some months into our time in Number 10, when Alex Allan, John

Major's PPS who had stayed on to shepherd us through the transition, was leaving to become High Commissioner in Australia, Robin offered me the position. He said I would have to resign from the Labour Party, but I hadn't been very political and he was sure he could arrange it. I declined. He had obviously been convinced I was plotting to get the job, and his concerns gave rise to a series of newspaper stories saying I had been seen off in my ambitions to usurp the prime Civil Service role. Instead when Alex left, we gave the job to John Holmes, the excellent Foreign Office private secretary.

Robin told us we needed a special Order in Council to allow Alastair and me to tell civil servants what to do. He thought perhaps Tony would want another similar political appointee so he suggested we allow for three positions with special powers. We went along with the idea, although it always seemed to me entirely unnecessary. After all, political appointees in Number 10 had been managing civil servants for decades, most recently the two heads of John Major's Policy Unit, Sarah Hogg and Norman Blackwell. This Order in Council later came to take on a totally disproportionate significance in the media and was used as a political hammer with which to attack Tony. Gordon Brown made a great play of abolishing it when he became prime minister. Later Robin graciously admitted that it was a mistake. In an excess of tidy-mindedness he had been advised by the machinery of government experts in the Cabinet Office that the existing position of special advisers was anomalous. The original provision in Harold Wilson's time had only allowed them to offer advice, not to make policy. Instead of adjusting the theory to reality, the officials wanted to protect the theory and make an exception for us. It was ludicrous, however, to suggest that we were doing anything different from what Ed Balls was doing in the Treasury as a special adviser to Gordon Brown or other special advisers were doing elsewhere in Whitehall.

Machiavelli writes that 'States suddenly acquired, like all else that is produced and that grows up rapidly, can never have such root or hold as that the first storm which strikes them shall not overthrow them; unless, indeed, as I have said already, they who thus suddenly become Princes have a capacity for learning quickly how to defend what Fortune has placed in their lap'. We tried to learn quickly. Our first-day briefs made it clear we would not be trapped by the machine.

We had planned out carefully what to do, including, for example, ensuring that Tony's first visit outside London was to Northern Ireland to demonstrate the priority we attached to resolving the Troubles. One of the symbolic changes that came to define the new informality of the early days was not, however, ours. The press made much of the 'New Labour decision' to drop the rule that ministers should refer to each other in Cabinet meetings by their titles rather than their names. It was captured by the press as 'Call me Tony'. Far from being the idea of some party apparatchik or spin doctor, it was actually the brainchild of Alex Allan.

We needed such symbolic changes after eighteen years of one-party rule. One step we took to mark the change of generation was not, in retrospect, a huge success. That was 'Cool Britannia'. Encouraging the creative arts in Britain was fine, but making it so easily prey to parody was not. I compounded the problem by insisting that, despite the doubts of my colleagues, we invite members of Oasis to a party in Number 10 to celebrate Cool Britannia. I did so because my teenage sons, as aspiring rock musicians, wanted Noel Gallagher's autograph. We paid the price for ever after with the endlessly repeated TV clips of the rock star walking into Downing Street every time something went wrong, just like the pictures of the Beatles visiting Harold Wilson. A prudent prime minister, however young, should avoid the temptation to appear trendy.

To prepare for our time in government, I had set up a planning group made up of Labour Party figures with experience of government or at least of planning the transition to government, together with retired mandarins. The group used to meet in the official Gower Street residence of the Master of Birkbeck College, Tessa Blackstone, and included Charles Clarke, who had been Neil Kinnock's chief of staff, and Patricia Hewitt, who together had planned for a transition that didn't materialise in 1992, and also Nick Monck, who had recently retired as Permanent Secretary of the Department of Employment. I established a similar group of former senior diplomats, including Michael Butler who had been the Permanent Representative to the European Union and David Hannay who had filled the same job as well as being ambassador to the UN – they could provide informal advice on foreign policy. With the help of Patricia, who was then at the consultants Accenture, we had constructed a programme to train shadow ministers for their new roles in government. Hardly any of them had any experience of government or indeed of running anything, and exposure to retired mandarins was supposed to accustom them to the relationship between politicians and civil servants. But most were suspicious of the mandarin class and cynical about the exercise, especially when Tony Blair, Gordon Brown and John Prescott refused to participate. Few really used it to prepare themselves for their new jobs.

Many Labour politicians had expected the civil servants they faced to be dyed-in-the-wool Thatcherites, yet after eighteen years of Tory government the civil servants were bored and desperate for change. We arranged for the Permanent Secretaries to start meeting their Shadow Cabinet opposite numbers six months before the election. Some, like Jack Straw, took to it so assiduously that they irritated civil servants with their repeated requests for meetings; but others refused. In some cases the Permanent Secretaries had to see two different shadow ministers. Andrew Turnbull at Environment had to meet Frank Dobson, who was Shadow Environment Secretary, and then sneak up to Yorkshire to meet John Prescott, who we had told Andrew would take over the department in government. The Permanent Secretaries themselves understood the suspicions that the politicians harboured and leaned over backwards to prove that they were not intrinsically right wing. They often pulled their punches by failing to tell shadow ministers how daft some of their ideas were. In the event, our major problem was not a wall of Conservative opposition from the Civil Service but having to restrain their new-found left-wing enthusiasm.

Tony only began to focus seriously on the Cabinet while he waited for the election results at his house in Trimdon. John Prescott came up from his Hull constituency to finalise negotiations over his new 'super ministry' combining Environment, Transport and the Regions, the three subjects that really interested him. Peter Mandelson came over from Hartlepool to offer advice, and Gordon Brown called several times to ask who would be getting which job. Very rapidly, we had to appoint one of Gordon's supporters, Doug Henderson, as Europe Minister because he had to go off to represent the country the next day in Brussels.

The appointment of the first Labour Cabinet in eighteen years was Tony's chance to set his stamp on the direction of the new government, and we should, in retrospect, have been more imaginative in our choice of ministers. The Labour Party rules, however, required that the elected members of the Shadow Cabinet should form the Cabinet in government, and so we were stuck with the people we had in Opposition. We managed to make some changes at the margin. In Opposition, Tony had persuaded Derek Foster, the elected chief whip, to stand aside, and with difficulty he persuaded Michael Meacher to accept a junior position under John Prescott rather than being in the Cabinet. We shuffled some of the portfolios, moving George Robertson to Defence and Donald Dewar to Scotland, for example.

As each of them came into the Cabinet Room to be appointed that afternoon, however, the new members were so ecstatically grateful that Tony almost certainly could have made more sweeping changes. By lacking the courage to do so, we found ourselves hobbled in our attempts at reform in the early years. Old Labour stalwarts like Frank Dobson, in the crucial portfolio of Health, and Gavin Strang at Transport, made it more difficult to bring about rapid change in the public services. A new prime minister should not worry about continuity with Shadow Cabinet positions. Whatever experience has been gained in Opposition is of little use in government, and in any case some politicians are better in Opposition than they are in government. Robin Cook was a brilliant House of Commons debater and, while we were in Opposition, used to come to my office on the ground floor in Speaker's Court in the Palace of Westminster to ask me if I had seen the reviews of his performances in *The Times*. If I said I had not, he would read them to me while I made appreciative noises. As Foreign Secretary, he was thrilled by his huge new office dominated by a twenty-foot portrait of a nineteenth-century Nepalese general and he invited me in on his first day and plopped down into the leather armchair, saying, 'Pretty good for a former Workers Education Association lecturer, eh, Jonathan?' Robin did not, however, apply himself to the grind of governmental work and found a lot of policy work boring. As a result, he never lived up to his true potential as a minister.

A new prime minister should think hard about who they want in each position in government, be ruthless in culling their Shadow

Cabinet, and then leave those they appoint in place as long as possible so that they can acquire real expertise, unless they are felled by scandal or incompetence. They should exclude from their mind the notion that the appointment of a Cabinet can be handled like a management exercise. It cannot. The appointment of a Cabinet is politics, not HR.

We were more radical in changing Prime Minister's Questions (PMQs) from its traditional two sessions of fifteen minutes each week on Tuesday and Thursday afternoons to half an hour a week on Wednesday at midday. PMQs serve as an essential tool both for Parliament to hold the prime minister to account and for the prime minister to find out what is happening in government by demanding explanations from departments and summoning officials. Questions on Tuesdays and Thursdays tied the prime minister to London all week, and because the two sessions were in the afternoon two full days a week were lost in preparation. Moving it to one session on Wednesday liberated at least one and a half working days a week. We had planned the move in advance while in Opposition, and we slipped it into place immediately after winning. Had we tried to make the change two years later we would have been met by a wall of resistance and it would never have got through. A prudent prime minister would always make such procedural changes in his first few days, before MPs have got their bearings.

Machiavelli advised others to follow the bold, decisive example set by Cesare Borgia: 'Whoever, therefore, on entering a new Princedom, judges it necessary to rid himself of enemies, to conciliate friends, to prevail by force or fraud, to make himself feared yet not hated by his subjects, respected and obeyed by his soldiers, to crush those who can or ought to injure him, to introduce changes in the old order of things, to be at once severe and affable, magnanimous and liberal, to do away with a mutinous army and create a new one, to maintain relations with Kings and Princes on such a footing that they must see it for their interest to aid him, and dangerous to offend, can find no brighter example than in the actions of this Prince.' The same applies to a new prime minister. An election victory, especially a landslide victory, provides a new government with political momentum. That momentum should be used to push through the most difficult and controversial measures a government intends to make as quickly as possible. Painful reforms only pay off over time and they should be introduced early so that their benefit is felt before the prime minister has to go to the people again, rather than introducing them as another election looms. Over time opposition will build up and it is harder to be radical. A leader should spend his political capital early rather than hoarding it.

Unfortunately it is easier to give this advice than to follow it. We had the opportunity to change British politics for ever after the 1997 election by bringing the Liberal Democrats into government and reuniting progressive forces for the first time since the nineteenth century. In the months leading up to the election, we had been engaged in secret talks with Paddy Ashdown, Roy Jenkins and other leaders of the party unbeknown to most of the Shadow Cabinet. We had agreed the two-against-one election strategy that had helped bring the Tories down, but when Paddy Ashdown phoned Tony at his constituency home on election day, our collective nerve failed. Tony did not invite Paddy to join the Cabinet, and Paddy insisted he would need immediate agreement to proportional representation, anathema to the Labour Party then, in order to be able to join. Tony told me at the time that he did not feel strong enough to force the issue in the Labour Party. Leaders often underestimate their power at this stage. They have a personal mandate at that point. They will never be so powerful again.

We carried on talks with the Liberal Democrats after the election, and they culminated in a dinner with Roy and Paddy on 21 October 1997 at Tony's flat in Number 11. We agreed we would go for the alternative-vote system followed by a top-up system after the next election, that two Lib Dem ministers, Ming Campbell and Alan Beith, would join the Cabinet in November and that Paddy Ashdown would join six months later. But once again, as in May, both sides chickened out, and the happy couple never made it to the altar.

In Roy Jenkins's phrase, government is a 'precious egg' carried by the prime minister in a thousand-mile egg-and-spoon race in bare feet over burning coals, and we didn't want to drop it; we felt we had too much to lose. This fear led us to be too timid on public service reform as well. Our strategic aim was to shift from producer-driven public services to health and education services driven by the patient, the parent and the pupil, but still free at the point of use.

We should have moved directly to radical reform to bring this about. But we were constrained by our promise to stick to Tory spending plans in the first two years to demonstrate that the Labour Party was financially competent and was not the profligate tax-and-spend party that had led to devaluation in the 1960s and the winter of discontent in the 1970s. As I noted in my diary in June 1998, throughout the early years we were terrified that an economic down-turn would make us just another predictable Labour government unable to manage the economy.

Once we started increasing spending on public services, we soon realised that more money was not a solution in itself. We then tried to impose reform from the centre through targets and ring-fenced budgets, but that didn't work either. Instead, it created perverse incentives in the system that held back improvement, and we realised that reform by central fiat was not going to work. Finally, after 2001, we started to introduce a mixed system of provision, using the private and voluntary sectors as well as the public sector. Such a mixed economy allowed the system to be driven by the user and brought about real, sustainable changes. Had we been able to introduce those radical changes straight away, we would have been in a position to reap the political benefits they brought, rather than leaving bene-fits to our successors. But we lacked knowledge of how the system worked and we did not want to frighten the party by moving too fast, and the battle we had to introduce reform later demonstrated that the opposition was real. A wise prime minister, though, would ignore the opposition and press ahead while they are strong, rather than advancing gradually and allowing resistance to build up. In the words of Isaiah Berlin, Machiavelli's advice was: 'if your action must be drastic, do it in one fell swoop, not in agonising stages'.

In the twentieth century, Labour had been merely a series of punctuation marks between long periods of Conservative govern-ment, and we were obsessed with the aim of becoming the first Labour government to serve two full terms. It had never happened before, and we were terrified that if we were too radical we would lose the second election or have our majority so reduced that we could not continue, as had happened to the Labour government of 1945. We therefore hoarded our political capital instead of spending it. We also had before us the spectre of Bill Clinton's first term, in

which he frittered away his support in a series of missteps over gays
in the military and health-care reform, allowing Newt Gingrich's
Republicans to win the 1994 midterm elections. To avoid mistakes
that might lead to losing the election, we imposed absolute discipline
in the party. Machiavelli would have sympathised. 'Virgil, by the
mouth of Dido, excuses the harshness of her reign on the plea that
it was new, saying: "A fate unkind, and newness in my reign, compel
me thus to guard a wide domain."'

A key question for a new government is whether it has a positive
or a negative mandate. Machiavelli warns of the dangers of a purely
negative mandate. He reminds 'the Prince who acquires a new State
through the favour of its inhabitants, to weigh well what were the
causes which led those who favoured him to do so; and if it be seen
that they have acted not from any natural affection for him, but
merely out of discontent with the former government, that he will
find the greatest difficulty in keeping them his friends, since it will
be impossible for him to content them'. That is the problem that
faces the current Conservative/Lib Dem government; the electorate
didn't vote for it but just voted to get rid of Gordon Brown. On the
other hand the problem with a positive mandate such as the one
Tony won in 1997 is that the new government faces exaggerated
expectations. We had deliberately kept our undertakings to the electorate modest, with five very limited pledges such as reducing class
sizes. We delivered on all these promises within a couple of years, but
they were soon forgotten. After eighteen years of Conservative rule,
people projected on to the new government all their hopes and aspirations, regardless of what we had actually promised. Many of those
hopes and aspirations were in conflict, and every time we had to
make a choice we alienated one part of our coalition of support. If
you do anything in government, it will not be long before you have
disappointed half your supporters, and, if you do nothing, you will
have soon disappointed all of them.

It would be better if the test of the first hundred days did not
exist. In an ideal world incoming prime ministers would take a rest
after an election and act only when their minds are clearer. But the
test has existed since the time of President Roosevelt, and the media
will judge any new leader on how much they have achieved by that
date. There is therefore no choice in reality but to move quickly and

boldly. The lesson from our experience is that a new leader has to have prepared in Opposition for that sprint in government and has to be ready to be bold in his first weeks so that he can reap the benefits of his actions before the next election, as President Obama, for example, has tried to do with his gamble on health-care reform.

The dominant sensation for a new prime minister on entering Number 10 will be how difficult it is to make anything happen. Constitutional theorists opine about the untrammelled power of the British prime minister in Parliament, but it doesn't feel like that when you get there. A new prime minister pulls on the levers of power and nothing happens. That feeling of powerlessness goes on. I recorded in my diary on one occasion, when we were under attack, how strange it was to feel so weak inside Number 10 when everyone outside appeared to think we were all-powerful.

In truth, political power does not reside in Number 10 but is instead widely diffused in the British elite, not just in government but outside it as well. The only way a prime minister can govern is by persuading that elite, by building coalitions of support and by carrying his colleagues with him. The little secret of the British constitution is that the centre of government is not too powerful but too weak. If a new prime minister wants to deliver on the promises they have made to the electorate, they will need to be a leader of remarkable skill, in fact the sort of prince whom Machiavelli was addressing: 'where the Prince himself is new, the difficulty of maintaining possession varies with the greater or less ability of him who acquires possession'.

CHAPTER TWO

'The Prince'

Leadership

I first met Tony Blair when he visited Washington DC in January 1993, accompanied by Gordon Brown, following Bill Clinton's first election victory. As the Embassy's political officer, I had spent some weeks working with Tony's long-time aide and confidante Anji Hunter to prepare the trip, as well as with her friend Sue Nye, Gordon's equivalent. The two men's main purpose was to study how Clinton had won and to harvest ideas from the New Democrats who had succeeded in dragging their party back into the election-winning centre ground. But they had another aim: to make a political point back in Britain about the direction the Labour Party should take, and they were accompanied by a TV crew filming their every move. John Prescott ensured that they were noticed by publicly attacking the 'beautiful people' chasing round America in search of new ideas. Tony's easy televisual manner was obvious straight away, and I noted in my diary that he seemed genuinely committed to radical reform of the Labour Party. What particularly struck me, though, were his finely tuned political instincts and the boldness that marked him out to me as a potentially great leader.

According to the Machiavelli scholar John Plamenatz, Machiavelli 'valued above all the two qualities which enabled a man to assert himself, courage and intelligence', and these are the two qualities at the heart of leadership in any field. What Machiavelli meant by courage is self-evident, but by intelligence he did not mean intellect but rather judgement or instinct – what we would now call emotional intelligence. This is the mysterious ingredient that allows great leaders to have a sense of where Fortune will lead and how best to take advantage of it. Unlike wisdom, for example, which can be acquired with experience, these qualities of courage and intelligence cannot be learned. A leader has to be born with them.

Roy Jenkins observed exactly these qualities in Tony Blair. In a backhanded compliment, he described Tony as a 'second-class intellect but a first-class temperament', borrowing the words of Oliver Wendell Holmes's famous description of President Roosevelt.

The relationship between Roy Jenkins and Tony Blair was both warm and distant at the same time. Tony invited Roy to Chequers in July 1997. Over drinks in the Long Gallery, sitting in old-fashioned leather easy chairs next to the cabinet containing Oliver Cromwell's death mask, Roy revealed it was the first time he had been there socially. Neither Harold Wilson nor Jim Callaghan had invited him. He clearly saw Tony as someone who could fulfil his own unrequited ambitions and someone who shared the same ideology. But he could not, in Churchill's words, 're-rat' and join Labour again now the party had moved in his direction. As time went on Roy was disappointed by Tony's unwillingness to be as bold as Roy wanted on Europe, and annoyed when Tony persuaded him to chair a commission on proportional representation as part of the rapprochement with the Liberal Democrats, but then was unable to support the alternative-vote system, which was likely to be the most palatable to the Labour Party, and which it had been agreed Roy should recommend. Tony admired Roy. He devoured his books, particularly his biography of Gladstone, on whom Tony modelled himself to some extent, and which he discussed at length with Roy. But having remained in the Labour Party at the time of the split with the SDP when Roy had not, Tony had a question mark over Roy's judgement, and thought his overemphasis on intellect rather than temperament made him less of a natural leader.

In politics the quality of courage is mainly demonstrated by the ability to make difficult decisions and the willingness to take risks when you can't be certain of the outcome. Let me illustrate the point by two contrasting styles of leadership, that of Tony Blair and that of Gordon Brown.

Tony's almost instantaneous decision to run for the Labour leadership when John Smith died in 1994 demonstrated his boldness. A more timid politician would have conceded to Gordon, his senior partner in the development of New Labour, but he felt that Gordon had missed his opportunity at first by agonising and then finally failing to stand against John Smith when Neil Kinnock stood down in 1992, as he had advised him to do. By 1994 Gordon's moment had passed and Tony was the candidate more likely to succeed both in the leadership contest itself and in winning a subsequent general election. Contrary to the myth, Tony told me that Peter Mandelson, far from supporting him straight away when John Smith died, had initially supported his rival and said to Tony on their first encounter after the news, 'This is decided for Gordon.'

In examining the lives of Moses, Cyrus, Romulus and Theseus, Machiavelli concludes that 'we shall see that they were debtors to Fortune for nothing beyond the opportunity which enabled them to shape things as they pleased, without which the force of their spirit would have been spent in vain; as on the other hand, opportunity would have offered itself in vain, had the capacity for turning it to account been wanting'. He believed that great leaders had both luck and the capacity to seize an opportunity when it presented itself without thinking twice, and that is what Tony had done when John Smith died.

It was soon apparent that this bold move was not a one-off. At his first party conference as leader in 1994, despite the advice of his colleagues including Robin Cook, and despite the record of what had happened to a previous Labour leader when he had tried, Tony decided to reopen the question of Clause IV, which constitutionally committed the Labour Party to public ownership. When he did so, he had no clear idea of what he wanted to replace it with, nor a plan of how to secure its change, and he ran every prospect of wrecking his brand-new leadership on the issue; but he could see the symbolic necessity for the party of breaking with the past. It is all very well to be bold, but you also need an organisation, and his staff rapidly pulled together a campaign within the party. The process of debating the new Clause IV itself helped convince people outside the party that Labour had truly changed. Tony was effectively using his popular support in the country to change the party. The wording we ended up with for the new Clause IV may not have been of the standard used in the United States Declaration of Independence – perhaps unsurprisingly, as the main drafting session took place with Tony and his staff perched on the double bed in his first-floor bedroom in Islington. Tony had forgotten when he invited us round for a drafting session that his daughter Kathryn's birthday party was being held that evening and Cherie exiled us upstairs away from the noise. The new wording served its purpose in committing the Labour Party to what it actually wanted to achieve rather than to some shibboleth of the past.

In government, however, you can't demonstrate courage merely by taking on your own side, as Tony had done earlier in taking on the unions over the 'closed shop' and toughening Labour policy on crime. You also have to take on the Opposition. Tony did so in the 2005 election campaign, on the issue of immigration, which is the potentially lethal third rail of British politics. Feelings ran very high, especially among the key group of swing voters we needed to win over. Michael Howard was following what the Tories described as a 'dog-whistle campaign' of trying to win back traditional Tory voters by exploiting the question. At first we weren't sure how to deal with it, but in the middle of April Tony decided to confront the matter head-on and sat down to write a speech on the subject. On 22 April he delivered the speech, extolling the remarkable advantages immigration had brought to Britain and denouncing Howard for trying to play to the seamy side of British politics, while carefully avoiding accusing him of racism. I was in the campaign headquarters on Victoria Street as he made the speech. For the first time during the campaign the whole place went quiet as they listened and, as he finished, they erupted into applause. It had been a high-risk strategy to address our greatest weakness directly, and do so in a positive way. It didn't win us any votes, but it blocked off the issue for the Tories for the rest of the election. Had we ignored it, we would have seen our vote gradually driven down.

Of course, blind courage is not enough. Guile is necessary too, as I shall explore later. I had noticed during Tony's delivery of the immigration speech that the teleprompter appeared to have stopped working at certain points and that he stumbled over his words. When he came back I asked what had gone wrong. He said the teleprompter was fine, but there were parts of the speech that he did not want the media to focus on and he had read out the words looking down at his typed text instead of using the teleprompter, so that the news bulletins would not report them.

Sometimes in government Tony metaphorically drove the car at the wall, daring others to give in and risking his leadership to secure the reforms he thought vital. He did so for example over the education reform bill in 2006 which controversially gave freedoms to schools like city academies and enshrined choice in education. At the beginning of the year, the whips told us there were fifty-six Labour rebels on the bill. Gordon Brown's shadow whipping organisation on the back benches was organising against. Bruce Grocott, Tony's former Parliamentary Private Secretary, said no one in Number 10 understood how bad it was in the Parliamentary Labour Party (PLP). We had just pushed them too hard on reform. Matthew Taylor, Tony's strategy adviser, wanted to make concessions, but Tony said to me the PLP had to understand that, while they could commit suicide if they wanted to, he was not going to concede on reform. Any concession would look like surrender and he was not prepared to do it. He would rather sacrifice his leadership than back down.

The Tories had agreed to vote for the bill so we thought we could get it through Parliament, but there are real dangers for a Labour leader in depending on Conservative votes. The ghost of Ramsay MacDonald hangs heavy over the Labour Party, and no leader wants to find himself seen as a Judas, clinging on to power by selling out. Tony wanted to attack the Labour rebels but was wisely restrained by Ruth Kelly, the Education Secretary, who argued that they should be wooed rather than savaged. The rebels started plotting with the Conservatives and Lib Dems to vote against the programme motion that timetables a bill so it can be considered in committee and passed within a reasonable time. The Conservatives, although supporting the substance of the bill, were happy to play this tactical game. If we lost, we would be left like the hapless John Major, going through all of the stages of the Maastricht bill on the floor of the House. The rebels secretly told the Opposition parties that we had a large delegation of MPs away campaigning in a by-election in Scotland, and they deliberately didn't let on to our whips that they themselves were going to vote against. Luckily, the whips were alerted to the skulduggery just in time and managed to see off the ambush, winning the programme motion by ten votes. In the end, we managed to win over enough MPs to reduce the rebellion on the bill itself to sixty MPs and forty abstentions. Gordon Brown voted for it, but his supporters in the PLP did not. If Tony had followed the advice to make concessions, he would never have been able to get the flagship reform through. In these circumstances, a wise leader must not blink; if they do their credibility is gone for ever. A leader's opponents have to believe they are mad enough to drive into the wall, or they won't give in.

There is of course a point at which such boldness turns into folly. Taking courage to extremes is not advisable, particularly under the influence of hubris dealt with later in this book. Just like a good skier, you want a leader to have a balance of courage and fear, each moderating the other. But if you have to choose between a chronic coward and an overconfident leader, I agree with Machiavelli (even if I don't agree with his implicit attitude to women) when he says: 'I am well persuaded, that it is better to be impetuous than cautious. For Fortune is a woman who to be kept under must be beaten and roughly handled; and we see that she suffers herself to be more readily mastered by those who so treat her than by those who are more timid in their approaches.'

Machiavelli was harsh on his former employer, Piero Soderini, the *gonfaloniere* of Florence, complaining that 'he could never make up his mind'. When confronted with problems, Soderini intellectualised, resisted when he should have yielded and gave way when he should have resisted. As the ambassador who had to wait for months at the French court in 1501 for instructions that never came because the Signoria (the Florentine government) couldn't make up its mind which policy to follow, Machiavelli's vitriol is understandable. The French cardinal Georges d'Amboise said to him in irritation 'we shall all be dead before the [Florentine] spokesmen come', adding ominously 'however, we will see to it that others die first'. Machiavelli generalised from his personal experience to conclude that 'irresolute Princes, to escape immediate danger, commonly follow the neutral path, in most instances to their destruction', and in *The Discourses* he added that 'their weakness does not allow them to arrive at a decision when there is any doubt; and unless this doubt is removed by some compelling act of violence, they remain ever in suspense'.

This warning is just as true in modern politics as it was in fifteenth-century Italy. Ironically, Gordon Brown put his name to a book entitled *Courage* just before taking over as prime minister in 2007, but his record made Soderini look decisive. When confronted by a difficult decision he would commission more advice, ask for more research and play for ever more time. This inability to take a decision seemed also to infect his immediate circle, with the exception of Ed Balls. Tony told me in 2000 that in his opinion Ed was running the Treasury rather than Gordon. Gordon was like that. He liked to have people decide for him. Tony had played a similar role when they worked together in Opposition. Ed's judgement may have been flawed, but at least he could reach a decision rather than putting it off indefinitely.

Gordon's influence on those around him was at times extraordinary. After a few years working with him his aides became changed people. Ed Balls, who had been a pleasant young man as a *Financial Times* leader writer, was transformed by his connection with Gordon. He reminded me of Quintus Fabius in *The Discourses*, who came under the influence of the tyrant Appius: 'though an excellent fellow, [he] was after a while blinded by a little ambition and, under the evil influence of Appius, changed his good habits for bad and became like him'.

Politicians have an instinctive desire to keep their options open and often delay making decisions till the last possible moment, and wisely so. Civil servants will push them into a premature choice when the politicians would be best served by keeping their options open. But there is a limit. The price of indefinite dithering can be catastrophic, as Machiavelli observed in *The Discourses*: 'where there is doubt as to which course to choose and it requires courage to decide, then ambiguity will always be found if on the point under discussion the decision rests with weak men'. He felt that 'slow and tardy decisions are no less harmful than ambiguous decisions'.

The truth of this maxim was demonstrated by Gordon's wavering on whether or not to call an election in the autumn of 2007. Going into the Labour Party Conference, he was ahead in the opinion polls and was seen as a refreshing change after ten years of Tony Blair. He had managed a couple of minor crises competently. His closest aides, Ed Balls and Douglas Alexander, were urging him to call a snap election not just privately but through the pages of the newspapers. The party greybeards, led by Jack Straw, were advising caution. Gordon was in an agony of indecision. The party machine cranked itself up, but still he couldn't decide.

Finally, he was forced to make a statement announcing that he would not call an election. He compounded his mistake by claiming in a press conference, totally unconvincingly, that he had never intended to call an election in the first place and hadn't looked at the opinion polls. The public, wisely, pay very little attention to politics; that is what they employ politicians for. But some special moments in politics 'cut through'. They provide a sudden window on to a politician's real character, and the public notice and form an opinion. This was such a moment. The public caught a glimpse of the real Gordon, decided they did not like what they saw and formed an opinion that they did not change subsequently. The polls turned down. He never recovered. Had he made an earlier decision, either for or against an election, he would have been in a far stronger position. This very public display of indecision cost him and the Labour Party dear.

A pattern began to emerge once Gordon was prime minister: first the announcement then, in the face of opposition to the announcement, retreat and finally the attempt to blame someone else for the original decision. In 2009, Gordon decided he could appear as a tough leader prepared to take on the trade unions by proposing the part-privatisation of the Royal Mail, but as pressure mounted and he faced a rebellion among the ranks of his own MPs he unceremoniously abandoned the policy and finally allowed his supporters to blame Peter Mandelson for pushing the idea in the first place. On Iraq, Gordon first decided in the run-up to the 2010 election to set up an inquiry on the basis of mistaken advice that it would be good for him in contrast with Tony Blair's record on the war. He announced the inquiry on 15 June and said it would be held in private, just as the post-Falklands Franks Commission had been. The next day, under political pressure, he reversed himself and said it would be held in public. And finally the media were briefed over the weekend that it had been Tony Blair's idea to hold the inquiry in private. Whatever Tony's views, he had been out of government for two and a half years and Gordon was prime minister and it was he who had made the decision.

Machiavelli believed that, in addition to the ability to make difficult decisions, successful princes need to be born with good political instincts. Some leaders have perfect pitch and others have a tin ear. Some can judge the public mood and help to lead it. Others just can't.

Tony Blair's reaction to Princess Diana's death on 31 August 1997 was an example of perfect pitch. At first the Number 10 clerk on duty that Saturday night, Nick Matthews, couldn't contact Tony when the news came through of the car crash. Tony was in his constituency home in Trimdon for the first time since that year's election, and there was no phone in the bedroom where he was asleep. Nick called the policeman on duty in the newly built hut outside the house, but the policeman was convinced it was a spoof and was not going to put his career at risk by entering the prime minister's house in the middle of the night without the authorisation of a senior officer. Nick then called police headquarters in Durham and persuaded them to order the policeman to wake the prime minister. The first Tony knew about the accident was being woken to discover a uniformed policeman in his bedroom. It had taken an hour to get him up.

Tony spoke to the private secretary in Number 10, to Michael Jay, the ambassador in Paris, and to Alastair Campbell. Alastair had had a crush on Diana, and Tony had met her a number of times privately in Opposition. He had also invited her and William to visit Chequers since becoming prime minister. When Tony was called again at five to be told that she had died, he was deeply shocked but had a clear instinct of where the public mood would go. It was he, not Alastair, who was the author of the phrase 'the people's princess', which captured the moment around the world. I recorded in my diary that 'he obviously feels real grief but also feels he needs to express it for the nation. The upswelling of sadness is quite extraordinary. Although she was a controversial figure, now everyone loves her.'

I missed the developments on Saturday night because I was staying on a farm in Dorset and my pager didn't work. The first I heard of it was on the Sunday-morning news, and by the time I got to London the royal court was in chaos. Those in London were disagreeing with those in Balmoral, and those on their way to Paris to collect Diana's body were disagreeing with both. The Spencer family wanted a private funeral, but it was clear that it had to be held in public to allow people to express their grief. We cancelled all Tony's meetings and put campaigning for the Scottish referendum on hold.

Donald Dewar wasn't keen, especially as the Tories had proposed postponing the referendum altogether.

It was not just Tony's skill at capturing and expressing the feelings of a nation that was evident during the Diana moment, but also his ability to identify at once the direction in which public opinion would go and then to corral and lead it. On the day after her death, he told me that he did not think the royal family would be able to manage as the public mood turned ugly. The Queen and the immediate royal family remained at Balmoral and refused to fly the flag above Buckingham Palace at half mast, on the grounds that it never had been before.

Tony instructed me to dispatch members of our staff to the planning meeting at the Palace, including Anji Hunter, Hilary Coffman, who as a press aide to Neil Kinnock had acquired plenty of experience at firefighting, and one of the private secretaries together with Alastair Campbell. The courtiers at the Palace welcomed them and were willing to make the funeral a more open affair, with ordinary people attending and not just the great and the good. At one morning meeting the chairman asked which of the people there hadn't been to a public school in the hope of finding a representative of the Palace without a plummy accent who could appear on television as their spokesman. Tony told me to find some lasting way of commemorating her death. In retrospect, one idea that I wish we had accepted came from the organisers of the Millennium Dome who suggested we scrap the Dome and replace it with a children's hospital dedicated to her.

The crowds in the Mall kept growing, and a groundswell of republican sentiment started to build. When Tony spoke to Bill Clinton on Tuesday, he was despairing about the ability of the royal family to see the mood, let alone to see it off. There were repeated clashes between the royal family and Diana's brother, Charles Spencer, who suggested that Tony should read one of the lessons at the funeral but that Prince Charles should not. Tony described to me the peculiar sort of melancholy he had come to associate with the royal family, trapped in their lives and condemned to do their duty. I thought that there was a serious danger they had put themselves in a trap that would finish off the monarchy. They blamed Diana for the fuss, and perhaps they were right; the republican backlash was her revenge from beyond the grave.

The Queen gradually came to accept Tony's advice. She agreed to look at the wreaths on a short walkabout and to fly the flag at half mast, and she took his advice to make her broadcast on the following Friday more personal and to refer to herself as a grandmother, allowing the public scenes of grief to be seen carrying on behind her as she spoke. The public mood turned, and the funeral on Saturday was a moving and unifying occasion. I watched it on the big screen in Hyde Park. Tony was applauded, but the real ovation was reserved for Charles Spencer when he attacked the press and the paparazzi.

Diana's death did not bring about a fundamental change in Britain, as it had seemed for a moment it might, but Tony's part in the events was remembered. Many years later he told me that when he was on holiday in Florida he went into a restaurant and was accosted by a diner who said, 'I just saw you in the film *The Queen* and you were great.' For politicians, reality and fiction sometimes merge.

Not all politicians have such well-developed instincts. Gordon Brown demonstrated his tin ear while trying in 2006, rather late in the day, to convince people that he was a reformer. He had told Tony in advance that he would use his Mansion House speech on 21 June to make it clear that he would be New Labour when he took over. We were rather taken aback when, instead of a commitment to public service reform, the evening news announced he had committed himself, and the government, to continuing with Trident, our submarine-borne nuclear deterrent. We had no particular problem with the commitment itself, but he had not consulted anyone before making his statement and it pre-empted the orderly discussions that were going on in government on the subject. The Cabinet Secretary, who was chairing the Committee of Permanent Secretaries preparing the advice for ministers, was particularly peeved.

The reason for this outburst – which had nothing to do with the rest of his speech – was that the previous weekend Gordon had been cast by the media as a traditional lefty after a speech he had made to the Compass Group, a left-wing pressure group. In response, he was desperate to convince Rupert Murdoch that he was in fact a centrist, in the hope of securing the support of Murdoch's papers. He was convinced that Murdoch held the keys to his becoming prime minister. His announcement on Trident did elicit a supportive editorial from the *Sun* and articles by political commentators Peter Riddell and Steve Richards saying that there was no longer any point in Tony Blair continuing as prime minister. But it was a purely tactical and short-term gain, because at the same time he upset the other Cabinet ministers involved in the decision, worried the military top brass by playing politics with an issue that they took very seriously indeed, and convinced his left-wing base that they could not trust him.

These innate qualities of courage and political instinct, while essential, are not enough by themselves to make a great leader. Leaders also need to acquire five other skills: competence, the ability to communicate, charisma, perspective and charm. As Machiavelli notes of new leaders: 'It is not to be expected that having always lived in a private station they should have learned how to command.' They need to learn the arts of leadership, and those 'who thus suddenly become Princes' need to 'have a capacity for learning quickly how to defend what Fortune has placed in their lap, and can lay those foundations after they rise which by others are laid before'.

The first and most important skill is competence, the ability to be both a chairman and a CEO; to be able to set out a grand vision and to master, at the same time, the complicated detail of policy and politics. In Machiavelli's words a prince must 'give striking proofs of his capacity'. Ronald Reagan could do the grand vision but not the detail. Jimmy Carter could do the detail but not the vision. Tony on the other hand combined both vision and an executive ability. Contrary to the myth about his lack of interest in detail, he had a barrister's ability to soak up vast amounts of paper, while at the same time remaining focused on the big picture. He could lay out a vision for public service reform and also spend hours worrying away in long meetings with health professionals and civil servants at the finer points of health-care delivery.

When ministers stay in a job for more than a few years, they tend to become more expert than the generalist civil servants advising them, who are apt to shift jobs every two years or so. By the end of her time in office, Mrs Thatcher knew more detail on most policy areas than the civil servants who briefed her, and the same was true of Tony after four or five years. Tony took a particular delight in going back to first principles and in trying to find the right answer. Again it was his barrister's training, and it helped him escape the trap of conventional wisdom.

The part of a prime minister's contract with the voters on which the electorate really expect them to deliver is crisis management. If they fail in that, they lose support very quickly indeed. The one time our poll numbers fell through the floor and the Tories overtook us came in September 2000 during the fuel crisis when a protest by hauliers nearly brought the country to a halt. Despite their dislike of the high price of petrol, the public didn't support the protesters, but they did hold the government responsible for resolving the blockade and keeping the petrol flowing to the forecourts.

Looking back, it is surprising that it took us so long to realise how serious the problem was. On the first weekend, we were anxious not to overreact to the hauliers' blockade of the refineries. John Prescott wanted to come down from Hull to chair an interministerial meeting, but we were afraid it would look like panic and we discouraged him. It was in any case difficult to take the protest seriously when the petrol price rise was so obviously due to international events rather than to a tax rise, and we thought the police would be able to handle it. It struck me in later crises how often this pattern was repeated. You may not see how serious a particular challenge is until it is right upon you.

On the Monday, Tony phoned me and told me to deal with the crisis; he would never forgive me if he had to come back from his regional trip to sort it out himself. I pulled every lever available and none of them seemed to be connected to anything. People began to panic-buy petrol, and when I called the oil company chairmen they told me that three-quarters of the petrol stations would be dry by the evening. The instinct to buy was perfectly logical individually but disastrous collectively. The experts told us that the petrol tanks in the cars on the roads in Britain hold many weeks of normal supply, but if everyone filled up at the same time the country would be without fuel within hours. The just-in-time delivery system is such that the country is constantly balanced on a knife-edge, and panic can tip it into crisis very quickly.

We were getting two different stories about what was happening at the refineries from the police and from the oil companies. The oil executives said the police were not taking the blockade seriously and were making no effort to hold the pickets back. The police said the oil-tanker drivers were refusing to come out of the refineries and there was nothing they could do; it was effectively a tanker-driver strike. The police and oil companies blamed each other. In desperation, we got the operational heads of all the major oil companies and the police representatives to come into the Cabinet Office and installed them in a small, chilly office equipped with computers, phones and TVs. Jeremy Heywood, the PPS, and I moved in there with them, and we kept them working day and night to try to get fuel out of the depots. Gordon Brown would call Tony from time to time and say that he was just about to get the Grangemouth refinery in Scotland reopened with the help of the Transport and General Workers' Union, but it never happened. In the end it was Shell and Exxon that managed to get fuel flowing first on the Wednesday morning, and on Thursday the police finally did a deal with the protesters at Chester. I was woken by a call at 6 a.m. to say that the blockade had been broken.

The public never realised quite how close we had come to shutting the country down on 13 and 14 September 2000. Ford had been about to close its European operations; hospitals were about to shut down for lack of fuel; and cashpoints were about to run out of money. We were considering taking 1920 emergency powers to run the country. The blockade broke down just in time. Once the immediate crisis was over, we persuaded Exxon and then Conoco to reduce their prices, and in the following budget we took off the automatic escalator that had driven up tax rates on fuel.

Tony held firm the whole way through the crisis and made no concessions. At the time I couldn't decide if it was our 'Black Wednesday', turning the public against us decisively, or if it was a 'Diana moment' that would pass. I thought it was probably the latter, and so it turned out; but no more than a thousand protesters, using mobile phones and the Internet, had nearly brought the country to a halt. In similar circumstances, a wise leader should refuse to make concessions during a crisis. If you try to buy off such protesters once, as the French government tend to do (their excuse being that full-blown anarchy is never more than a few inches below the surface in

French society), you will never be able to stand firm against them again. Your credibility will be shot. You should only make concessions after the crisis has passed, when you can do it from a position of strength and in order to demonstrate that you understand the root of the grievance and are willing to address it.

Several months later, in early 2001, we faced an even greater test of our competence in the foot-and-mouth outbreak. Again, it is surprising how long it took us to grasp the seriousness of the problem. We had not really been paying attention to the first reports of cases of foot-and-mouth, assuming that they were part of the usual agricultural background noise. Tony and I were at breakfast at the ambassador's residence in Washington on Friday 23 February as part of a North American tour when I got a call from Nick Brown, the Agriculture Secretary, saying that he was going to stop all movements of sheep and cattle throughout the country. It seemed at the time to be an extraordinary overreaction, but actually it was already too late.

At first we left the handling of the crisis to the Ministry of Agriculture, Fisheries and Food (MAFF) and of course the chief vet since he was the expert, but by mid-March Tony had lost confidence in them and they knew it. They were punch-drunk, and they suspected, correctly, that Number 10 was trying to take over running the crisis from them. At a meeting on 22 March, I tentatively suggested putting a firebreak around the foot-and-mouth outbreak in Cumbria and slaughtering livestock in a wide swathe across the country to prevent it spreading further. To my alarm, the chief vet said, 'Oh, that's a good idea. Let's try that.' He told us it might be possible that foot-and-mouth was already endemic in the sheep population. Tony started comparing foot-and-mouth to the fuel crisis. Again we pulled on every lever and none of them was working. The focus groups made it clear that the public blamed the government. We were beginning to lose hope.

A saviour appeared in the unlikely form of the government's chief scientist, David King. He produced a mathematical model that purported to show how the epidemic would grow and how it would decline, closely following the lines of the 1967 foot-and-mouth outbreak. He appeared to have absolute confidence in the model, and the upswing certainly seemed to confirm his predictions.

Meanwhile, we were facing demands to vaccinate the entire cattle and sheep population, an idea strongly supported by Prince Charles who had first started giving Tony advice on the outbreak in early March. The problem with vaccination was that it would make it impossible for farmers to sell their meat in the UK or export it to Europe for the foreseeable future. The National Farmers' Union (NFU) was strongly opposed, and it wasn't at all clear that vaccination would halt the epidemic. So we faced the toffs clamouring for vaccination on one side and the farmers opposed to it on the other. The farmers unfairly accused us of wanting vaccination because it would allow us to rush into an election that we would otherwise have to postpone. To try and keep a grip on reality, I maintained contact with a farmer in Cumbria whom Tony had met on a visit there. I phoned him most days to get a farmer's eye view of the problem. The Scottish and Northern Ireland farmers were keen to separate themselves from what was happening in England. Ian Paisley even came to see Tony in Downing Street to argue that Northern Ireland should be exempted from UK controls because 'our people may be British but our cows are Irish'.

On the morning of 17 April Tony was in favour of going for vaccination. Luckily Ben Gill and Richard Macdonald of the NFU came to see him that afternoon and persuaded him that we should stick to the policy of slaughter and rely on the mathematical pattern holding. David King reassured us that the corner had been turned and gradually foot-and-mouth did come under control, possibly as much as a result of the improving weather in late April as because of all that we had done. Had we given in to the pressure for vaccination, the British food industry would have been set back by years. We had learned that science can play a central role in solving problems as long as you can work out who is giving the right scientific advice.

The tourism industry had suffered terribly as a result of the outbreak, and Alastair insisted we send Tony on holiday in England. We dispatched him for a few days to Cornwall and he hated it. It rained every day and reinforced his view that he needed to go abroad if he was to get any sun and relaxation. Again we had plunged in the opinion polls but came back up as we resolved the emergency and fulfilled the crisis management part of the prime minister's contract with the people.

In managing the outbreak, we also rapidly learned how weak MAFF really was. It simply could not manage the logistics of a mass slaughter of animals. Serious backlogs meant that huge piles of dead cows were building up all over the country and the department could not move or dispose of them. MAFF desperately needed a culture change, and we merged it with the Department of the Environment into a new department called DEFRA. The only body that seemed to be capable of dealing with such a severe logistical problem was the army. We deployed them in the middle of March and they made an almost immediate impact. We soon came to respect the army 'enablers', the engineers and logisticians who can deploy troops and equipment rapidly whatever the difficulties and are one of the parts of the British army held in the greatest esteem by the American military. In the case of a really serious crisis facing the country, they are the one group that a government could depend on.

Sometimes you can get crisis management wrong the other way round. In common with most other countries in the world, we over-reacted to the threat of a shutdown of all computer systems from the 'millennium bug'. Margaret Beckett in particular put a huge amount of time and effort into preparing for it, but at midnight on 31 December 1999 nothing happened. Similarly in 2006 we were worried that the outbreak of avian flu would pose another foot-and-mouth epidemic, and we demanded that the new chief vet came back from her holiday. We went straight into crisis management mode rather than waiting to see how things developed, and we even debated whether all domestic birds should be vaccinated – all the parrots in Holland had already been. It turned out to be another false alarm, and if we had decided to vaccinate every chicken in Britain, we would have done extraordinary harm. A prudent leader will learn to distinguish between the false emergencies and the real crises; but, if in doubt, it is better to err on the side of overreaction than underpreparation.

There seems to be a pattern to crisis management. First is the failure to realise how serious the crisis is. Then comes the panic and the setting up of COBR, the emergency unit that operates from a suite under the Cabinet Office twenty-four hours a day, whether you are burning dead cows or dealing with a terrorist incident. And there is also a grim pattern to the statistics in any crisis, brought home to me by the tsunami in 2004. Initial reports indicate relatively small numbers of deaths, but the numbers start increasing dramatically after a few hours and then continue growing in the days following the disaster. Everyone who is uncertain of the whereabouts of loved ones thinks they may have been there. The authorities have to keep checking through long lists of possible victims and the numbers begin to decline again gradually as they sort out who was present and who was not. In the end, you usually end up with a number that is a bit higher than the initial estimate but much lower than the enormously inflated figure on offer a few days after it took place. Yet it is the high number that is always remembered by the public. The same pattern held true of 9/11 and 7/7 and all the other disasters I encountered.

The second skill crucial to a strong leader is the ability to communicate. Machiavelli puts particular emphasis on the importance of presentation, saying that above all a prince 'should strive by all his actions to inspire a sense of his greatness and goodness'.

Bill Clinton's advice to Tony when he became prime minister was never to stop communicating. He said he had forgotten the lesson in his first year as president, with disastrous consequences. Tony took his advice to heart and saw it as a key part of his job to interpret and explain momentous events to the British people.

On 11 September 2001, Tony went down to Brighton to give a speech to the TUC, and I was left behind in Number 10 expecting a dull day. When Tony was away, I used his den for meetings, and I was just going in with Maarti Ahtisaari, the former president of Finland, who had helped us on decommissioning weapons in Northern Ireland, when the first aircraft hit the Twin Towers. It looked like an accident involving a small plane. The duty clerk popped his head round the door after a few minutes and said another plane had flown into the second tower. I told him not to be silly: it was just the TV running the film again. He returned almost immediately to say that it was indeed a second plane and that the situation was serious. Ahtisaari said he would leave, and I went back into the Private Office to start coordinating the response with Jeremy Heywood, while staring at the TV screens on the wall in horrified fascination as events unfolded. It was two o'clock, and most of the mandarins were still out to lunch. Our first thought was about the danger of a coordinated attack somewhere in Britain. We checked that Whitehall security was being strengthened. The Department of Transport assured us that City airport in London had been closed and flights over the capital banned. The police had raised security in Canary Wharf. Tony called from Brighton seeking reassurance that he was right not to go ahead with his speech to the TUC. Instead he said a few words and returned to London. While he was on the train we set up a series of conference calls for him with Stephen Lander, Director General of MI5, and John Stevens of the Met. Richard Wilson, who had succeeded Robin Butler as Cabinet Secretary, rushed back from his lunch and into our office.

Tony asked us to get President Bush on the phone, but we couldn't. He was flying around the US on Air Force One incommunicado because the secret service were afraid that there might be another plane about to attack the president. Chirac, Schroeder and Putin called. The latter in particular, while supportive, wanted to say 'I told you so' about Islamic extremism after his war in Chechnya, which had drawn fierce criticism from the West. The whole afternoon was characterised by uncertainty. Our main worry was that the Americans would lash out wildly rather than taking time to consider what to do.

When Tony returned to Number 10, we convened COBR. The room was crowded with ministers and officials, but no one could tell us much other than that the attack was likely to have been carried out by al-Qaeda. Tony returned from the meeting with a handful of ministers to discuss what to do next and began to prepare his public statement. At first he was unsure how to react, but when he went upstairs to deliver his broadcast from Downing Street's grand Pillared Room, he was the first world leader to make a public comment and he caught the mood perfectly. He reassured the British people that we were not under attack, offered solidarity to the American people, expressed grief and signalled our willingness to take action together with the United States. He was speaking for most of humanity. Many Americans are still grateful for his ability that day to articulate the fears and hopes of so many millions. Most British prime ministers are unknown to the American public. This occasion brought Tony to their attention. From time to time, I am stopped at the border entering the US because my visa, for bizarre reasons, indicates that I worked for Tony Blair, and the immigration official will ask me how he is doing, convinced that he is still prime minister. When I tell them there is now a new prime minister of the United Kingdom, they think I am pulling their leg. Very few world leaders break through into American consciousness.

We managed to reach President Bush on the phone at lunchtime the next day. He was clearly shaken but said he had no intention of retaliating by just 'pounding sand' with cruise missiles as President Clinton had done in the case of previous al-Qaeda attacks. He would take action only after reflection and planning. After the call, Tony sent him a long note detailing his proposals for building a global coalition of support, delivering an ultimatum to the Taliban, addressing the Arab/Israeli dispute and suggesting a second phase of dealing with global terrorism.

Even in the television age, oratory is a necessary skill of leadership, although the nature of oratory has changed. Bill Clinton was an execrable speaker in his early years, and the only cheer he got as the keynote speaker at the Democratic Convention in 1988 was when, after an interminable speech, he said 'and finally'. I accompanied him in July 1991 when he made his first exploratory visits to New Hampshire and he was still a weak speaker then, but he learned through practice and is now one of the best public speakers in the world. His ability to empathise with people and convince them he is interested in their concerns is second to none. Tony, too, had to learn the art of public speaking. When he started out as a politician, he read aloud the texts of his speeches rather than actually delivering them. While he was never a big-hall demagogue in the Welsh tradition of Neil Kinnock and Lloyd George, he did have an ability to paint in light and shade and was unafraid of moments of silence as a way of gaining an audience's attention and giving emphasis. He could hold the audience in a big hall and over an hour or so take them on an exhilarating roller-coaster ride.

At every Labour Party conference Tony fought a duel of speeches with Gordon. As early as September 1998, I noted in my diary that there was a competition between them to see who could get the longer standing ovation. Gordon's speeches were powerful but always delivered throughout in one mode, spraying the crowd with a machine gun. Tony would sit through Gordon's speech on the Monday, and it would galvanise him into making his speech for the next day even better.

The speech-making process for conference was always miserable, and in the early years Tony would virtually have a nervous breakdown as he secreted himself away to work on it. I identified a sort of annual 'J curve'. He would start off in early September with a reasonable first draft, but each new redraft would then make it worse. Only when we got to the conference hotel the weekend before the speech and the clock was ticking would it start to improve and round the bend of the J. The last frantic efforts on the Monday night and Tuesday morning would finally lift it to a new high. He drafted most of the speeches himself. Alastair Campbell and Peter Hyman, one of Tony's long-time aides who wrote beautifully, drafted excellent passages of purple prose, but for me they sat oddly with the rest of the speech and left a series of false endings rather than building up to one crescendo. We had the habit of trying to cram too many ideas into the speech and could never work out what to do with the long, arid passages on policy through which the audience would sit in anaesthetised silence. The final stages of the speech preparation were painfully rushed, and Tony rarely had time to rehearse on the teleprompter. I noted with delight in 2005 that for the first time in ten years we had enough time for a proper run-through, even marking up the applause lines for supporters in the hall.

Politicians need the ability to make speeches even when they have nothing to say. I used to marvel at Tony's ability to attend ten or more events each evening at the Party Conference and make a speech at each of them. On the basis of only an oral briefing as he walked between the events, he would make a perfectly judged and witty speech referring to all the key people and making all the main relevant points.

Of course, not all speeches are triumphs. Tony's most memorable disaster was his speech to the Women's Institute in June 2000. I noted in my diary on 31 May, before the event, that he had produced his worst draft speech ever. The whole theme was misplaced, and he had asked for ideas for it from Paul Johnson of the *Spectator*, who was a friend and a closet supporter. The combination was diabolical. Tony delivered it on 7 June and was slow-handclapped. In his defence, it was just after Leo's birth and he wasn't really concentrating as he normally did. But even those who are brilliant speakers can misjudge their audience or have an off day.

The third quality required of a leader is charisma. It may seem strange to suggest that this is something that can be acquired rather than an inherent quality that you are born with, but it is. Even such personally unprepossessing men as Mikhail Gorbachev and John Major can turn heads when they come into a room by virtue of their high office, through what Max Weber described as the 'routin- isation of charisma'. Personal charm is necessary as the foundation, and charisma flowers if the politician is a natural performer or an actor manqué. Tony's pretensions to be a pop star when he was at Oxford are well known, and that desire to be on stage and the centre of attention were essential to his charisma. He used to light up when the spotlight fell on him. His father used to tell a story of their time on the ship out to Australia where he was briefly a law lecturer. Tony, a toddler, stood up in front of the whole ship's company and danced and danced until his nappy fell off.

Politicians are required to be performers and have to remember they are always on the stage. Tony used to worry about sitting through long military parades or official events because he knew the paparazzi would be waiting for a yawn or for him to pick his nose. You have to remain on duty the whole way through the event to deny them the shot they are looking for. Politicians now generally understand that the most important thing about a performance is their demeanour rather than what they say. Since the era of Richard Nixon through to the British election TV debates in 2010, politicians have been more worried about perspiration than making a mistake in their words, and rightly so because the voters do not pay close attention to what comes out of their mouths. What they notice is the way politicians look and behave.

An essential ingredient of charisma is optimism. Generally speaking in politics it is the optimistic candidate who wins and the pessimistic one who loses: Blair versus Major, Bush Jr versus Gore, Obama versus McCain, Clinton versus Bush Sr, and so on. Tony had an optimistic spirit that people took to and that made them comfort- able having him in their living rooms. The public quickly pick up on the awkwardness of a politician who feels uncomfortable in their own skin. It makes them distrustful.

The fourth quality required of a leader is the ability to have a sense of perspective, to see things in a wider context rather than being caught up in the moment. It is too easy as prime minister to be sucked into tactical manoeuvres or to become obsessed by a particular crisis rather than seeing events in a longer time frame. Tony commented to me after a few years as prime minister that he wished he had studied something useful at university for his career. Instead of law he should have read history. Machiavelli would have agreed. 'As to the mental training of which we have spoken, a Prince should read histories, and in these should note the actions of great men, observe how they conducted themselves in the wars, and examine the causes of their victories and defeats, so as to avoid the latter and imitate them in the former.' And his disciple James Harrington went further in *Oceana*: 'No man can be a politician, except he be first a Historian or a Traveller, for except he can see what must be, or what may be, he is no politician . . . but he that neither knows what has bin, nor what is, can never tell what must be, nor what may be.'

Politics is lived with tremendous intensity. When you are at the centre of a feeding frenzy it feels as though it will never end, but if you can see that things will not always be this way, it makes it easier to keep your head even if your advisers are losing theirs. That was the point of Harold Wilson's phrase 'a week is a long time in politics', and given how often it is repeated it is surprising how few people appear to know what he meant. A sense of perspective tells you that there is a cycle in politics and that things go up as well as down. What history teaches above all else is that politics is never a straight line; you cannot project from the way things are now to how they will be in the future. There are always discontinuities and surprises, and all a leader can do is to be ready for them rather than assuming things will continue unchanged for ever. Every few months the media would tell Tony that it was his worst week ever and I appointed myself the resident optimist to reassure him and the team that everything would work out in the end. Bill Clinton's advice to Tony in 2003 when things looked grim, based on his darkest moments in the Monica Lewinsky controversy, was just to keep showing up for work with a smile on your face and hope that something would turn up.

Last, and in many ways most importantly, a successful leader requires charm or sinuousness. Machiavelli advises that a prince should be both a lion and a fox, 'for the lion cannot guard himself from the toils, nor the fox from wolves. He must therefore be a fox to discern toils, and a lion to drive off wolves.' A leader 'must have all the fierceness of the lion and all the craft of the fox'.

Tony was the master of constructive ambiguity. In a meeting, he would impart his meaning but in such a way that people didn't realise what it was until afterwards. I remember a conversation in Opposition with Jack Cunningham, in which Tony was relieving Jack of part of his Shadow Cabinet job. If Jack had married together something Tony said at the beginning of their half-hour conversation and what he said at the end, he would have grasped what he was being told. I certainly did, sitting in on the meeting. But he didn't, and the penny only dropped as he walked out of Tony's room and saw the television news in the outer office announcing that his job had been changed. It was for that reason that people would become convinced they had a deal with Tony when in fact they did not.

Perhaps the most impressive demonstration of Tony's fox-like qualities was his handling of Northern Ireland, where he charmed both the Unionists and the Republicans into an agreement that they never originally intended to accept. In 1997 and 1998 Tony managed to carry David Trimble and the leadership of the Ulster Unionist Party through a series of painful steps – particularly Sinn Fein's participation in all-party negotiations on the future of Northern Ireland which would have caused them to pull out of the process if the persuader had been someone less skilful. Later he managed to charm Ian Paisley into a remarkable friendship based on their common interest in the Scriptures. I used to listen at the door of the den to their laughter and come in to discover them discussing the concept of 'grace' rather than the political crisis at hand. Sometimes I would find little religious tracts that Paisley had left behind for Tony's son Leo. These conversations helped to build a trust between the two of them that allowed us in the end to deliver Ian Paisley and the DUP into a lasting peace in Northern Ireland. On the other side, he persuaded Gerry Adams and Martin McGuinness to take a major risk not just with their political careers but also with their lives to lead the IRA into an agreement the movement would never have accepted if they had understood its terms at the beginning of the process. In other words, if Tony had approached the negotiations 'lion-like' rather than 'fox-like', there would have been no agreement. He had to talk the two sides gradually into doing things they did not want to do, and to lead them from A to B, not in a straight line, but by a very circuitous route.

This ability to woo is sometimes regarded by commentators as a sort of black magic and disparaged as trickery. It is in fact an essential tool in the repertoire of a leader. Bullying can work for a while as a method for getting your way, but unless you can also charm people with you, you will fail in the end. Machiavelli went as far as to say: 'He who has best known how to play the fox has had the best success.'

As part of their repertoire, it is essential that a leader also knows how to use anger. At one particularly difficult negotiation with the Orangemen of Drumcree in Mo Mowlam's office in Castle Buildings in Belfast, I completely lost my temper. One of the Orangemen, a lawyer with a loyalist background, started insulting Tony and accusing him of lying. I leapt from my seat and reached over the table to grab him by the lapels with the aim of punching him. Tony pushed me back into my seat and told me to behave. Afterwards he said to me that it was crucial never to lose your temper, except on purpose.

The big dividing line among political leaders is between those who are conviction politicians and those who are not. At one of his first meetings after he became Foreign Secretary in 1989, I was told that John Major asked the officials present to write down the pros and cons of a particular course of action. At the end of the meeting he took his decision on the basis of which list was longer. Strong leaders go into meetings knowing what they want the outcome to be and have a sense of direction, while weak leaders are merely buffeted by events. It is extraordinary that people who want all their lives to be prime minister should have no idea what to do with the office once they have got there.

Conviction politicians are generally endowed with unusual amounts of self-belief. Tony certainly believed that he could resolve most problems, and that is what helped him to be so successful in bringing peace to Northern Ireland. Unlike his predecessors, he believed both that it could be done and that he personally could do it. He would repeatedly tell me that he could sort out a particular problem that he had delegated to me and that I was struggling with if only he had the time to sit down and focus on it. He liked difficult challenges. Indeed, he often seemed to get bored when things were going too easily and would cease to pay attention. He would only perk up when the going got tough.

Machiavelli wrote: 'It should be borne in mind that the temper of the multitude is fickle, and that while it is easy to persuade them of a thing, it is hard to fix them in that persuasion.' He thought that great leaders like Moses, Cyrus, Theseus and Romulus could never have ensured that their ordinances were observed for any length of time had they been 'unarmed', by which he meant they needed to have the means to keep the believers steadfast in their belief or to make unbelievers believe. He observed that 'all armed prophets have been victorious and all unarmed prophets have been destroyed. Such persons have great difficulty in carrying out their designs; but all their difficulties are on the road and may be overcome by courage.'

Great leaders are both born and bred. They need to be brave and endowed with extraordinary political instincts, but they also have to be armed with a range of skills if they want to carry people with them. In order to come to power, they need to be blessed with fortune and to know how to take advantage of her. But, if they are to stay in power, they have to have steel in their soul. In a democracy, that does not mean arms and soldiers but the ability to carry people with you. For unlike Machiavelli's prince, democratic leaders cannot rule by themselves but, as we shall see, only as part of a collective leadership.

CHAPTER THREE

'The Best Form of Government'
Cabinet, the Civil Service and Making Things Happen

Machiavelli observes that 'in the actions of all men, and most of all of Princes, where there is no tribunal to which we can appeal, we look to results.'

This is true of democratic leaders as well, but in a democracy it is harder to achieve results. A prime minister is not a president, let alone a prince. He cannot govern by himself, however good he is. He has no separate democratic legitimacy, and government in Britain is collective. The prime minister depends for his power on the support of the members of his party in Parliament, and at any moment they can get rid of him (although the Labour Party is notably more loyal than the Conservative Party and has never got rid of a leader in anger but always waited for them to resign even when the price of leaving them in place is disastrous electoral defeat).

The manifestation of collective government in Britain is the Cabinet. The prime minister continually has to ensure that they are with him if he is to remain in office. It is the loss of their support that most commonly brings down a prime minister between elections, as Mrs Thatcher discovered to her discomfort in 1990. In this, they are quite unlike the Cabinets of presidential systems in the US or France, where the members have no separate power of their own but depend on their leader.

In Britain, the government only remains strong as long as it remains united. If the prime minister loses control and factions develop, it will soon collapse. Machiavelli observes that 'together all are strong, but when each begins to consider the danger he is in, they become cowardly and weak'. The government's coherence is maintained by the doctrine of collective responsibility. In order to continue to serve in the government, ministers have to support all government policies, not just those in their own area of responsibility, and if they do not they have to resign. They therefore, at least implicitly, have a say in the policies adopted by the government even if they are not directly involved in their elaboration. They can raise objections and, if their objections are not met and they feel strongly enough about them, they can resign.

That is the current role of the Cabinet in the British system of government. It is not a policymaking body but the political manifestation of a united and strong government based on collective responsibility. A dangerous myth has, however, been built up around the idea of Cabinet government in recent years, propagated by a number of retired mandarins. Their argument, somewhat simplified, is that Tony Blair murdered Cabinet government and replaced it with something called 'sofa government'. Before him, everything was well regulated, the big issues of state were discussed in Cabinet on the basis of papers provided by the civil servants in the Cabinet Office, and good decisions were reached and properly recorded. No one was kept in the dark about anything and the Cabinet Office strove to make sure that all departments had an equal say and that there was fair play. In their doctrine, it is the Cabinet that has the power, not the prime minister. He is simply a *primus inter pares* who chairs the Cabinet.

This is nonsense. As I have said already, Machiavelli is right to observe that 'many Republics and Princedoms have been imagined that were never seen or known to exist in reality'. And to me, as to him, it seems 'better to follow the real truth of things than an imaginary view of them', because if a prince tries to live by myths he 'is more likely to destroy than to save himself'. The supposed golden era of Cabinet government was the 1970s when Cabinet would meet sometimes for two days at a time to discuss thorny issues. The Civil Service were in control as a series of weak and short-lived governments, Labour and Conservative, succeeded each other. They were the years of Jim Hacker, Sir Humphrey and *Yes, Prime Minister*, not a decade we naturally associate with the success of Britain as a country. The reason that Cabinet meetings took so long was that the Labour Party in particular was riven with severe ideological splits, and the two wings slugged it out round the Cabinet table, rather than having the dignified, inclusive, evidence-based policy discussions suggested by the proponents of the golden age.

Cabinet government of that sort, if it ever existed, died before Tony Blair went into politics, and it was finally buried under Mrs Thatcher, to whom, ironically, Robin Butler, leader of the mandarin tendency, was both private secretary and then Cabinet Secretary. She did not have much time for her Cabinet colleagues, she did not want lengthy discussion, and she usually knew what she wanted out of a meeting before she went into it. She would often make the most important decisions in her sitting room upstairs in Number 10 rather than round the Cabinet table. The difference between her and her predecessors was not the degree of her commitment to Cabinet government but that she was a strong prime minister who knew her mind and could get her way. This is the key question in Machiavelli's view, 'whether the Prince is strong enough, if occasion demands, to stand alone, or whether he needs continual help from others'. The division is not therefore between Cabinet government and no Cabinet government but between a weak leader and a strong one. Each time weak prime ministers succeed strong ones they invariably announce they are reintroducing Cabinet government, but all they really mean is that they do not have the power to lead their government effectively by themselves.

There is a good reason why the mandarins' conception of Cabinet government doesn't exist in reality: it would be a singularly bad way of making decisions. Any discussion that involves twenty-five people or more, many of them uninformed about the subject under discussion unless their department is directly involved, and with many of the right people whose voices should be heard not present, will give you at best an unfocused political discussion of a subject. So Cabinet is the right place to ratify decisions, the right place for people to raise concerns if they have not done so before, the right place for briefings by the prime minister and other ministers on strategic issues, and the right place to ensure political unity; but it is categorically not the right place for an informed decision on difficult and detailed policy issues.

The clue to the threadbare nature of the argument put up by the critics is their focus on furniture. It doesn't matter whether decisions are made sitting on a sofa or round a coffin-shaped table.

It doesn't matter if the participants call each other President of the Board of Trade or Margaret. I was a civil servant for sixteen years and a political appointee for thirteen years, so I have seen both sides. I can tell the difference between an ad hoc committee and an Ad Hoc Committee of the Cabinet, but I don't think it matters. Those who suggest that it does are stuck in an old-fashioned mindset that cannot distinguish between form and substance. The series of set-piece attacks by retired Cabinet Secretaries and other senior civil servants on the modern system of government in reports and speeches are essentially the death rattle of the old mandarin class.

I don't pretend that all the decisions that were taken in government from 1997 to 2007 were right. We made many mistakes, but they were generally made not because of process, not because we did not have the facts in front of us, not because a particular minister or Cabinet Secretary was absent, but because we collectively made the wrong decision. That is why the propagation of this mandarins' myth is so pernicious. It is designed to mislead new governments into thinking that, if only they follow the old ways, somehow they will not make mistakes. Prudent prime ministers do not think about the rooms they meet in, the furniture they sit on or the formal titles of those present, but about whether they are making the right decisions, have been adequately challenged, and whether they know clearly what they are trying to achieve.

Decisions are well made if the right people are in the room and they have all the available facts before them, on paper or orally, if those in the room feel free to challenge propositions and argue, and if the decisions are properly recorded and disseminated. Of course, lots of other people would like to come to momentous discussions so that they can say they were in the room at the time, but much of my job was keeping out of the room those who had nothing to contribute other than rank. Most of the important decisions of the Blair government were taken either in informal meetings of ministers and officials or by Cabinet committees, not by a bunch of ill-informed cronies sitting on a sofa. Unlike the full Cabinet, a Cabinet committee has the right people present, including, for example, the military chiefs of staff or scientific advisers, its members are well briefed, it can take as long as it likes over its discussion on the basis of well-prepared papers, and it is independently chaired by a senior minister with no departmental vested interest. For example the Constitutional Cabinet committees chaired by Derry Irvine were exactly the right places to take the crucial decisions on Scottish and Welsh devolution in 1997 and 1998.

On the other hand the banning of beef on the bone early in government was an example of how not to make a decision. SEAC, the expert committee advising the government on BSE, was preparing recommendations on T-bone steaks and oxtail, and their draft advice was leaked to the BBC. Jack Cunningham, the Agriculture Secretary, and Ron Davies, the Welsh Secretary, panicked and demanded to come and see Tony immediately for a decision. He was caught off guard and hadn't focused on the issue. He asked if it meant that spare ribs would be banned (of course not since they are pork) and allowed himself to be bounced into the wrong decision. Later we discovered that the committee predicted that only six cases of potentially infected meat a year might enter the food chain, and that was not sufficient grounds for the extreme action that was taken. It took us years of hard political grind to get beef on the bone back into the shops.

The lesson is clear: prudent leaders should never allow themselves to be rushed into decisions and should always demand to see all the available facts and hear all the arguments before they decide.

One of the most difficult things in government is to get a decision, once taken, to stick in face of the pressures to unstitch it. There is an apocryphal story about Bill Clinton, who was clever enough to see at least four sides to every question, that illustrates the problem. As Governor of Arkansas, he was persuaded to veto a particular bill one Friday evening and had his state troopers shove the bill under the door of the office of the Speaker of the State Legislature, which was closed by then. But on Saturday he was convinced by arguments that the bill should instead be allowed to pass, and he dispatched his state troopers to retrieve the bill from under the door, which they succeeded in doing with the aid of a wire coat hanger. In that case it didn't matter, but political leaders are terribly susceptible to changing their minds, which often leads to disaster. Machiavelli correctly believes that a leader's 'decisions should be irrevocable, and his reputation such that no one would dream of over-reaching or cajoling him' or he will be considered fickle or irresolute.

None of this is to say that Cabinet meetings are unimportant. It is just that they are about politics, not policy. We prepared intensively for each Cabinet meeting. Sally Morgan, and later Ruth Turner, in charge of government relations, would ring round all the members of the Cabinet beforehand to see what was on their minds. Before the meeting itself, we would shuffle people in and out of Tony's den to resolve last-minute problems and agree on when Gordon Brown or John Prescott should be invited to intervene in the subsequent discussion. It was only when the discussion had not been properly prepared that things could go wrong.

In December 2005, we made one such mistake when Tony tried to raise, without preparation, both the future of the 'Wilson Doctrine' and the issue of judges' pensions at the end of a Cabinet meeting. The Wilson Doctrine was Harold Wilson's statement in 1966 that there would be no tapping of MPs' phones. He undertook that, if this situation ever changed, he would inform the House at the first moment compatible with national security. Such a moment had never come, although anyone who has read the transcripts of my and Mo Mowlam's phone conversations with Martin McGuinness, which had been leaked to the *Sunday Times* by a disaffected member of the Royal Ulster Constabulary, would have had a shrewd appreciation of the truth of the situation. Finally, in 2005, the Intelligence Services Commissioner proposed that the situation should be regularised. In the light of rigorous new rules on phone tapping, he advised that MPs should be put on the same footing as everyone else in the country rather than having a special status. So, logically, dropping the Wilson Doctrine should have been relatively easy to agree.

But logic didn't have much to do with it. John Prescott, having been wound up by Peter Hain, the Northern Ireland Secretary, who had strong opinions on such issues, came to see Tony grumpily just before Cabinet and said he understood we were about to start bugging MPs. I tried to explain that we weren't, we were just trying to deal with the awkward historical legacy of the Wilson Doctrine, but he said Tony always did his own thing and harrumphed off. I asked Tony if it wouldn't be more sensible to put off the discussion, but we had put down an 'inspired parliamentary question' (in other words one that we had asked an MP to ask), and it would have been slightly embarrassing to give it a holding rather than a substantive reply, so Tony decided to push ahead. He tried to raise the matter in passing at the end of Cabinet, but John Prescott and John Reid leapt in, objecting strongly to putting MPs on the same footing as everyone else as the Commissioner proposed. They argued that MPs deserved a special status when it came to intercepts. Tony had to retreat rapidly and postpone the discussion. In the event we abandoned the attempt to reform the doctrine, and as far as I know it is still unreformed. Immediately after that setback, Charlie Falconer, the Lord Chancellor, raised the issue of judges' pensions. Judges wanted to be exempted from the new ceilings on tax-free pension contributions, and Charlie had promised them that he would get the matter resolved. He was worried that there might be a mass judicial resignation if we did not. Whatever the rights and wrongs of the matter, trying to bounce Cabinet was a mistake. Gordon and others raised strong objections, and after the disaster of the previous discussion we had to postpone that decision too, although the judges did get their exemption in the end.

Tony was not a natural chairman. He didn't as a rule feel bound to follow an agenda or sum up the discussion. There were never any votes in Cabinet, and usually any dramatic differences had been resolved before they got there. The one time early on in government that discussion became heated was when Gordon unilaterally capped ministerial salaries in 1997. After the summer break, the press had focused on the £44,000 pay increase that Tony would get as prime minister that year, having surrendered his increase the year before when we were in Opposition. They contrasted this increase with the tough line we were taking on public sector pay. Tony, who was about to depart for Washington, called Gordon, who was in Mauritius, to say that he thought he would have to turn down his salary increase in light of the criticism. Gordon said he wanted to turn down his increase as a Cabinet minister too and started shouting at Tony when he resisted the idea. Immediately after the call, Gordon briefed the papers that he personally would not be taking any increase. In Gordon's absence, Alistair Darling, as Chief Secretary, had to make the statement to Parliament on our approach to the public sector pay review bodies and he added that he didn't want to take an increase either.

When the rest of the Cabinet heard, they were not happy. John Prescott, who had appointed himself shop steward, called to shout at me, saying that Tony had broken the deal that they had made the previous year and that he himself was taking the rise. I then had to ring all the members of the Cabinet to break the news to them that they were not getting an increase for yet another year. They were overwhelmingly hostile. One told me about her overdraft. Another said Gordon didn't have any children and didn't understand other people's family responsibilities. A third told me about his alimony payments and how his wife had cleaned him out. When Tony came back, he calmed John Prescott down and we rang round the Cabinet again. When it came to the Cabinet session on the following Thursday, they all complained and, as Gordon wasn't there, they made it clear who they blamed for the debacle but they disconsolately went along with the decision.

The Cabinet discussion on the Millennium Dome in June 1997 illustrated perfectly why the Cabinet should not be a policymaking body. '*Grands projets*', the big buildings or events that bring lasting glory in the way that ceremonial games and triumphal arches did for Roman emperors, are irresistible to prime ministers. Machiavelli understood this, saying that 'Nothing makes a Prince so well thought of as to undertake great enterprises.'

The trouble is that the British, unlike the French, are not good at delivering or appreciating such spectacular projects. The British media and the public are cynical about overblown promises that invariably accompany them. The government usually tries to deliver them on the cheap, and they go wrong, massively exceeding their budget. In Opposition, we had been persuaded by Michael Heseltine and his team to keep the Dome alive, but once in government our doubts reappeared and we had to decide if we would finish building the Dome or cut our losses and drop the idea.

Tony thought it was right to be ambitious and that to give up would smack of defeatism. He was, on balance, in favour. He raised the question at Cabinet and set out the arguments. John Prescott supported Tony out of loyalty and Gordon hedged his bets. The next few ministers seemed in favour, but then a long list, led by David Blunkett, strongly opposed the Dome. Tony had to leave early to attend a church event in Parliament, and he handed over the chairmanship to John Prescott, convinced that the project was lost. I watched in wonder as John listened to all the contributions and then concluded that everyone seemed to be opposed, so he would tell Tony it was a 'Yes, but' if he wanted to go ahead.

We did go ahead, and we might have got away with it as only a moderate failure if it were not for a last-minute disaster on New Year's Eve 1999 itself. Everyone who went to the Dome that evening had to go by a special Tube service. Unfortunately, the security system didn't work, resulting in thousands of people being stuck in the Underground. That would not have mattered so much, but those stranded included all the newspaper proprietors and editors invited to the party. They telephoned frantically demanding to be released, and Tony, already at the Dome himself, tried to get them freed, while being assured by Charlie Falconer, the minister in charge, that everything was under control. The editors who missed the midnight festivities took their revenge with uniformly negative coverage of the celebration and of the Dome itself. The Dome would probably have bombed anyway, but that mistake sealed its fate.

Political Cabinets are designed to give the government more coherence by giving ministers a chance to have a wider political discussion than they can in the formal Cabinet. They usually take place after regular Cabinet meetings. Officials withdraw, leaving only politicians and special advisers behind, and the party General Secretary slips in. Ours would normally begin with a briefing by Philip Gould, the party's pollster. There might or might not have been an opinion poll conducted in the previous few weeks, but either way Philip could instinctively express the views of the population. Then Tony would give a presentation setting out the political strategy for the next few months. Gordon would follow immediately with a completely different, and generally more left-leaning, political agenda. There would then be a political ramble around the table where everyone felt the need to talk even if they had nothing to say. Meanwhile, Gordon would scowl and scribble furiously on a dog-eared pile of papers with a black marker pen to demonstrate his contempt for what they all had to say. The whole was topped off with a rousing if incomprehensible political send-off by John Prescott that left everyone feeling warm but confused.

Mrs Thatcher famously observed that 'every prime minister needs a Willie', referring to the role of her deputy, Willie Whitelaw, in steadying the Conservative party. John Prescott was Tony's Willie. He was in charge of the Labour Party's heart and soul. Gordon had favoured Margaret Beckett as deputy party leader in 1994, but Tony had always wanted John because he thought he could help achieve a balance in the party between old and new, left and right. I was fond of John, even though his greeting to me when I came to work for Tony in Opposition was not exactly friendly. Anji Hunter took me up to see him in his rather nicer office above Tony's suite of offices in the Palace of Westminster. He looked at me disdainfully and, having been told that I had come to be Tony's chief of staff, said, 'So I suppose we can start now, can we?' in order to put a toffee-nosed outsider like me in my place.

John was an excellent chair of Cabinet committees and could win all sides round to a sensible solution but his stream of mangled syntax tended to leave everyone befuddled. Tony sometimes came out of his weekly one-on-one meetings with John saying that he felt as though he had been in a tumble dryer. In 1997, John chaired a meeting in Robin Butler's office on Cabinet pay with Ann Taylor (Leader of the House), Alastair Campbell and me. He was at his incoherent worst. None of us had any idea what he was going on about, and the civil servants trying to take notes looked nonplussed, their pens hovering over their notepads. Robin Butler, trying to be helpful, intervened to explain that we were proposing that the Cabinet give up their 'catch-up' pay award for the year. John latched on to this and started talking about the 'catchment area'. Alastair and I got a fit of the giggles. By the end, he had talked himself into the right conclusion, that the Cabinet should give up £16,000 each for another year, although it had taken an hour and a half to get there.

Some of John's idiosyncratic phrases were truly wonderful, like repeatedly referring in Cabinet to the leader of the firemen's strike, Andy Gilchrist, as 'The Andy', questioning the enforcement of the 'Bargo on the China' (the EU–China arms embargo) and inventing a new figure from the classics called 'Dame Osthenes' (Demosthenes, a fellow rhetorician) in his final session of PMQs with William Hague when Tony was away. Despite his incoherence and however ungrammatical he was, you always caught the drift of what John wanted to say. I remember being moved at the Cabinet discussion of education reform in October 2005 by his plea on behalf of those who had failed their eleven-plus, where he was isolated but spoke with real passion. His argument was 'the trouble is if you create good schools people will want to go to them', which was really the point of what we were trying to do. When the education reform package was agreed four months later, John went along with it while uttering a cry of pain. We had sent our education adviser, Conor Ryan, up to Hull to explain the city academy programme, and that had helped win him over. Gordon, who had wound John up to oppose the reform in the first place, left the Cabinet meeting early so that he would not be implicated in the decision. Tony had intended to challenge them all to say whether or not they supported the reform package in order to smoke Gordon out on the issue, but without Gordon there was no point. John's rows with Tony about policy were often tempestuous but always good humoured. Part way through one of his arguments with him on education reform John said he was getting confused: 'Look at the Tories, they are saying the same as you' on the issue. In response Tony asked 'And what does that tell you?' hoping to make the point that even the opposition were supporting the policy because it was popular. After a moment's thought John replied, 'That you're a Tory.'

I prided myself on being a good and well-trained negotiator, but John Prescott could negotiate me into a cocked hat. Several times I had to agree with him what his ministerial portfolio would be and ended up conceding more than he had asked for in the first place, including before the 1997 election when we created a huge super-department for him. After the 2001 election, we wanted him to give up his ministry and settle for being just deputy prime minister. The Cabinet Secretary was not keen on having him rampaging around the Cabinet Office with nothing to do, but John wasn't having any of it anyway. Tony was in despair when I ended up conceding a large new department even after 2001.

John had a chip on his shoulder, as he recognised, and we had to spend a lot of time managing his feelings. The first mistake I made was arranging a secret strategy session in the country with Tony and Gordon and their teams in Opposition in 1995. I couldn't find anywhere else so we held it at my brother Chris's house in the New Forest. When John discovered he wasn't invited, he was furious.

He briefed my future brother-in-law, the journalist Toby Helm, for a front-page story in the *Sunday Telegraph* about having been excluded from the meeting in 'the Hunting Lodge' (a slightly odd description of my brother's house). From then on, we had to hold pretend strategy meetings to include him and then have the real ones later. John insisted on having one-on-one meetings with Tony every week and sulked if they were ever cancelled, but by 2002 he was getting fed up with them and complained to me that nothing ever happened as a result of their discussions. He was always feeling left out and complained about being excluded from the meetings of the Third Way Policy Network because he 'was not clever enough'.

John dreaded having to do PMQs in Tony's absence. He would start preparing at the beginning of the week and had huge teams in to help him. A good deal of the time was spent with him trying out attack lines on the assembled cast. Despite his worries, he would do very well and I would get Tony to call from abroad to congratulate him. His speech at the end of the Labour Party Conference was an annual event. Alastair used to help him write it, and he would take on board any jokes that we had decided were too offensive for Tony to use. He resented it when I had to tell him not to attack the CBI chair when he had made some derogatory comments about unions, and in 1998 he objected strenuously when I said that he had to take jokes about Peter Mandelson out of his speech, after he had famously compared Peter to a crab in a jar (to the crab's advantage).

A prudent prime minister would always have a John Prescott figure. The leader needs a deputy who can reach parts of the party that he cannot and who can help ensure loyalty in the Cabinet and more widely.

Because government is collective not absolute, leaders have to spend a lot of time meeting their colleagues and keeping them happy. In Opposition we had a weekly meeting of what we called the 'Big Guns', with Tony, John Prescott, Gordon Brown, Robin Cook and Tony's staff plus Peter Mandelson. They were fairly fraught occasions, given the relationships among those in the room, and they led to a good deal of door-slamming and drama, but they were essential to providing some agreement on the direction of the party. In government we abandoned the four-way sessions, but Tony had to see each of the participants separately pretty much every week.

It is also important to see loyalist ministers, and Tony would have regular sessions with John Reid, Alan Milburn, Tessa Jowell, David Blunkett and others, in part to reassure them that he was not giving in to Gordon. Of course, they didn't always get on with one another. In 2004, David Blunkett collaborated with the publication of a book in which he was exceedingly frank about what he thought of his colleagues. He was particularly harsh on Tessa Jowell, who had been extraordinarily kind and supportive of him. I noticed Tessa going into PMQs the following day with red and swollen eyes. When I got her to come and see Tony afterwards in his rooms behind the Speaker's chair, she burst into tears. David's comments had knocked her sideways. David sent her a huge bunch of flowers to try and make up.

As Machiavelli observed: 'To keep his Minister good, the Prince should be considerate of him, dignifying him, enriching him, binding him to himself by benefits, and sharing with him the honours as well as the burthens of the State, so that the abundant honours and wealth bestowed upon him may divert him from seeking them at other hands; while the great responsibilities wherewith he is charged may lead him to dread change, knowing that he cannot stand alone without his master's support. When Prince and Minister are upon this footing they can mutually trust one another; but when the contrary is the case, it will always fare ill with one or other of them.' A prime minister should give ministers a salary and a car and make them responsible for real work, but not let them be too independent. Sometimes they should be required to take the blame when things go wrong.

Cabinet members took a lot of managing. Anji Hunter, Sally Morgan, Ruth Turner and I would have to spend a good deal of time ringing round imparting some bit of news or eliciting opinions. Ministers were, naturally enough, very susceptible to believing negative stories in the newspapers about themselves. If such a story appeared, we would debate whether or not it was a good idea to call them to reassure them. If you didn't, they might be resentful; but, if you did, you might be drawing their attention to the report and making them believe it. Of course it was possible the story was true and that they were about to be sacked and you didn't want to lie to them. Anji Hunter called Chris Smith in November 2000 after a story that he was to be sacked. He was fairly phlegmatic, but I am not sure he believed the reassurance. In 2005, we had to call Charles Clarke after the historian and journalist Anthony Seldon had alleged that Tony thought he was 'a duffer'. It was untrue, and Charles took it perfectly cheerfully, having been a chief of staff to the leader of the party himself and knowing how such things worked. Jack Straw was very upset when it came out that Tony had offered his job to Gordon in June 2005, and, because it was true, there was not much we could do to reassure him.

As well as being solicitous of ministers, you also need to be ruthless with them. Machiavelli identified this problem in his time: 'As to how a Prince is to know his Minister, this unerring rule may be laid down. When you see a Minister thinking more of himself than of you, and in all his actions seeking his own ends, that man can never be a good Minister or one that you can trust. For he who has the charge of the State committed to him, ought not to think of himself, but only of his Prince, and should never bring to the notice of the latter what does not directly concern him.' All too often ministers are subject to self-absorption, and as Douglas Hurd observed rather coyly when announcing his intention to run for the leadership of the Tory Party after Mrs Thatcher stood down: 'We all think we have field marshals' batons in our knapsacks.'

Gerald Kaufman points to the two modern-day sins that ministers fall prey to almost the second they are appointed: 'ministerialitis' and 'departmentalitis'. When they acquire the first, they assume they have become a minister as the result of some unique virtue of their own rather than because their party won the election through the hard work of their party activists and fellow MPs. They lose interest in contact with other MPs and concentrate on their red boxes and ministerial cars and diaries rather than thinking about the politics that got them there and will be essential to keeping them there. That is someone else's job. The result of the second is that ministers think their job is to defend the interests of their department rather than those of the government as a whole. They will fight to the death to defend their budget and their agenda but do not think about the bigger picture. Ministers like to pander to their interest groups, whether they be farmers or the arts lobby, and they think there is very little benefit for them in standing up to such vested interests and promoting the overall good of the government.

Of course, finding a solution is harder than identifying the problem. Gerald Kaufman correctly says ministers need to remember that they are politicians and party members first. They should be ready to pay party visits in parallel to official visits in regional towns, and they should turn up to national policy forums and openly debate policies with their party colleagues. But it also requires the prime minister to bring the government together and make each member feel part of a common project. We would arrange for groups of junior ministers to meet Tony every other week so he could hear their views and give them pep talks. He normally recognised most of them. We arranged training sessions so that they had opportunities to get together and talk about the government's overall objectives. Cabinet ministers were also supposed to meet regularly with their ministerial teams, but it was amazing how few did so in practice. The best way of all to make the government unite, however, is to have an effective Opposition. Being under sustained attack can do remarkable things to bring ministers together and make them think collectively.

The purpose of government is to make things happen. However, actually making something happen is extremely difficult in a well-developed democratic system. Checks and balances are built in to prevent radical change, and among the most effective of the brakes is the Civil Service.

One of the first things a prudent prime minister has to do on coming to office is to capture civil servants' attention. Mrs Thatcher succeeded in doing so. A possibly apocryphal story is told about how, on her arrival in office, she asked for a paper on how to implement the Conservative Party's undertaking to privatise the British National Oil Company (BNOC). Several months later she was presented with a hundred-page 'submission', the curious expression used by the Civil Service to describe a memo going up the hierarchy, explaining why privatisation would be impossible. She sacked Ian Bancroft, the head of the Civil Service, and a few weeks later she received a much shorter submission explaining exactly how the BNOC could be privatised. I have no idea if the two events were connected or even if the story is really true, but, if it isn't, it should be.

We had a similar experience of the fatalism of the Civil Service soon after we arrived in Number 10. A Home Office team came to make a PowerPoint presentation to the prime minister in the Cabinet Room on crime, complete with multicoloured graphs showing that the crime rate would rise inexorably. When Tony asked why crime would rise, the officials replied that it was because the economy was growing and that put more temptations in the way of criminals. We scratched our heads. I asked the team what would happen if the economy were to go into recession. Without missing a beat, the officials replied that crime would rise because people would be deprived and more of them would have to resort to robbery to survive.

This deeply engrained fatalism is a serious problem in the upper reaches of the Civil Service. Having been a civil servant myself, it is easy to understand how it develops. When you have been wrestling with a problem for decades and you are familiar with how difficult it is to resolve, when you know there are no easy answers and are reconciled to failing again and again, it is difficult not to be cynical about the fresh-eyed, bushy-tailed aspirations of a new minister who knows next to nothing about the problem and whose 'new' policies are not new at all. It is this cynicism that gives rise to the *Yes, Prime Minister* parody of civil servants who, as the greatest possible criticism they can make, tell the minister that the course of action he proposes would be 'very brave'. It is a culture where the word brave is a warning rather than praise.

Now it is the job of civil servants to warn their ministers of the elephant traps into which they are about to walk. They have the experience, and they know where the traps lie, unlike their minister, and they should be listened to carefully. But from a minister's point of view their negativism can become tiresome. He looks for a can-do spirit which instead of incessantly pointing out the difficulties, will come up with solutions. It was for this reason that Tony Blair famously spoke about bearing 'the scars on my back' in a speech in Islington in 1999. He had come into office promising action and found himself banging his head against a brick wall of difficulties. Thinking the thought was understandable, but saying it out loud wasn't wise. You need the civil servants to help you implement your promises, and attacking them simply makes them defensive rather than more willing to take risks.

The system is stacked against civil servants who might want to get things done. There is very little upside gain for an individual official who succeeds in resolving a problem and a huge downside risk for permitting something to go wrong. We tried to change this blame culture in the context of our plans to cut back on red tape. As things stand, no civil servant gets praised in their annual report for removing a piece of unnecessary bureaucracy that complicates life for teachers or for businessmen, but if they scrap an existing regulation and as a result disaster strikes, then they will take all the blame. Newspapers will campaign to know why the regulation was relaxed that allowed paedophiles to get into schools, or reduced fire precautions at work leading to many deaths, or whatever the rule was. The accusation against the Blair government that it introduced a 'nanny state' is extraordinarily unfair. We tried hard to give civil servants an individual incentive to scrap unnecessary rules and to protect them in the event they were blamed for having got rid of them. We even considered 'regulation budgets' for departments so they would not be allowed to introduce new regulations without scrapping old ones, but our efforts had few noticeable results. The accretion of regulation upon regulation seems to be almost irresistible. Unless a war or revolution sweeps them away, you are stuck with the gradual furring up of the system, which the economist Mancur Olson called 'sclerosis'.

It is not just the mindset of civil servants that is the problem: it is also the skill set. The upper reaches of the Civil Service are still staffed with policy advisers when what is needed are project managers. I remember my boss in the Foreign Office in 1989, John Fretwell, telling me with horror that the Permanent Undersecretary now expected him to take responsibility for a budget and for the personnel under his jurisdiction; he said it was like asking a brain surgeon to become a hospital administrator. He was not alone in taking this attitude to the role that civil servants should play.

A prudent leader would introduce a new bargain whereby the government reduced the number of civil servants substantially, kept the best ones, ensured that they had the right skills and paid them properly. Such a policy would come under fierce attack from the *Daily Mail*, which used to weigh in every time we appointed a highly paid expert to run a failing part of the bureaucracy, complaining about the waste of taxpayers' money. Actually, employing an outsider to sort out the Immigration and Nationality Division in the Home Office would save the taxpayer massively more than even a £1 million annual salary.

The Civil Service is akin to a monastic order, where people still enter on leaving university and leave on retirement. Their attitudes change slowly, and their powers of passive resistance are legendary. Part of the answer is to open it up. We introduced five-year contracts after which civil servants have to compete for new jobs inside or outside the system, but there is still very little interchange with the outside world and it is still too much a cradle-to-grave career. There should be an assumption that a civil servant will leave the public sector after one or two five-year terms and work outside. Outsiders should be actively recruited to work for short stints in the Civil Service. Again, the issue of pay would need to be addressed. To attract outsiders into the service, higher salaries would need to be paid, and to persuade civil servants to go outside, Civil Service pensions should be more comparable to private sector ones, i.e. lower.

Individual named civil servants should be made responsible for particular projects so that they can be held accountable and be empowered to get them done. They should be rewarded if they succeed and take the blame if they fail, instead of everyone just blaming the system. The silo structure of departments gets in the way of making things happen and it would be better to try and get away from it by building time-limited cross-departmental teams around solutions to problems with their own budgets. Such teams could be disbanded once the problem has been resolved.

These are not new ideas, but they desperately need someone to be brave enough to put them into place. It may not matter to a Conservative administration which wants government to do little, but for a progressive party that wants government to change things it is essential to reform the system.

We repeatedly looked for new ways of making things actually happen in the real world as opposed to on paper. We tried to use crisis management skills invented for tackling a foreign policy crisis or a terrorist attack to resolve practical problems in domestic policy. To deal with an upsurge in knife crime, in March 2002 Tony opened up COBR, bringing together the police, the courts service, the Home

Office and all the other bodies that needed to cooperate, so that the problem could be addressed with the same sense of urgency as if it were a foreign crisis. By removing the bureaucratic barriers between departments, it paid off and produced a rapid reduction in attacks.

After the 2001 election we made one innovation to the system that significantly improved our chances of getting things done. In the first term Michael Barber had been a successful special adviser to David Blunkett in the Department of Education, introducing numeracy and literacy hours into primary schools. He asked to come and see me during the election campaign, and we met in the coffee shop at the foot of Millbank Tower. He put to me the idea of creating a new unit that would ensure that the top priorities of the government were actually implemented rather than remaining on paper. After the frustrations of our first term, I could immediately see the attractions of the idea and put it to Tony, who launched it at a press conference during the campaign. After the election, we set about creating a prime minister's Delivery Unit staffed with bright young McKinseyites. We set it a series of specific, concrete targets, like ensuring the punctuality of rail journeys, reducing waiting times in the NHS and reducing crime levels in particular categories of crime. It was their job to monitor the departments' efforts to meet these targets and ensure their full implementation according to the timetable we had set. They operated a traffic-light system so that the prime minister or ministers could see at once from their regular presentations whether or not we were on target to meet our goals.

A key element in making the Delivery Unit a success was giving it the personal authority of the prime minister. Although it wasn't housed in Downing Street, it reported directly to him, and ministers knew he cared about its work. That made them and their senior civil servants pay attention. Another was adopting a collaborative approach with departments rather than being perceived by them as threatening. Michael made it clear from the beginning that they were there to help ministries resolve interdepartmental problems that were blocking progress. If they needed a regulation removed or more money from the Treasury, then the Delivery Unit could help to secure it. The Delivery Unit would work through stocktake meetings with departments in the cabinet room every two or three months. Tony would be in the chair, and all the top civil servants and ministers from the department concerned would attend. They would last two or three hours, starting with a presentation by the Delivery Unit on where we stood on each target and what needed to be changed to make sure that we met them. Tony would worry away at the details until he was satisfied that the problems had been resolved and then set out what needed to be done over the next three months.

These systems only work if they are confined to a handful of targets. You cannot run the whole government in this way. The targets need to be concrete and measurable, not just aspirations, like better education for five-year-olds. Within those constraints a Delivery Unit can make a real difference in ensuring that at least some promises are implemented in practice, and now the idea is spreading around the world as other governments realise the importance of producing results if they want to maintain public support.

But no such scheme will transform the ability of government to deliver unless the Civil Service changes, and that requires a new approach to its management. The Cabinet Secretary should have management control of the Permanent Secretaries of the departments. He should be able to set their objectives and rewards, move them between departments and manage the senior Civil Service down at least three grades below the top. But at present he cannot. Senior officials' bonuses are set by an independent assessor, they report to their Cabinet ministers, and the weekly meetings of Permanent Secretaries are dignified senior-common-room chats about the failings of ministers rather than operational discussions of how to make sure that the government's priorities are implemented. In 1997, it was put as a serious proposition to Tony that he should promote a Permanent Secretary who had been a disastrous failure in order to remove him from his department. That is still too often the approach to failure in the Civil Service. When we insisted instead that he should be sacked, it took the Civil Service two years and cost some millions of pounds. There should be no reason in the modern world why you should not be able to sack someone who is incompetent even if they are a civil servant.

We wanted successive Cabinet Secretaries to focus on the task of reform but they kept slipping back into policymaking and crisis management because that was what they had been trained to do and was what they found interesting. Andrew Turnbull made a noble effort at starting to move the Cabinet Secretary's job in this direction, but had difficulty gaining the support of the other Permanent Secretaries. Gus O'Donnell, the first modern Cabinet Secretary in my view, with more sinuous political skills, has begun to get a grip of the system, but it will take more than one person to make the centre of British government effective. It would help if an outsider was brought in to shake up the Civil Service as a genuine chief executive devoted full-time to managing it rather than dabbling part-time in policy and ethics.

One demonstration of the ability of the Civil Service to resist change was the opposition they mounted to the idea of the recruitment of an outsider for the job of Cabinet Secretary when Richard Wilson retired. We proposed there should be an open competition so that outsiders as well as insiders could apply but Richard was opposed. Richard proposed that he interview all the applicants and put up a shortlist of two. It was, he said, the only way to settle down the Civil Service. We had a shrewd idea of who he wanted to fill the post, while we wanted a reformer. We counterproposed splitting his job into two, one the traditional Cabinet Secretary and the other a new CEO for the Civil Service. Richard agreed but kept a close grip on the process to ensure that it didn't really happen. I managed to sneak Michael Bichard in to see Tony as a possible candidate. Michael was Permanent Secretary at the Department of Education, but he was seen by the Civil Service as an outsider because he had previously been a local government chief executive rather than working his way up the Civil Service hierarchy. When Tony revealed to Richard that he had seen Michael, Richard flew off the handle and spoke in intemperate language he later regretted: Number 10 was a mess, we were trying to interfere in the work of all the departments, we needed to return to collective government. Tony gave as good as he got, and Richard retreated through the green baize door (actually now an electronic door controlled by a swipe card) to the Cabinet Office. Tony thought the outburst had arisen because Richard detected political weakness in Tony's position, but I thought he had been wound up by the other Permanent Secretaries who always gave him a hard time. Richard saw off our idea of an outsider as head of the Civil Service in a way Machiavelli would have been proud of, but a prudent prime minister would return to the idea and insist on it if they really wanted to shake up the Civil Service.

Gerald Kaufman described the Cabinet Office as a Ferrari compared with the lumbering Humbers of the departments of state like the Home Office or the Department of the Environment. If so, it is now a very ancient and dilapidated Ferrari. Despite more than a decade we spent trying, the Cabinet Office is still not a command, control and communications centre for the government as a whole, and some in the Civil Service do not accept that it should be. They think it should be a referee between departments ensuring fair play and a way of brokering agreements between departments. The trouble with this attitude is that it leads to a lowest common denominator approach. The government can only do what no department objects to, rather than the centre of government setting an objective and the Cabinet Office coordinating efforts to achieve it.

I got into trouble while we were in Opposition for suggesting that we wanted to move from a feudal to a Napoleonic system. I had agreed to brief an off-the-record seminar of constitutional academics and civil servants chaired by Peter Hennessy, and someone unkindly leaked my words to the press. The tabloids, with their vestigial hatred of 'old Boney', managed to translate what I thought was my subtle argument into the suggestion I wanted us to be more French, but I think my analogy still holds good. The British system of government is traditionally a feudal system of barons (Cabinet ministers) who have armies and funds (civil servants and budgets), who pay fealty to their liege but really get on with whatever they want to do. There is very little that the prime minister can do to make the government consistent or coherent. The only weapon he has in his armoury, a very blunt one, is hiring and firing people. My proposition was that, if the New Labour government was going to succeed in delivering, we couldn't rely on the old ways. We needed to have greater coordination at the centre on both policy development and implementation.

Machiavelli likewise saw two alternative systems: 'A sole Prince, all others being his servants permitted by his grace and favour to assist in governing the kingdom as his ministers; or else, by a Prince with his Barons who hold their rank, not by the favour of a superior Lord, but by antiquity of blood, and who have States and subjects of their own who recognise them as their rulers and entertain for them a natural affection.' He drew a contrast: 'States governed by a sole Prince and by his servants vest in him a more complete authority; because throughout the land none but he is recognised as sovereign, and if obedience be yielded to any others, it is yielded to his ministers and officers for whom personally no special love is felt', whereas, in the French system, 'The King of France, on the other hand, is surrounded by a multitude of nobles of ancient descent, each acknowledged and loved by subjects of his own, and each asserting a precedence in rank of which the king can deprive him only at his peril'. In his view, the former system is much more efficient if you want to get things done. It was in this sense that I wanted more central drive, and the point of the Cabinet Office was to provide the transmission system between the will of the centre of government and what departments actually do.

One of the problems in doing this, of course, is that Number 10 and the Cabinet Office are not the entirety of the centre of government. There is also the Treasury, and the Treasury decides the budgets and sets their own targets for departments. The power at the centre is split, and the two parts often contradict each other, allowing departments to play them off one against the other. I therefore proposed in January 1998 that we create an Office of Management and the Budget at the centre of government modelled on the American system and those existing in a number of other European governments. The public spending part of the Treasury would be split off, leaving behind a Ministry of Finance, and joined with the management functions of the Cabinet Office. That would produce effective machinery at the centre of government uniting financial and management objectives instead of having Number 10 and the Treasury setting rival and conflicting targets for government. The Office would be headed by a powerful Chief Secretary in Cabinet.

We didn't push the idea at the time, mainly because it would have led to a fight to the death with Gordon Brown who was busy turning the Treasury into a giant Policy Unit of his own, and he would never have surrendered control of public spending. We returned to it in 2005, however, and the Cabinet Secretary did some initial work on how the split in the Treasury could take place, but again we shelved it for fear of pouring petrol on our simmering dispute with Gordon Brown. I understand that Gordon Brown and Ed Balls looked at the idea again themselves once they took control of the government but didn't pursue it. In calmer times, a prudent prime minister would revisit the idea if he wants to make government more effective.

Because of the weakness of the Cabinet Office, we looked on a number of occasions during Tony's decade in power at creating a separate Department of the Prime Minister. There is an argument for the prime minister having a larger office, with a proper staff and budget, capable of taking on departments in argument, but when we first considered the idea in February 1999 Richard Wilson threatened to resign. Fearing we were trying to create one by the back door, he went even further the next month by refusing to allow us to appoint any more staff to Number 10. Two years later, prior to the 2001 election, Richard himself proposed that we merge the Cabinet Office and the Prime Minister's Office into one department so that he would become my boss and the rest of Number 10 would be integrated into the different divisions of the Cabinet Office. He went round Downing Street interviewing people about who would stay and who would go after the election. Tony never took this proposal seriously, and was more focused on a radical paper on a Prime Minister's Office drawn up by John Birt who had become a strategy adviser in Number 10, but he neglected to tell Richard who worked up a grand scheme of his own. Eventually, it was left to me to break the news to him of what we were really going to do after the 2001 election, and he did not react well, particularly to the notion that we move the heads of the European and Foreign Policy secretariats of the Cabinet Office into Number 10 and make them also the prime minister's advisers. He said it was a perversion of the constitution. But, once he got over the shock of his own ideas being rejected, he did come round to the concept.

The relationship between Number 10 and the Cabinet Secretary is often fraught. The Cabinet Secretary wants to become the prime minister's closest adviser, but the prime minister doesn't always want that, and if the Cabinet Secretary feels excluded from meetings it can rankle, and naturally enough he blames the chief of staff for keeping him out. Richard had made his career by making himself useful to Mrs Thatcher as a deputy secretary in the Cabinet Office, and he then became indispensible to Michael Howard as Energy Secretary, so much so that Howard took him with him as Permanent Secretary when he was reshuffled to the Home Office. When Richard succeeded Robin Butler, he thought that Robin had allowed himself to become too distant from Number 10 and he wanted to play the role for Tony that he had for Thatcher and Howard, but Tony wanted him deployed elsewhere. Finally, this rejection got to be too much for him, and in 2001 we had to deal with a heartfelt outburst about how Alastair Campbell had been briefing the press against him. I liked Richard and admired his political and bureaucratic skills, and I had not seen this outburst coming. We later paid a price by incurring his lasting enmity. This tension underlines the need for a prime minister to put his relationship with his Cabinet Secretary on a clear footing from the beginning so that he is not disappointed and resentment does not build up. For a Cabinet Secretary, as Richard's successors realised, the secret is that if you do not try to force yourself on the prime minister, then it is more likely rather than less that they will seek your advice and support. As Machiavelli put it, 'men are more inclined to throw themselves on your lap the more averse you appear to be to have them there'.

As for Number 10, although I could see the argument for more muscle inside Downing Street, I was always opposed to the creation of a large prime minister's department. In 2001, a young member of the German Kanzleramt, the centre of the German government, joined us for a month and did a study of Number 10 for the German government in order to pick up lessons for the reforms they were considering. He came to see me before he went back to Berlin and said that the one thing we should never do was imitate the German system. The Kanzleramt is huge, divided into different functional departments with many layers. It replicates the whole system of German government in miniature, in part because coalition governments require intensive co-ordination on every policy front. As a result it is ossified, slow and overly bureaucratic. Number 10 has the advantage of small size, personal contact and nimbleness. It would be a terrible thing to sacrifice that.

A prudent prime minister should always realise that Number 10 is, in the end, a court and not the HQ of a multinational corporation.

CHAPTER FOUR

'That Flatterers Should be Shunned'
The Court

All leaders are surrounded by courts, in business and NGOs as much as in politics, even if they are called something different in the modern world. The nature and organisation of the court is crucial to their ability to lead. One of the key dangers a leader must avoid is '*pensée unique*', a consensus where everyone in the inner circle is of one opinion and no one questions the leader.

Machiavelli says, 'One error into which Princes, unless very prudent or very fortunate in their choice of friends, are apt to fall, is of so great importance that I must not pass it over. I mean in respect of flatterers. These abound in courts, because men take such pleasure in their own concerns, and so deceive themselves with regard to them, that they can hardly escape this plague.' Machiavelli argues that in resisting the temptations of flattery a prince must show that he is not afraid of hearing the truth.

He therefore gives advice that holds good to this day, saying that 'a prudent Prince should follow a middle course, by choosing certain discreet men from among his subjects, and allowing them alone free leave to speak their minds on any matter on which he asks their opinion, and on none other. But he ought to ask their opinion on everything, and after hearing what they have to say, should reflect and judge for himself.' It is important 'that each and all of them may know that the more freely they declare their thoughts the better they will be liked'.

I used to laugh when the press suggested that Tony was surrounded by 'yes men'. I doubt there was ever an occupant of Number 10 less prone to flattery. In fact, if anything, the danger was that Alastair Campbell and I and some of the others were too robust in making fun of Tony to his face, to the extent of undermining his confidence from time to time. The crucial bargain was that, however rude we were in private, however strongly we argued for a particular course of action, once the decision was made we would all tuck in behind it and not express a word of disagreement in public or indeed outside the inner circle. Frank advice will only be welcomed or accepted if it is given entirely in private. If it is repeated in public, it undermines the unity of purpose of the government in pursuing a particular course and attracts contempt for the leader – the very worst thing in Machiavelli's view that can happen. Loyalty and confidentiality are therefore the first requirement of any member of a court. If that is ever in doubt, those courtiers are of no further use.

Machiavelli argues in *The Discourses* that the aim should be to ensure that the prince's 'reputation was greater than his strength', and in *The Prince* he advises that the prince should strive 'to bear himself so that greatness, courage, wisdom, and strength may appear in all his actions'. A leader must then be seen in public to be a superman, although of course he is an ordinary mortal like anyone else. It is the job of the court to make him appear other than he really is. In fulfilling this task I was always reminded of the scene in *The Wizard of Oz* when Dorothy finally meets the 'great and powerful Oz', who is capable of solving all the problems of his people. Merely to be in his presence is terrifying. When Dorothy's dog Toto pulls back the curtain hiding the great wizard by mistake, Oz is revealed to be an ordinary old man from Kansas. Our job as courtiers was to stop the curtain from being pulled back and to keep the bellows and pulleys going so that the myth of the great and all powerful leader was maintained.

A prime minister is therefore never allowed to be sick. Tony as a result had to give speeches with a sore throat that made speaking in a normal voice almost intolerable, and we had to find strong anaesthetics so that he could speak at all. He had to carry on with foreign trips although half dead with flu and having to be propped up. He fought the 2005 election not just with a recalcitrant Gordon Brown making his life a misery but with an inflamed disc in his back. He could not stand up straight, and his face grimaced with pain. I phoned him early on in the campaign unaware of the disc and told him to stop limping. He got quite short with me and explained his predicament.

The job of the prime minister's close staff is to be a barrier between his anger and fear, and the rest of the world. When he is panicked you cannot let on to even his wider office or despondency will rapidly spread. Just as dogs can smell fear, if a leader lets his doubts seep out, his opponents will attack and savage him. But leaders need people to whom they can express their inner concerns. Mrs Thatcher for example confided in Crawfie, her dresser.

Anji Hunter and Sally Morgan, two strong women, provided Tony with a reassuring antidote to Alastair's and my own abrasiveness, and they took on much of the burden of sitting in the den listening to him complain and building him up. They knew his wishes and could convey them confidentially to ministers and others. Anji was a friend from his teenage years who had joined him as an aide when he became an MP. She could silkily deal with Cabinet members and journalists on his behalf and sat in almost endless sessions with Tony and Alastair in the early years, giving him counsel and succour. Sally was an experienced, modernising, Labour Party official who helped keep Tony's compass pointing in the right direction inside the party. She knew her way through all the factions. One of the comic duties that both had to deal with was Tony's habit of asking repeatedly what was happening on an election day from eight o'clock in the morning onwards. Since the polls had only just opened, there was no way of knowing what was happening, so they took to making up formulaic answers, such as 'It is sunny in Birmingham so there will be a good turnout in the key swing West Midlands seats.' He never seemed to get wise to the fact that the answers were pure invention.

Prime ministers get used to their staff and have a tendency to try to keep them on when they ought to go or even when they want to go. Tony put a huge effort into trying to persuade Anji not to leave No 10 after the 2001 election. She relented for a few months but it was a mistake, and she sensibly insisted on leaving in the end. It is good to have a turnover of staff and fresh blood coming in, but leaders grow familiar with the people around them and they don't like change. They should be persuaded in most cases to relax their grip on people.

I decided in Opposition that it would be necessary to create the position of a chief of staff in government after studying previous Number 10s. Under John Major and his predecessors, there was no one below the prime minister who brought together all the different parts of the office, and the prime minister himself had to arbitrate between competing factions. It led to an unseemly competition on Friday nights to get the last note on some vexed subject into the prime minister's red box. The head of the Policy Unit and the political secretary, both political appointees, would try to add memos on top of the policy papers, and the PPS and the Cabinet Secretary, both civil servants, would stay late to ensure they could have the last word on top of that of the political part of the office. Number 10 needs someone who can coordinate the political and the Civil Service sides, the press and policy, and the domestic and foreign. As a political appointee who had been a civil servant and a former diplomat now focusing on domestic politics I had a foot in both camps.

The title chief of staff comes from the United States, but the job exists in most Western democracies. The chief of staff in the Elysée is a very grand figure, almost a prime minister, sitting in the corner office of the Palace. In Germany the chief of staff is crucial in keeping the eternal coalition government going by chairing the meeting of deputies prior to the Cabinet itself to remove disagreements between the two parties. It is a full time job, and I remember Frank Walter Steinmeier, Schroeder's chief of staff, opening a cupboard door in his office when we first met in Bonn to show me the bed where he slept most nights because he couldn't go home. Downing Street was definitely not the West Wing, although *The West Wing* came to Downing Street in 2002. John Spencer, the actor playing the White House chief of staff Leo McGarry in the series, asked to come and see me. I was suspicious, but his agent assured me that the visit wouldn't be used for publicity, so I agreed. In preparation, I watched a DVD of the show, which I had never seen before. Spencer was charming, and we had a chat about the pressures of our jobs, mine real and his fictional. He asked for a photo together and we had it taken in front of the fireplace in Tony's den. Predictably enough, they used the photo in a PR release, although they scarcely needed more publicity.

The chief of staff must have the prime minister's complete confidence and that can only come with time. The natural fear of anyone in that position is going out on a limb and having it sawn off behind him. I found it particularly difficult at first when I did not have Tony's full trust. In 1998, I was telephoned by Michael Levy, the chief party fund-raiser, who told me I was about to be sacked. It was late at night and I didn't know what to do, but my partner, Sarah, suggested I go and see Alastair, a neighbour, and so we gathered up our newborn baby and went to consult him. He was mildly reassuring, and when I spoke to Tony the next day he said he had no intention of sacking me. Even so, the scare made me anxious for months. Like any courtier, you fall out of favour from time to time, and looking back at my diary it is embarrassing to see how often I was on the verge of resigning. The leader naturally wants to keep his courtiers from becoming overconfident and so plays off one against another, and courtiers have to learn to live with that.

It is not possible to do the job properly if you are constantly worrying about your back. I came to understand that it was inevitable that some of my decisions would be reversed by the prime minister, and I noted in my diary in 2004 that it is crucial that a chief of staff does not mind being countermanded by his boss. It is his job to absorb pain. On a number of occasions, I sacked members of staff or outside advisers at Tony's request only to have them reinstated after they appealed to Tony.

At first I travelled incessantly with Tony when he went abroad as a manifestation of my own insecurity. Tony used to try to throw me off the plane and send me back to Downing Street, saying I was a curious mixture of self-doubt and overconfidence and he and Alastair would tease me mercilessly. Over time I realised that he was right, as I used to find myself spending my whole time on trips on the mobile phone sorting out problems back in London, so I increasingly remained in place as he travelled unless there was an important negotiation I could be involved in. One well-deserved cause of mockery was my decision to have an official box made up with the title 'Chief of Staff to the Prime Minister' emblazoned on it. Alex Allan had told me that all Principal Private Secretaries had such boxes and suggested I have one too. On its first outing on a foreign trip, however, it led to such utter humiliation at the hands of Tony and Alastair that on return I stuffed it under my desk and it remained there gathering dust for the following ten years.

Gradually you become intimate with the leader. In the morning when Alastair and I would go up to Tony's flat, I would be reminded of a levee in Louis XIV's Versailles. We watched Tony eat breakfast more times than I care to remember, and often he would issue instructions when in his bath or with me passing him his shirt in his dressing room. My brother had had a similar experience, having his breakfast regularly cooked for him by Mrs Thatcher in the Number 10 flat while she issued her instructions. You listen in to most of the leader's phone calls with Cabinet members and foreign leaders. Tony could never get the hang of this. When I would refer to something from one of those conversations, he would look stunned. At the beginning he tried to stop officials being patched in to calls, particularly those with Gordon, and he tried to make his own phone calls without going through 'switch', the Number 10 switchboard. But he got used to it. As prime minister, you live your whole life in a goldfish bowl. I never, however, became a friend. A chief of staff needs to maintain a certain distance from the principal so that he can have at least some objectivity. In fact, as Machiavelli observes, it is very difficult for leaders to have real friends or to maintain those friendships that pre-exist their coming to office.

You obviously need to trust one another. One of the penalties of working on Northern Ireland was that I had to have a bomb alarm fitted to my car. It almost never worked properly and would go off for no reason, but it was difficult to be blasé about it, and I always had a frisson of fear and a tingling in my legs when I turned on the engine after the alarm had sounded. One Saturday afternoon in 1999 I had taken my family for a walk in Regent's Park, and when we got back to the car and opened the door the alarm sounded. I scrabbled around on my knees looking under the car but couldn't see anything unusual. The choice was either to risk it or wait several hours for the bomb squad to turn up. I was for starting the engine straight away, but Sarah didn't agree. I decided to call Robbie, Tony's driver, who understood the workings of the alarm mechanism. Unfortunately, he was driving Tony down to Chequers, so I had to talk to him through Tony on his mobile phone in the back of the armour-plated Jag. Robbie told me to check various lights, which I did, but Tony soon got bored of relaying instructions and said he thought it would probably be all right and rang off. I got my family to stand a few hundred yards away and then started the engine. Nothing happened. Tony called a few minutes later to see if I had blown myself up.

Over time I grew to think a bit like Tony and even inherited his hand-me-down shirts and ties. Unfortunately, I couldn't take his suits. In Opposition, he once spilled some tea on himself just before appearing onstage and we had to swap suits. He was fine, but I was left with three inches of calf exposed to the wind because his legs were so much shorter than mine. I used to think that in my brother's time in Number 10 he grew to look increasingly like Mrs Thatcher and his hair became whiter and more bouffant. Maybe just as dogs grow to look like their owners, advisers come to look as well as think like their bosses.

It is crucial that a chief of staff comes to know the leader's mind and can make lesser decisions for him. I was a point of contact for ministers and senior civil servants, and of course the staff of Number 10, when they needed a decision taken rapidly. I got to know when I could safely speak on the prime minister's behalf and when I needed to nobble him as he came out of the den between meetings and get an instant decision from him, or when I should hold off for a proper discussion later. That is one of the reasons it was a mistake for Gordon Brown to abolish the job of chief of staff when he became prime minister — as another way of differentiating himself from his predecessor. The absence of someone who could make decisions gummed up the whole system.

Of course I made mistakes. When Mike Jackson retired as Chief of the General Staff, the MoD sent over to Number 10 the CV of his proposed successor, asking for the prime minister's agreement. Tony's foreign policy and defence adviser Nigel Sheinwald came to see me and we agreed that it wasn't worth consulting Tony about such a trivial subject, and Nigel wrote back to the MoD agreeing to the appointment on the basis of Mike Jackson's recommendation. A few months later we faced a serious problem with the new Chief, Richard Dannat, when he chose to attack the government through the pages of the *Daily Mail* while we were in St Andrews engaged in crucial Northern Ireland peace talks. Tony complained about him to me, and I, forgetting what had happened earlier, said that it was his fault as he had appointed him. He denied that he had and said he had never been consulted. I went back to the files and discovered that he was right and had to confess to Tony.

I made plenty of other blunders too, especially in the early years. At the time of Princess Diana's death in 1997 I was staying in rural Dorset, out of range of mobile phone signals. I drove up to Eggardon Hill to take a walk with friends, leaving my briefcase full of confidential papers in the boot of the car. I noticed two likely lads eyeing us as we parked but didn't think much about them. When we came back, the car had been broken into and my briefcase was gone. I called the security people in Number 10, and they told me I needed to go and see Special Branch in Dorchester. It was news to me that there was a Special Branch in Dorchester, but I drove there and an officer saw me through a little window at the side of the police station. He took notes. He appeared not to be entirely certain where 10 Downing Street was and then asked me if there was anything people would have noticed as we got out of the car. I said, yes, the woman with me was pregnant. He asked, so that would be your wife? I said no, she was my partner. He wrote that down slowly and deliberately. Was there anything else? I said yes, there were two other women and their children with us. He paused and asked if they were with their husbands. I said no, they were a lesbian couple from Hollywood. At this point he gave up. Special Branch sent the Dorset constabulary to scour the fields but we never recovered the briefcase or the papers. The incident gave me a certain sympathy for all those exhausted civil servants who are crucified for unintentionally leaving briefcases full of secret papers on the train.

Peter Mandelson jokingly described my role as being that of 'Jeeves'. There is something to that. It is not just the shoe polishing and waiting at table, but the job is also to help the master out of scrapes and to think ahead. He will listen to your advice because he knows your loyalties are undivided and the advice that you give is private and is given exclusively in his interest. I used to write occasional notes to Tony on particularly thorny issues from Iraq to managing Gordon, giving him a different view from the conventional wisdom he was receiving from officials and ministers. Having looked back at the notes in the files, some of them were remarkably prescient and others, unfortunately, plain daft. Tony once complained to me that I was writing them for posterity, but I wasn't. The aim was to ensure that the formal advice he received was challenged. My tuppenceworth was not always gratefully received and sometimes I must have been infuriating. I would put provocative points to Tony and he would roundly insult me in return, but I couldn't help noticing that he was absorbing them anyway, and sometimes the suggestions would pop up later in speeches or in his conversations with ministers.

It helps for the chief of staff not to have a huge, or very obvious, ego − it gets in the way − nor to crave the limelight. For my first few years in Downing Street, the press didn't have my photograph. Instead, they would include a mysterious black silhouette alongside any story they ran, or a photo of another Jonathan Powell, the famous TV producer. Eventually Anji insisted that I have a photo taken by the Press Association, but I wish I hadn't. It is only possible to do the job properly from behind the arras. You must be able to move silently if you are to carry out confidential tasks and you do not want yet another actor on the stage.

It is also desirable that Number 10 staff should not be directly answerable to Parliament. There was a precedent that protected staff from appearing before select committees which helped my brother, for example, during the Westland Helicopters scandal that led to the resignation of Michael Heseltine from Mrs Thatcher's government in 1986. Unfortunately, Alastair Campbell killed this off by volunteering to appear before the Foreign Affairs Select Committee during the Gilligan row. I tried to persuade him not to do it, but he dismissed my opposition by saying it was just because I was afraid of appearing before the committee myself. A prudent prime minister would re-establish the precedent. The public sparring should be left to elected politicians rather than courtiers, who should not be turned into political figures.

Some back-room boys aren't satisfied with remaining in the back room, however, and want to go on stage in their own right. As Machiavelli put it, 'nature has so constituted men that, though all things are objects of desire, not all things are attainable; so that desire always exceeds the power of attainment, with the result that men are ill content with what they possess and their present state brings them little satisfaction'. It is usually a mistake to make the transition from back-room boy to onstage performer because the skills required for the two roles are very different. Ed Balls, for example, who as a back-room operator was extremely effective (in the Cesare Borgia sense), was awkward onstage. The other strange phenomenon in this respect is that those who are good at giving advice to others often seem unable to follow the advice themselves when they go onstage, sometimes with disastrous consequences. As I noted to myself in 1997, 'If you want to do this job don't start looking for your name in the indexes of books', or think your part will be played by a movie star when the film is made of events.

The main skill needed for the job is the ability to keep a very large number of balls in the air at the same time and not to allow even one of them to fall to the ground. My rule of thumb was that six simultaneous crises were manageable but the seventh would usually prove too much. I used to sit at my desk surrounded by TV screens with different news channels on, with the Press Association news tape streaming across the bottom of my computer screen and endless emails and phone calls coming in with requests and problems from intelligence on troop movements in Serbia to a decision on whether ministerial Jaguars should be replaced with BMWs. It felt like being a first mate on a supertanker, scanning the horizon and avoiding small boats while steering the course set by the captain. You are constantly on duty. Sarah could tell when I was nearly home because the phones would start ringing five minutes before I got there. Evenings and weekends were the same as weekdays, except that you were at home rather than in the office. You were answering the phone or dealing with faxes, trying to joggle small children with one hand while your mobile was pressed to your ear with the other. When I started in Number 10, I would work regularly from seven in the morning to eleven at night, but unless you are planning to spend a very short time in the job that is not a good idea. I watched successive White House chiefs of staff wipe themselves out within months by trying to work from 5 a.m. to 10 p.m. every day. You cannot take rational decisions if you are tired the whole time. My advice to future chiefs of staff would be to pace themselves, to get enough sleep and aim for a marathon rather than a sprint.

A can-do spirit is necessary. It is not the job of the chief of staff to tell the prime minister why something can't be done. He has a whole Civil Service to do that. The chief of staff is supposed to make his wishes come true, but it is important to avoid being too literal in implementing the prime minister's instructions. I always had in front of me the example of a distant ancestor who had rushed to put his master's instructions into practice too precipitously. That was Sir Hugh de Morville, one of the four knights who took Henry II's words at face value when he said: 'What miserable drones and traitors have I nourished and brought up in my household who let their lord be treated with such shameful contempt by a low-born cleric.' The four rushed off to murder Thomas à Becket in Canterbury Cathedral as they thought their master wanted them to do but then found themselves denounced. Morville was sent by the Pope to do penance fighting with the Crusaders and is buried under the floor of the al-Aqsa Mosque in Jerusalem. It is always better to stop and think before you carry out the leader's more intemperate instructions too quickly, at least until they have had an opportunity for second thoughts.

Political leaders are, as a rule, pretty hopeless at management. They have a tendency to appoint two or three people to the same job and to forget that they have asked one person to carry out a particular task and then to ask another to do it as well. They are not always good at personnel judgements, and many of our choices of people for senior jobs over the years were mistakes. If possible, the chief of staff should relieve his boss of any management responsibilities and leave him to concentrate on setting a vision, deciding policies and making speeches.

It is also the job of the chief of staff to break bad news to the prime minister. Tony used to accuse me of taking great relish in this task and said I had a particular look in my eyes whenever I came to tell him of some terrible development. I remember approaching him with Alastair in 1998 in the corridor at Number 10 just as he came out of the Gents with the news about Peter Mandelson's loan from Geoffrey Robinson, which led to the resignation of both of them. As often with bad news, it took some time for it to sink in. We usually had to go back into the den, cancel other meetings and explore the full ramifications.

From time to time the problem arises of bad news arriving late at night. Andy Card, George W. Bush's chief of staff, told me that he used to go to sleep with his BlackBerry on his chest set on vibrate, so that if it rang it would not wake his wife. And John Podesta, Clinton's chief of staff, told me that his problem was not having to wake Clinton but being woken by the president in the middle of the night. He would want to chat about something he had just seen on the cable network C-SPAN or about something he had read. In Downing Street, we had pretty efficient machinery for deciding when to wake Tony, but occasionally it would go wrong. In 1999, the Number 10 duty clerk decided on her own initiative to wake Tony to tell him that a plane had been hijacked by Afghan refugees and was coming in to land at Stansted. He really didn't need to be woken for something he could not influence, and he spent the next day grumpily complaining to me. There is an increasing tendency to wake leaders just so that their press spokesmen can tell the media the next day that they have been woken rather than because they need to be. My advice would be to let sleeping leaders lie wherever you can. They don't get enough sleep as it is.

The most important task of a chief of staff is saying 'no'. Politicians always like to say 'yes', and it is important that they continue doing so if they are to remain popular. But it is not possible to see everyone who asks for a meeting, nor to attend every event they are invited to, so someone needs to refuse and to take the flak for doing so. Likewise, not all advice should be accepted and someone has to send it back asking for more work or even rejecting it. As Machiavelli says, 'Princes should devolve on others those matters that entail responsibility and reserve for themselves those that pertain to grace and favour.' The trick for the chief of staff is doing so without becoming a hate figure and being sacrificed – or worse, as Rasputin found out. You have to learn to be nearly as sinuous as the political leader you serve if you want to survive in the long term. Some argue that diplomats are not ideal material for such a job because they are too inclined to compromise, and it is true that you need a bit of steel if you are going to be effective as a chief of staff. But you can go too far, as some recent White House chiefs of staff have discovered, if you wield only the bludgeon and never try to charm.

Chiefs of staff do not last for ever and you have to decide when to leave. I opted to remain to the end so that I could go down with the burning ship, like the boy in the poem about the Battle of the Nile ('The boy stood on the burning deck, whence all but he had fled'). Michael Heseltine caught me by the coat sleeve as I was leaving Wiltons restaurant one evening in 2003. He was having dinner with his wife, and he said to me, 'Mark my words, quit while you are at the top, young man.' Perhaps he was right. One thing I am confident about, however, is that the job of chief of staff will continue to exist in the British system. Gordon Brown abolished it to make a political point, but it is necessary for the smooth running of No 10 and David Cameron has restored the post.

However wise the chief of staff is, the leader should never rely on just one adviser, or, as Machiavelli points out, he will become his victim one way or another. Equally, if the leader has a cacophony of advisers giving different views, it is easy for him to get lost. Machiavelli says, 'If he listens to a multitude of advisers, the Prince who is not wise will never have consistent counsels, nor will he know himself how to reconcile them.' Tony was wise enough to take advice from lots of different people: from Alastair Campbell and Peter Mandelson, but also from John Burton, his constituency agent, Gail, his mother-in-law, and Jackie, his children's nanny. Far from being confused by the different advice, he used it as a series of reference points by which to orient himself, or triangulate, and synthesise the conflicting views into a coherent strategy.

Tony had many strong characters around him and yet it was an unusually harmonious Number 10. The staff were complementary rather than competitive. I didn't want to do Alastair's job and he didn't want to do mine, and nor did the others. Each had their own function and stuck to it. Of course there were personal dramas, but they tended to be confined to spats between individuals rather than affecting the overall work of the machine.

We introduced a new structure into Downing Street, dividing it into five departments or functions: Policy, Strategy, Private Office, Politics and Press.

The Policy Unit had existed since the 1970s to give the prime minister political advice on policy. At the beginning of an administration, it is largely staffed by political appointees, but as administrations get tired and run out of steam it tends to become populated by civil servants. The people who work in it should be big figures who carry weight with ministers and are experts in their fields. We had some excellent heavyweight advisers like Conor Ryan on education and Simon Stevens on health, who were politically in line with Tony and easily able to hold their own with ministers and experts. Later on we had some younger advisers who would see Tony only rarely and did not really know his mind. We then had a problem of lots of different people from Number 10 calling departments and giving different messages, which led to confusion and complaints from Permanent Secretaries. The great US senator Daniel Patrick Moynihan had a good way of dealing with this problem. Whenever a young staffer would rush into his office saying breathlessly that he had 'the White House on the line', he would stop them and say, 'The White House is a building. Go back and find out who is on the line.' The same applies in the British system. It is not important in itself that someone is calling you from Downing Street; what matters is *who* is calling and whether they really represent the prime minister's thinking or their own. The people who should carry weight are those who say, 'The prime minister wants . . .' – and you know they really mean it.

Tony refused to make David Miliband head of the Policy Unit when we moved from Opposition to Downing Street, but insisted he remain as acting head. This was in part because he felt that David was too young, but also because he wasn't convinced he was New Labour enough. He grew to trust David completely, however, and became deeply impressed by his political instincts. When Tony and Sally persuaded him to become an MP in 2001, we had trouble replacing him. Some mad ideas were put forward for the post including Richard Wilson's suggestion of Terry Burns, the outgoing Permanent Secretary pushed out of the Treasury by Gordon Brown in 1998. Andrew Adonis, who took over, had been a brilliant education adviser and did a remarkable job as Head of Policy. He was a little too New Labour for the taste of the parliamentary party and some of the Number 10 staff at the time, but he never let that worry him. Later, when Tony sent Andrew off to be an education minister, we opted for a technocrat head of policy in David Bennett. As a scientist and ex-McKinseyite he brought a rigour and discipline to policymaking, but he was undercut from time to time by political tricks from the Treasury and elsewhere in government. The perfect head of policy would be very close to the prime minister, politically astute, a rigorous and disciplined policymaker not too anchored in one field, but taken seriously by civil servants and ministers alike. I am not sure such a person has yet been born.

The PPS sat in the outer office with me, and we had a number of assistant private secretaries from different departments, although much slimmed down from John Major's time. It is essential to have people in Number 10 who can work the Whitehall network of ministerial private secretaries, take notes of meetings and issue official instructions; but they can easily become demotivated and restless if they are removed from policymaking entirely, which will tend to happen if there is a strong Policy Unit. We tried at one stage to remedy this by merging the Private Office and the Policy Unit, but that didn't work because the two functions are critically different and you run the risk either of politicising civil servants or of being accused of having taken the politics out of policymaking. For five years, the function of PPS was filled by Jeremy Heywood, an outstanding civil servant for whom the word 'Stakhanovite' might have been invented. He enjoyed it so much that he went back again to fill the role of running Number 10 for Gordon Brown and now David Cameron.

One of the PPS's functions is to liaise with Buckingham Palace and the royals, which means preparing an entirely theoretical agenda for the prime minister's weekly meeting with the Queen – theoretical because neither party ever refers to it and they very sensibly have a gossip instead – and going for a glass of warm white wine in the office of the Queen's private secretary while the Queen and prime minister meet. Occasionally there are royal scandals to sort out, although that is mainly a press issue, and abdications are few and far between.

The other royal-related task is to accompany the prime minister on the annual visit to stay with the Queen in Balmoral at the beginning of September. This was something I had always avoided but foolishly agreed to do in 2001 when Jeremy tired of it. It resulted in my becoming a republican. I had a chance to explain to President Bush that it was the only sense in which I was a republican when I attended a royal dinner at the American ambassador's house during his presidential visit in 2003. He asked Tony the next day what was 'up with Jonathan and the Queen', and Tony tried to explain. I had accompanied Tony with my whole family to attend the famous Balmoral barbecue in which Prince Philip cooks and the Queen serves and which the Number 10 private secretaries are invited to attend each year. When we arrived the Queen's private secretary took us for a walk in the grounds up to John Brown's statue on a small hillock above the castle. As the walk went on and on, I began to wonder how we were going to get to the barbecue in time. Being properly brought up, I couldn't possibly bring myself to ask our host what was going on, but Sarah was not so squeamish. The private secretary replied, oh yes, he had decided to buy a nice bit of salmon and we were to have dinner in his house on the estate instead. We were nonplussed but realised we were not going to the barbecue after all.

The next morning as we were getting ready to leave we were told that we had been disinvited because one of the ladies-in-waiting had discovered that my partner and I weren't married and had told the Queen. She supposedly felt that she should not set a bad example for Charles when Camilla was still not allowed at the Palace by inviting an unmarried couple to the barbecue. So we ate salmon instead. I have no idea if the explanation was true, but I found it pleasingly comic. Tony was more concerned by the fact that attending the barbecue meant that he missed the England vs Germany World Cup qualifier, which amazingly England won 5–1. As he was watching the replay in the castle, one of the junior members of the royal family wandered in and asked, 'How long do these games normally last?'

Perhaps the most under-recognised part of any leader's office is the scheduling and advance team. The huge scheduling office in the White House is by far the most powerful department in the building. No one can get face time with the president unless the office agrees to it. We had similarly fierce diary secretaries, starting with Kate Garvey, who knew what the prime minister wanted and enforced it. They were the ones who had to say no to all the meetings the prime minister himself had agreed to as people lobbied him when he was away from Downing Street. The petitioners would insist, truthfully, that the prime minister had told them he really wanted to see them, but the diary secretary knew better. Saying no was not always possible so they invented the technique of 'FOFEing', which stood for 'fob off for ever'. If people insisted on meetings they would just say of course but we need to wait a few months till Tony is less busy. When they contacted us again in a few months' time the diary secretary would repeat the exercise until the petitioners eventually gave up.

One of their jobs was to stop people crashing into meetings uninvited, which led to impressive stand-offs on the threshold of his den with ministers and senior officials. It was also their job to go into the den and break up a meeting when it was supposed to end. Tony would never terminate a meeting himself. He wanted it to appear that, as far as he was concerned, the session was so enjoyable it could go on for ever, and he would wave the diary secretary away repeatedly before finally agreeing, apparently reluctantly, to move on to his next appointment. It wasn't really possible to have a meeting for less than half an hour if you allowed the visitor to sit down, so we would try what the White House calls 'drop-bys', when Tony would pop into the Cabinet Room from his den next door and see someone waiting there. As long as we didn't allow them to sit down, we could get Tony out in fifteen minutes. A prime minister who doesn't have a well-organised and well-run schedule cannot be effective.

I had a dream of an efficient speech-writing department in Number 10 like the one in the White House, effortlessly turning out deathless prose in the leader's style full of historical allusions and new policy announcements, but we could never replicate it, despite going through a string of speech-writers. Number 10 is not the White House and cannot attract that quality of talent, and prime ministers are not presidents. They are brought up in Parliament and live or die by their speeches. Writing and delivering them is their bread and butter. Tony could never get comfortable with other people writing his speeches. For any major event, he sat down and wrote it out himself in longhand, and for some reason he had to do it at the last minute, getting up at four in the morning to write a speech for delivery at lunchtime. Like a teenager he seemed destined always to pull an all-nighter. That meant everyone else had to get up early to type the speech, proofread it and check the policy.

The worst example was Tony's very successful speech to the European

Parliament in 2006. He kept changing it right up to the last minute, so I had to stand by the printer in the hotel room pulling off the final pages as he was walking out of the door already late for his appearance in the chamber. There were of course exceptions; Tony would on occasion deliver speeches written by Andrew Adonis and Phil Collins, both extremely good writers, but the vast majority were his own. I wanted to liberate the time he devoted to speech-writing for political and policy work but it was never to be; and given how much of the job of prime minister is about communicating, maybe it is right to devote all that time to expressing the ideas rather than simply having them.

The media and the Opposition complained about the politicisation of Downing Street, but actually it is not nearly political enough. The criticism is in any case ahistorical. Until recent decades, Number 10 was staffed with the prime minister's cronies and political side-kicks. It wasn't subject to the Northcote Trevelyan reforms of the nineteenth century which established a politically neutral and professional Civil Service. Even Jock Colville, Churchill's private secretary, wasn't a traditional Civil Service appointee but more a friend of the family. Harold Macmillan had political allies working for him in Number 10, and it was only in the 1960s that Number 10 became a Civil Service preserve; and, quite soon after that, Harold Wilson changed it back again by bringing in political appointees. Number 10 always has been political and always will be, and I have never been clear why it is thought to be a bad thing for the prime minister to have political advice ready-to-hand. After all, the Exchequer pays for all political parties, including the Opposition, to have advice, so there is no issue of principle. The question is really the relationship between the political and the Civil Service parts of Number 10. The neutrality of the civil servants working there should be preserved, and they should not be asked to carry out political tasks. In Mrs Thatcher's time, there was a problem because civil servants like Bernard Ingham were politicised by their long tenure and by their alignment with Mrs Thatcher's wishes. In our time, the existence of a strong political team meant that civil servants did not drift into party political terrain, and all the political advisers could be removed as soon as the regime changed.

The real core of Number 10, though, what actually makes the

place work, as we discovered soon after arriving, is the support staff. The quaintly named duty clerks, Garden Room girls, messengers and 'switch' keep the office working twenty-four hours a day. The duty clerks are young, junior civil servants who choose their own successors. The clerk on duty sits at a desk in the outer office with a little dumb waiter behind which goes down to their office below with official papers and intelligence coming in and going out. If we were out of the office, they would take the calls and find us if necessary. And most of all they ran the place at night and on holidays. Over Christmas 2004 it was the duty clerk who managed the brunt of the immediate aftermath of the tsunami almost single-handed.

One of the Garden Room girls (so called since Lloyd George's time when they were recruited to provide the extra secretarial assistance necessitated by the First World War, and who were sited in basement rooms overlooking the Number 10 garden) accompanies the prime minister at all times and acts as a point of contact. When Tony had his heart scare in 2003, it was the Garden Room girl on duty who called me to tell me he was going off to hospital and kept me in the picture as events unfolded. She let me speak to Tony just before he went under the anaesthetic and I was perhaps a bit breezy; he was decidedly nervous. Bearing in mind the rule that Prime Ministers are not allowed to be sick, the incident needed to be carefully managed. I got Jeremy Heywood to speak to the Palace and the Cabinet Secretary and got Sally Morgan to talk to John Prescott. I asked Jack Straw to make the parliamentary statement on Europe the next day in place of Tony, and we had a debate on what should happen to the nuclear button while he was indisposed. Jack Straw came into the office the next morning so that he could say he had seen Tony alive when he made the parliamentary statement; it reminded me of Mao having to be filmed swimming the Yangtze in 1966 to prove he was still going. A few days later Tony told Bill Clinton he had had an irregular heartbeat for some time. Clinton inadvertently made this public, but Tony's consultant insisted he did not have an irregular heartbeat at all. Cherie was convinced that the condition had been brought on by too much coffee and forbade him to drink the stuff, but he had withdrawal symptoms and would keep having cups sneaked through to him when he was in the office.

Above all, there was 'switch', the disembodied voices we heard every minute of every day. Over the years we built up a long-distance relationship. They got to know our wives and children and the events in our lives, but the medium was radio rather than TV because they were sitting in the Cabinet Office rather than Number 10 and we couldn't see them. They had an unparalleled database and could get anyone on the phone anywhere in the world at any time of day or night. Their iron rule was that they would not pass on any telephone number they had been given even if asked for it by the prime minister himself, but they would put you through to the person concerned. After the hauliers' blockade in 2000, the *Sun* mischievously handed out switch's private number and our lines were jammed. Ministers couldn't get through and the business of government nearly came to a halt. We complained to Rupert Murdoch, and the paper's editor, David Yelland, looked distinctly nervous for the following few days. We had to change the number.

I was at my desk at eight thirty on 21 July 1997 when an older member of switch called to say she had William Hague on the line for the prime minister. I was a bit taken aback. Leaders of the Opposition have perfectly cordial relations with the prime minister, but an early-morning call was not routine. I told her to say we would call back. I checked with Tony, who was willing to take the call, and I asked her to get Hague back. Instead of calling the office of the Leader of the Opposition, she phoned the number the caller had given her and put him through. I listened with mounting horror as it became clear that it was a radio hoaxer who didn't even sound much like Hague. Staying on the phone, I asked the private secretary to tell switch to cut the hoaxer off mid-call. Tony was cross with me because he had been handling the conversation with good humour and said he had realised it was a hoax from the first. I was mortified by my mistake, and all day the call was rebroadcast complete with switch saying, 'You don't sound like yourself, Mr Hague.'

Any prime minister who mistreats or alienates this cadre of dedicated support staff is making a terrible and probably fatal mistake.

Number 10 settled into a routine after our first year. Tony would fire off a note on Sunday evening to the senior staff setting out the issues he was worried about or proposing a new strategy. Some of them were pretty substantive. I clocked one strategy note in January

2000 that weighed in at twenty pages. I had to decide who it would go to, not least because anyone left off the circulation list would make a fuss. We often had to send them out by fax or email to external advisers, and I lived in fear that one would leak, but Tony reassured me that he had drafted them with that danger in mind. On Monday mornings Tony would chair a staff meeting in the Cabinet Room and run through the points in his note and what was happening that week. On the other weekday mornings, I would chair a meeting of the senior staff to deal with the issues of the day, and every month Tony would have a strategy meeting including our pollsters and outside advisers. Tony was obsessed with grabbing any moments in the sun he could, so we held many of our meetings on the terrace outside the Cabinet Room or in the Number 10 garden. He loved it, but the vision of buttoned-up Ulster Unionists sweltering in their suits in the glare as Tony urged them to compromise still haunts me.

Tony liked to retreat upstairs early to put Leo to bed or, before Leo's birth, to watch *The Simpsons* with the other children. We had almost no grand diplomatic or official dinners, and, if he had to go out and make a speech at a function, it had to be made after the starter so that he could get away or at least have a drink with the rest of the meal. During the week Tony could rarely do his red boxes. We made sure he saw any urgent papers during the day but saved up long policy papers for the Friday box. The pattern became set, and he would have three or four huge boxes at the weekend. Jeremy Heywood and I would always have to stay late on Friday as Whitehall emptied their out trays into our in trays, and we had to choose what he needed to see and flag it up with comments. Tony got through vast amounts of paperwork down at Chequers at the weekend, and Monday mornings were spent deciphering his scrawled comments.

In the end the leader needs to trust his court if he wants to set a constant course, just as he demands loyalty and confidentiality from them. Machiavelli describes talking to Father Luke in the court of Emperor Maximilian, who said of his ruler 'he seeks advice from none, yet never has his own way. For being of a secret disposition, he never discloses his intentions to any, nor asks their opinion; and it is only when his plans are to be carried out that they begin to be discovered and known, and at the same time they begin to be thwarted by those he has about him, when he, being facile, gives way. Hence it happens that what he does one day, he undoes the next; that his wishes and designs are never fully ascertained.'

Effective leaders have to get the balance right between trusting their staff too much and too little. Machiavelli writes that 'The new Prince should not be too ready of belief, nor too easily set in motion; nor should he himself be the first to raise alarms; but should so temper prudence with kindliness that too great confidence in others shall not throw him off his guard, nor groundless distrust render him insupportable.'

Above all, it should always be clear it is the role of the staff to take the blame while the prime minister takes the credit. Machiavelli argues that 'those who think that every Prince who has a name for prudence owes it to the wise counsellors he has around him, and not to any merit of his own, are certainly mistaken; since it is an unerring rule and of universal application that a Prince who is not wise himself cannot be well advised by others. It follows that good counsels, whencesoever they come, have their origin in the prudence of the Prince, and not the prudence of the Prince in wise counsels.'

CHAPTER FIVE

'Of Those Who by Their Crimes
Come to be Princes'

The Prime Minister and the Chancellor

The key relationship at the centre of the British government is that between the prime minister and the Chancellor. One controls the appointments, and the other controls the money.

There is an inbuilt institutional tension between the two offices. Number 10 wants to spend money to win political support, and the Treasury wants to cut spending and preserve the fiscal position. If left to themselves, prime ministers would spend like there was no tomorrow, and the Treasury's tightfistedness is necessary to save them from themselves. Machiavelli agrees that for a prince 'it may be a good thing to be reputed liberal', but he warns that 'A Prince of liberal disposition will consume his whole substance in things of this sort, and, after all be obliged, if he would retain his reputation for liberality, to burden his subjects with extraordinary taxes.' A prudent leader will save the purses of the citizens by listening to the Treasury.

The relationship is at its best when there is, in addition, a construct-ive political tension between the people holding the two jobs. When the Chancellor is weak, as Alistair Darling was from 2007 to 2009 (only gaining some room for manoeuvre after Gordon's abortive attempt to replace him with Ed Balls), the prime minister makes the spending decisions. Mrs Thatcher was at her best when in harness with a strong Chancellor like Nigel Lawson who would stand up to her and less good when operating with weaker Chancellors like Geoffrey Howe and John Major. Of course, with constructive tension, as with everything else, there can be too much of a good thing. And we had much too much of a good thing from 1997 to 2007.

In all organisations there is rivalry between the leader and the number two, particularly if the number two is also the expected successor. In politics, finance ministers are often the obvious person to take over from the prime minister and relations between them are not always warm. The Canadian prime minister Jean Chrétien faced a campaign by his finance minister, Paul Martin, to force him to retire. When Martin did succeed Chrétien as leader, he distanced himself from the *ancien régime* by, Chrétien felt, allowing Chrétien's name to be blackened by corruption allegations. The Liberal Party under Martin's leadership suffered an election setback the following year and had to stagger on as a minority government until losing power a few years later.

In Australia, Peter Costello, the Treasurer, was constantly snapping at prime minister John Howard's heels. He had hoped to take over as leader during Howard's second term and kept pressing him to set a date according to a deal that reportedly existed between them going back to 1994. Howard denied the claims and denounced the 'hubris and arrogance' of those pushing them. He said the leadership was the party's to decide, not a prize to be handed over by leaders to their successors. Howard eventually announced he was going in 2007, and the Liberal Party lost the subsequent election, with two-thirds of those questioned saying they did not want Costello as prime minister.

Tony Blair's predicament was therefore not unprecedented, and the eventual electoral outcome of the rivalry at the top was also all too predictable. His Chancellor was also his rival and the dauphin, unwilling to wait his turn. Gordon insisted that Tony had agreed that he should take over but was unwilling to cooperate with Tony's programme in government and was keen to distance himself politically from most difficult things the prime minister had to do. All the ingredients were present for a very Shakespearean tragedy.

What made the tragedy particularly poignant was the fact that the friendship between the two men went back a long way. They came into the Commons together in 1983. Gordon, the elder of the two, was the dominant figure throughout the 1980s. Tony told me that their relationship then was extraordinarily intense. They shared an office, and Gordon used to call him first thing in the morning and last thing at night as part of an endless circular conversation. It sounded more like a romance than a traditional political partnership.

When Gordon moved to a new office in the early 1990s, Tony declined to move with him so that he could finally escape his orbit. He said that Gordon divided the world into those who were for him and those who were against him, and drove everyone around him mad in the process. Tony felt he had to break out as he too was becoming increasingly paranoid.

They had already begun to drift apart by 1994, but Tony's decision to run for the leadership in that year tipped Gordon into an outright hostility from which he never emerged. By the time I came over from America to be interviewed by Tony for the job of chief of staff in September 1994, their relationship was in trouble – so much so that on my way back to Washington from my interview I was horrified to stumble across Gordon Brown and Ed Balls in Terminal 4 at Heathrow on their way out to Washington for a visit I had arranged for them. I was under strict instructions not to let Gordon know that I was being considered for the job, and I had to dart into WH Smith's to hide, and I made no mention of being in London when I met them the next day at the other end.

Gordon never got over Tony's leapfrogging of him. At a political Cabinet session in September 1998, I was amazed when a couple of Cabinet members told me they thought Gordon had come to terms with being number two. I did not think he would ever accept his former junior partner as his boss. Machiavelli's warning about what happens in these circumstances is absolutely clear: you have to deal with those who do not accept the new status quo severely and straight away. 'He who establishes a tyranny and does not kill "Brutus", and he who establishes a free state and does not kill "the Sons of Brutus" will not last long.' (This is not Julius Caesar's '*Et tu, Brute?*', but Junius Brutus who helped rid Rome of its monarchy, founded the republic and presided over the execution of his own sons for trying to overthrow the republic and bring back the monarchy.) In *The Discourses* Machiavelli writes from his own experience:

> Piero Soderini thought that by patience and goodness he could quell the desire of 'Brutus's sons' to return to another form of government, but in this he was mistaken. Though, being a prudent man, he recognised the need for action, and thought the type of ambitious men who were against him gave him ground for getting rid of them, yet he

could never make up his mind to do this. For, in addition to thinking that he could by patience and goodness extinguish their malevolence, and by distributing rewards put an end to some of their hostility, he was of the opinion – and often told his friends so in confidence – that, if he were to take vigorous action against his opponents and to fight his adversaries, he would need to assume extraordinary authority and introduce laws disruptive of civic equality.

Soderini's mistake, according to Machiavelli, was failing 'to realise that malevolence is not vanquished by time, nor placated by any gifts. With the result that, through his inability to emulate Brutus, he lost both his position and his reputation, a loss in which his country shared.' Machiavelli pointed to the experience of ancient Rome as 'a warning to all Princes that they can never live secure in their principality so long as those live who have been despoiled of it . . . a reminder to all potentates that old injuries are never cancelled by new benefits, least of all when the benefits are of less importance than the injuries previously inflicted'.

This, in a nutshell, was Tony's problem. His way of managing Gordon was to string him along indefinitely without ever addressing frontally the difficult issue of who was in charge. Tony knew him intimately so I deferred to his judgement of the correct tactic in dealing with his troublesome number two. I was surprised in September 1997 when he accused me of setting him against Gordon. I explained that I just disagreed on how to deal with him; with a spoiled child or a bully, you have to be firm early on or you are lost. Machiavelli advises that 'there are to be found numerous cases in which humility is not only no help, but is a hindrance, especially when used in dealing with an arrogant man who, either out of envy or for some other cause, has come to hate you'.

Machiavelli also sets out very clearly what Gordon's strategy should have been. Those, he says, who are ill-content with a prince should first measure their strength: 'if their position is such that they have not sufficient forces to make war openly, they should use every endeavour to acquire the Prince's friendship; and to this end should avail themselves of every opening which they think necessary to attain it, by becoming obsequious to his wishes and by taking pleasure in everything in which they see that he takes pleasure. Such familiar intercourse in the first place assures that your life will be safe and, without entailing any danger, allows you to enjoy the Prince's good fortune just as he does himself. It also provides you with ample opportunity for fulfilling your intentions.' If only Gordon had been content to cooperate with Tony on his reform programme and to wait patiently for his turn, he would have been able to succeed to the job of leader peacefully and the New Labour government would have enjoyed much greater political success. It wasn't that he prevented Tony getting his way in the end on policy; it just slowed him down. And it was not a matter of weakness on Tony's part, just an unwillingness to deal harshly with an old friend.

After a brief attempt by Gordon to woo me when I first came to work for Tony, for example taking me out to the Soho Club, I got my first taste of his modus operandi in 1995 when Paul Hamlyn, the publisher and philanthropist, generously donated money to set up Tony's office as Leader of the Opposition. Gordon got to hear of it, summoned me to his office in Millbank and sat me down in front of his desk. He told me in stern terms that he had Tony's agreement that all income was to be shared half and half with his office. I knew there was no such understanding and could not stop myself bursting out laughing. It must have been very irritating, and Gordon never forgave me.

His tactic of bullying weaker people often worked, but not always. In 2005, he tried to browbeat Adair Turner into modifying his proposals for pension reform. Adair stood his ground despite the shouting and carrying on. In November, Gordon asked Tony to get John Hutton, the Secretary of State for Welfare, to water down Adair's proposals. When I passed this on to John, he asked me why Gordon wouldn't talk to him about it directly. I told him he was asking the wrong person: Gordon hadn't spoken to me for nearly eleven years. Not only would he not talk to me in person, but he refused to talk on the phone. I had to call Ed Balls to negotiate any point, and I could often hear Gordon standing behind him telling him what to say. From 1999 onwards, I handed over my Balls duty to Jeremy Heywood, who as a former Treasury official handled the difficult negotiations toughly and brilliantly for nearly six years without poisoning his relations with either Brown or Balls.

Having failed at bluster, Gordon summoned Adair to the Treasury and tried to charm him into submission. When that too failed, he tried to get John Hutton to announce that the proposals would cost four pence extra on tax. John declined, and the Treasury briefed that story to the papers instead. Adair, however, held his nerve.

Later, in 2007, Gordon tried the same tactics with David Freud over his proposed reforms of the welfare system. Freud was summoned to the Treasury and hectored for forty-five minutes and then put into a room with Treasury civil servants and Shriti Vadera, Gordon's fearsome business and banking adviser, and told to amend his report. David stood up to them and wrote to Gordon later in the day, accepting one of his amendments, rejecting all the others and telling him that he had sent his report to the printers.

A good deal of the angst between Tony and Gordon revolved around Peter Mandelson, the third corner of the triangle that had existed since the early 1980s. Tony told me that before 1994 Gordon used to speak to Peter at least twice every day before 9 a.m., and Tony lamented that now he didn't speak to him at all. The friendship between the two of them had been turned into intense hatred (and of course turned back into friendship again once Tony left, or appeared to do so), but Gordon remained obsessed by him. He saved a particular intonation of voice for ringing Tony to complain about what Peter 'Mendelssohn', as he called him, had been up to in briefing the papers. He saw Peter behind every negative story about him in the press and would demand that Tony 'call the dogs off'. After making a conference speech in 2003 that was widely seen as an attack on Tony and a defence of 'Real Labour' as opposed to New Labour, Gordon bizarrely complained to Tony that the speech had in fact been supportive and had only been made into a potential leadership bid by briefings from Number 10. It was all 'Mendelssohn's' fault. Even after Peter had left for Brussels to become the EU Trade Commissioner, Gordon remained convinced that he was behind every bad story in the media.

Tony made repeated attempts to bring the two of them back together, but it never worked. In September 1999, Tony asked them to cooperate. Gordon's response was to set up two committees, one for government and one for the party, the first for him and the second for Peter, so that they would not have to be in the same group.

Not that Peter was blameless. When he felt that Tony and Gordon were getting back together again, he would complain that Tony was no longer talking to him and try to pull them apart. This drove Tony mad, and in November 2000 he asked me to draft a furious letter to Peter telling him to stop, although in the end he didn't send it. Usually Peter was only responding to some outrage perpetrated by Gordon, but Tony wouldn't permit tit-for-tat attacks. In October 2000, Tony warned Peter that he would sack him if he retaliated against Gordon for his latest act of war. Peter looked crestfallen and had to retract a briefing by 'friends of Peter Mandelson' given to the *Mirror*.

In the first two years of government, the arguments between Tony and Gordon were generally about the tight spending ceilings we had imposed on ourselves by agreeing in 1997 to stick to the Tories' plans. Tony was for spending more, and he eventually managed to squeeze an extra £300 million out of Gordon in 2000 to prevent a repeat of the winter health crises that had become a pattern under the Tories. Tony told me it was the most important battle of his prime ministership. If he couldn't get more money into the public services, we couldn't improve delivery by the time of the next election. If Gordon didn't agree, it was because he wanted Tony to fail. In these arguments, Gordon had some legitimate gripes, such as when Tony committed the government to matching average European Union spending on health in an interview on the *Frost* programme in 2000 without agreeing that line with Gordon in advance. He did it deliberately to force Gordon's hand, but Gordon had every right to feel aggrieved.

Budgets and spending rounds continued to be the focus of disagreements for the next decade. Gordon's Budgets were usually well received on the day but tended to unravel thereafter. I wrote in 1999 that Gordon got the credit for the apple but then we had to deal with the maggots hidden inside. Jeremy Heywood used to spend the afternoon of Budget day ploughing through the small print of the Red Book to find the double-counting and the exaggerated claims. The Opposition wouldn't get to them on Budget day, but they would have found them by PMQs on the following Wednesday and throw them at Tony.

Each Budget exercise began in the Cabinet Room with a briefing by the Treasury's economic experts, which I said in 1998 reminded me a bit of Michael Fish's weather forecasts and were about as accurate (actually, to be fair, Fish's were more accurate). Gordon normally kept us well away from Treasury civil servants and made a fuss when I chaired a meeting of Treasury officials in 1998 on our ideas for the reform of the Bretton Woods institutions. He and Ed Balls saw off the two Number 10 economic advisers, Derek Scott and Arnab Banerji, by starving them of information and forbidding Treasury officials to meet them. Of course, rows between Number 10's economic advisers and the Chancellor were nothing new, but in our case the battle was very one-sided.

In their bilateral meetings Gordon would drip-feed Tony with elements to be included in the Budget, but we knew there would always be a hidden surprise. Tony described the process of trying to find out what the surprise was as a game of twenty questions in which you had to eliminate all the alternatives until you were left with the actual proposal. Gordon would always end his Budget statement with an '. . . And finally', which presaged a treat for the Labour backbenchers, allowing him to sit down to tumultuous cheering. We knew Gordon would have 'a back pocket' to pay for that surprise somewhere within the spending limits, and Tony's constant quest was to find it first and spend it on something else. His priority was to devote resources to health and education while Gordon wanted to devote it to tax credits, an idea imported by Ed Balls from his professor at Harvard, Larry Summers, later US Treasury Secretary. We got so desperate in 2004 to find out what Gordon was up to that we refused to set a date for the spending round until he would tell us the content.

The Budget statement would be sent over in little chunks of impenetrable prose, all capitalised, as Gordon typed it up himself. He would make a scene if anyone else saw it other than Tony. When Jeremy circulated it to a few people in Number 10 in 1999, Gordon flew into a rage. Geoff Mulgan, our strategy adviser, had referred to the draft statement when talking to a Treasury official. Gordon sent Andrew Turnbull, then the Treasury Permanent Secretary, over to Number 10 to demand a leak inquiry. I observed at the time this was a bit bizarre since it appeared to be the habit of the Treasury to leak most of the contents of the Budget to the media in advance in any case.

Tony would suggest amendments to Gordon's statements to make the prose more comprehensible and the policy more palatable. These were usually accepted. When they weren't, things tended to go wrong, as they did in November 2001 when Gordon ignored Tony's suggestions and the Pre-Budget Report was interpreted as a tax-raising Budget. Gordon blamed the Health Secretary Alan Milburn and Charles Clarke for generating this impression via their media appearances, not himself. Luckily Tony usually prevailed, at least on the big issues. In 2002, he had to threaten to take the spending round to the Cabinet as a way of forcing Gordon's hand, and Gordon gave in because he knew he would enjoy little support there. Gordon would come to the special Cabinet on the morning of Budget day and rattle through the statement in a low monotone at Gatling-gun pace. No one ever commented, and I was at a loss as to how they could understand a thing he said unless, like me, they had been allowed to read the draft in advance. At the end there would be a ceremonial but rather unenthusiastic banging on the table by the assembled Cabinet members.

On the whole Tony and Gordon agreed on tax. In Opposition, I was the inadvertent source of a story by Robert Peston of the *Financial Times* that a New Labour government was not going to introduce a 50p tax rate. It served the useful purpose of getting our policy out into the open even if Gordon wasn't quite ready for it, and Tony was firmly of the view that we should stick to that pledge. There weren't really big ideological differences between the two over economic policy, just a refusal on Gordon's part to involve Tony and Number 10 in the process. I was worried about the spend, spend, spend nature of some of our Budgets and noted in my diary that, without reforms to save money in the public sector, we would have no cushion if the economy turned south.

Gordon's reluctance to agree to a Fundamental Savings Review (FSR) in Tony's last years in office was probably the most damaging example of the stand-off. Tony's aim was to use the FSR to cut out some of the waste that had inevitably built up in the years of increased public spending. Gordon refused to allow it to happen while Tony was still prime minister. When we argued with him, he announced publicly in the *Financial Times* that it would not happen till he was leader, and, when he briefed the Cabinet, he declined to refer to it being finished in the course of 2006 with the strong implication it would be finalised only after Tony had left. Tony kept asking to see the plan for it and even had formal letters sent to the Treasury by the Principal Private Secretary demanding to see it. Eventually Gordon turned up in Tony's office and threw the document on the table saying, 'You asked for a fucking document, so there it is.' Tony suggested that they collaborate on the plan, but Gordon wouldn't. As a result there was no FSR and we missed an opportunity to put the country into a better fiscal position going into the economic crash of 2008.

Gordon's refusal to share any information didn't just apply to Number 10. It led to endless rows with his Cabinet colleagues. In 2000, Alan Milburn, the Health Secretary, complained to us about not having been consulted in the Comprehensive Spending Round. He quietened down, however, when Gordon told him quite how much money was going to be stuffed down the throat of the Department of Health. But when David Blunkett, Education Secretary, found out how much Health had got he refused to settle on the education budget. Two years later, Gordon failed to tell either Alan or David what was in store for their departments, and they responded by refusing to participate in his public roll-out of post-Budget announcements. Against a background of rumours that he was moving to the Foreign Office in 2004, Gordon complained at Cabinet about how difficult it had been to resolve the spending disputes with departments. David Blunkett, by then Home Secretary and whose desire to succeed him was well known, cheerfully chimed in, 'Oh well, you won't want to remain as Chancellor then.'

The most difficult disputes were usually those over defence spending. Gordon resented the fact that the military briefed the media against him, and he genuinely thought it better to spend on domestic priorities and international aid than on defence. In Number 10, we took the side of the MoD, in part because they were such hopeless negotiators themselves. They never seemed to have the same figures as the Treasury from which to start negotiations, and Gordon often ended up debating directly with the admiral who was the financial adviser to the Chief of Defence Staff rather than with MoD ministers or civil servants. In 2000, Clare Short threatened to resign because she felt her Department for International Development budget was too small, and, when Gordon bought her off with more cash, Charles Guthrie, the Chief of Defence Staff, threatened to resign in order to secure more money for the MoD. In the end, he won an extra £130 million. This became a regular occurrence and his successor, Mike Walker, demanded to see Tony in 2004 so that he could tell him he was going to resign unless there was more money for the military. In 2007, Gordon proposed to us that we 'stage' the pay increase for the forces even though they were engaged in Afghanistan and Iraq. Tony managed to talk him out of it, and Gordon promptly positioned himself in the tabloids as the squaddies' champion.

Gordon made much of his claim to be, in effect, the prime minister for domestic policy, but in fact there were whole areas of domestic policy that he simply wasn't interested in or where he had merely a negative interest in blocking Tony's reform agenda. Throughout the ten years Tony was in office, Gordon argued that there were subjects the government shouldn't talk about, including crime and immigration. Every time Tony planned a speech on one of these subjects, Gordon, Ed Balls and Ed Miliband would try to talk him out of it, saying that they were Tory issues: we shouldn't be moving on to their terrain. Tony tried to persuade them that, with the decline in unemployment, crime and asylum were now the main issues on the doorstep and they could not be ignored, but Gordon wouldn't agree. He appeared to believe that it was possible to wish away difficult issues by not talking about them.

In June 2006, Gordon organised a session with Al Gore and a screening of his climate change film in Number 11 and was terribly upset when no minister would come because it clashed with a meeting of the Cabinet environment committee. We changed the time of the meeting, and the ministers all came to the screening and then went straight on to their postponed meeting. In a fit of post-film euphoria, they agreed to raise the target for the cut in carbon emissions from the 4 million tons we had been contemplating to 10.5 million tons. Gordon was distraught when he found out, because of the likely effect on the economy, and he immediately tried to reverse the decision. David Miliband, then Secretary for the Environment, came round to Number 10 and urged us to stand up to Gordon, which we did. But David then blinked himself and settled on a compromise of a cut of 8 million tons. Comically, Gordon went on to present the resulting target as evidence that he was greener than anyone else in the Cabinet.

Gordon's real skill lay in political tactics rather than strategy. Strategy meetings chaired by him would be about what pamphlet to launch tomorrow or what mini initiative to propose next week, rather than about any long-term vision. In 2000, as part of a rapprochement between the two of them, Tony asked Gordon to produce a strategy paper for the government. It didn't appear for months, and Tony kept asking Gordon for it. When it was eventually disgorged, in February 2001, the biggest idea in it was the slogan 'working hard for hard-working families', already well worn by Clinton and other Democrats. Gordon tended to get stuck either with abstract concepts or micro policy initiatives with nothing in between. His campaign on Britishness was an example of the former. At one level, it was an interesting conversation topic about the identity of people living in these islands, but with no practical policy ramifications. At another, it was a crude political assertion that the next prime minister could be a Scot despite devolution. What it wasn't was a political vision for how to change the country. Gordon had an irresistible attraction to complicated phrases that sounded erudite, like the great moment in Opposition when, on the advice of Ed Balls, he used a speech to talk about 'neo-endogenous growth theory', allowing Michael Heseltine to make fun of him at the following Tory Party Conference saying that his speech was 'not Brown but Balls'.

Gordon frequently unsettled Tony by complaining that there was no 'political operation' in government. A repeated complaint was that, following his latest successful Budget, Number 10 had cocked everything up. If he wasn't involved, he would tell Tony it was all a mess, particularly during an election campaign and, if there really was a prospect of things going wrong, he would make sure he couldn't be blamed. In 2006, he told the press that Number 10 had kept him out of the launch of the local election campaign whereas in fact we had gone to great lengths to involve him, but Sue Nye had refused on his behalf. If he didn't get his way he would go on strike, for example refusing to campaign in the 2003 local elections saying that he hadn't been consulted. In 2004, he attended only those press conferences devoted to economic issues. He avoided the Scottish elections in 2007 altogether, even though he was about to become leader, so that he couldn't be held responsible for a defeat.

Any idea that was not Gordon's own would be rubbished. Eventually, we got wise to the need to present the things that we wanted to happen as being his idea. I had been arguing that we should speed up progress in developing a Persian TV service for the BBC World Service, but there was no way I was going to get more money for the World Service from the Treasury. One of Gordon Brown's special advisers approached me and said he thought he could sell the idea to Gordon as his own, and then it would be possible to get it funded. I willingly surrendered authorship, and a proposal duly came from the Treasury for funding rapid progress on a Persian TV service (to which, needless to say, we readily agreed).

A turning point for me came in 2001 when 'switch' mistakenly plugged me into a phone call between Gordon and Nick Brown, who was abroad. The call was in the context of the foot-and-mouth outbreak, and Gordon peppered it with pleas to Nick to be careful in what he said in case someone was listening. Gordon said all this presidentialism was terrible. 'We have to stop him taking foot-and-mouth away from you.' Nick Brown complained that he had to waste his time coming to Number 10 to hear Tony blather on about the disease for an hour a day. They agreed that they should not discuss the issue with Number 10 policy people but would talk again with Ed Balls later in the day. I simply could not believe the disloyal way in which Gordon talked about Tony and I saw him in a new light.

Despite all this, Gordon had real strengths as a politician. He was highly intelligent, interested in policy detail, a brilliant political tactician and driven by an enormous force of will. These talents were in the end, however, tragically overwhelmed by his flaws. The bullying and the control freakery I have described were not really the problem – they are a common enough part of politics. It was the lack of courage that was the real issue.

Although Andrew Turnbull, who had been his Permanent Secretary at the Treasury, may have been unkind to describe Gordon as 'Macavity', it is true that Gordon always disappeared when things got rough. In Number 10 we used to joke that we could always tell when a crisis was over because Gordon would reappear. He would even walk out of meetings to avoid taking responsibility for a decision, as he did from a meeting with Tony and Jack Straw on whether or not we should hold a referendum in 2005 on the European constitution. When we were deciding whether to deploy more troops to Afghanistan in 2003, Gordon arrived at the beginning of the relevant Cabinet meeting, announced the date of the Budget and then left to make a speech in Scotland, so that no one later could say whether he had supported or opposed the decision to deploy more troops. Alistair Darling was left behind as his surrogate to complain about the costs and to lament the fact that we didn't have an exit strategy. Afterwards, in private, Gordon told Tony that it was 'his decision' – that is, Tony's decision. Tony had already ruined his coming premiership by spending all the money. Tony replied, 'So we know that I will get the blame for your prime ministership going wrong already.'

Gordon was not at his best when he came under attack. Papers on the decision to abolish the payment of tax credits on Advance Corporation Tax for pension schemes in our first year in office were released in 2007 under Freedom of Information (FOI) legislation, and the government was accused of having carried out a raid on pensioners. Instead of robustly defending the decision, Gordon refused to go on TV and sent Ed Balls instead, who blamed civil servants. Privately, Gordon blamed Tony for the attacks and demanded to know where the FOI Act itself had come from. Who had thought of it? He said threateningly that there would be much more on Iraq to come out. Tony replied that he thought that pretty much everything that could come out about Iraq already had done. Tony said to me that it reminded him of when Gordon had been attacked in Opposition for having been too supportive of the European Exchange Rate Mechanism, thereby limiting Labour's ability to attack the Tory government for Black Wednesday. Whenever under attack, Gordon froze.

Sometimes Tony would invite me into the den with him and Gordon to keep a note of their conversations. He hoped my presence would moderate Gordon's behaviour. It did help keep the volume down, but it didn't stop Gordon getting carried away by his own arguments. He would even contradict himself between sentences. He would first say that a policy he disagreed with would cost £200 million. When Tony persisted, he would say that in fact it would cost £2 billion. I would interrupt to say he had just said £200 million, but he would say 'No I didn't' and get cross. Gordon once put to the Cabinet as an example of waste in government a Department of Culture, Media and Sport website that had supposedly cost £58 million and had had only fifty-eight hits. Later investigation showed that in fact the website had only cost £58,000 and had had thousands of hits. It wasn't Gordon's fault. His staff had been misled by a typo.

In March 2005, when we finally got Gordon to meet John Hutton and Tony to discuss pensions policy, we asked John to pretend not to have seen Gordon's paper on the subject since Gordon had insisted that we not show it to him, and John faithfully kept quiet about it. As Gordon got more and more heated during the meeting, John's adviser Gareth Davies shook his head in exasperation. Gordon turned on him, shouting, 'Who are you?' Not that it did Gareth any harm as Gordon hired him when eventually he became prime minister. Gordon was caught out in a later meeting in the Cabinet Room on the same subject, when he said he had never seen a particular Number 10 paper. His accompanying staff actually had it in front of them and turned their copies over amid an embarrassed shuffling of feet.

Robin Cook took me out to lunch at Wilton's in February 2000. As he plied me with wine, it became clear that he was trying to find out how Gordon was seen in Number 10 at the time. I hadn't realised that he had known Gordon since he was a teenager. He told me that Gordon had wanted to stand in the Hamilton by-election in 1978 but had been told by his father, a local minister, that he couldn't because he and his wife were Tories and his mother had a weak heart. He didn't want to kill his mother, did he? Instead, he had to spend the campaign travelling around the constituency with Robin campaigning for George Robertson. An awful lot of wasted effort has been put into cod psychology concerning Gordon's personality, but Robin's analysis seemed convincing to me. Gordon's parents were very strict, and Gordon simply could not admit to doing anything wrong or making mistakes. That meant that he had to eschew any responsibility. If he was accused of anything, he would simply deny it was him and point the finger at someone else. It made it difficult for him to make decisions.

David Bennett, the ex-McKinsey consultant we brought in to head the Policy Unit in 2005, later told me that when he arrived in Number 10 most things in the government seemed to him to be better than portrayed in the press, but Gordon's behaviour and his relationship with Tony was far worse. He was puzzled why we had never let the outside world know. In retrospect, we probably should have made it public, but the moment never seemed quite right. We were fighting a form of asymmetric warfare. Gordon seemed to be prepared, if necessary, to burn down the citadel in order to capture it. We couldn't respond in kind because we were responsible for the government as a whole. If Tony mounted a reciprocal attack on his Chancellor, he would be damaging the entire Labour government, not just Gordon. We constantly had to hold our own side back. When Ed Balls published a paper on foundation hospitals in 2004, which was a frontal attack on the government's policies and was seen as a surrogate leadership challenge, Alan Milburn was incandescent and was poised to respond in kind. But we stopped him. We were continually fighting with one hand behind our backs.

Not that we were without blame. It takes two sides to keep a fight going, and I am sure that Tony's staff and supporters allowed their irritation to reflect itself in their conversations with the press, and it may well have seemed to Gordon, sensitive as he was to any slight, that he was under attack. We certainly came to think of him as the enemy. When Alastair Campbell and I were sitting next to each other at a 9/11 memorial service in St Paul's, he nudged me in the ribs and pointed to figures seated two rows ahead of us. Gordon was sitting alongside Iain Duncan Smith and William Hague. Alastair whispered in my ear, 'Look, the Leaders of the Opposition.'

Gordon often acted as if he were in Opposition. He would sit in policy meetings and blame the government. When challenged, he could not offer ideas of his own. He opposed the introduction of tuition fees for universities, and when Tony asked him what the alternative was he said he had a plan. On his behalf, Ed Balls worked up a graduate tax, but they could never quite bring themselves to put it forward because they knew how unpopular it would be, and so they continued to oppose without offering any alternative. When the Cabinet Secretary Andrew Turnbull announced a deal on Civil Service pensions that was unpopular with civil servants as a cut and also with commentators as unfair to those in the private sector,

Gordon publicly opposed the deal. When asked if he would reverse it, he had no answer.

Gordon could be easily wound up into believing that he was being done down. On one occasion, Piers Morgan, the editor of the *Mirror*, ran into Gordon in the hall of Number 10, having just completed an interview with Tony. Jokingly he told Gordon that Tony had over-ruled him by supporting the *Mirror*'s campaign for a special medal to be struck in memory of Princess Diana. When Gordon came into Tony's den, it took thirty minutes to calm him down and convince him that Morgan had been teasing him and that we had no inten-tion of agreeing to do what the *Mirror* wanted.

Gordon didn't like having meetings in Tony's office in Number 10, or going to the Number 11 flat, in case he ran into Cherie, so Tony would often go and see him in the Chancellor's Office in Number 11 where he would feel more comfortable. Gordon would occasionally refuse to turn up for meetings just to show who was boss. On one occasion, he said he could not come to a planned meeting because he was giving TV interviews, but, when Tony got hold of him on the phone, it was evident from his puffing and the other sound effects at the end of the line that he was on an exercise bike. By 2003, Tony had had enough. When Gordon refused to return from Scotland for a planned meeting on the euro and other issues, Tony sent him a message saying that if we were defeated on the parliamentary vote on foundation hospitals, which Gordon's supporters were opposing, he would be sacked. That got his attention. He started turning up for meetings. We won the vote.

Tony made repeated efforts to mollify Gordon. He saw him regu-larly, and, unlike most other ministers, alone. He would often spend hours on the phone talking to him at weekends. I would sometimes listen in. Once you were on the call, it was impossible to ring off because, for some technical reason I did not understand, doing so would leave a continuous loud beeping noise on both Tony's and Gordon's phones. In April 2003, I got so bored after the first hour of one of their circular arguments that I put the phone on mute and carried on with my walk with the shouting blaring away in my breast pocket. Sarah, who once overheard a snippet of one of the regular Sunday-evening calls, couldn't believe the tone of the argu-ment. She compared it to a jilted girlfriend, complete with high emotion, threats of blackmail and tears. On another occasion, Tony called me on a Sunday evening to say he had just completed a three-hour meeting with Gordon. I asked what on earth they could have to talk about for three hours. In response, he asked if I had ever been in love. 'Not with a man,' I replied.

From time to time Tony would tell me that Gordon had come to see him and seemed chastened. I said I didn't believe he was capable of feeling chastened, but periods of armistice did punctuate the continuing trench warfare. In 1999, after Peter Mandelson and Geoffrey Robinson had resigned from the government, Gordon made a major effort to be friends again. When he came into our outer office the next day, he even managed to address Tony's diary secretary, Kate Garvey, by her name and to say hello. It was followed by a meeting between the two teams, with Ed Balls, Ed Miliband and Sue Nye on his side, to make peace. I noted in my diary that I doubted it would last, and it didn't. During the 2006 rapprochement, we had managed to get Gordon to drop his opposition to education reform. Gordon said plaintively to Tony, 'I suppose, after education, you will want me to go along with you on health as well?' Tony said he did. Tony offered to give Gordon John Prescott's position as chair of the Constitutional Affairs Committee, as Gordon had requested, if only Gordon would cooperate on the issue of pensions in the Budget.

At root, the difficulty was that what Gordon really yearned for was Tony's undivided attention and his unlimited time, on the same basis as in the early years of Opposition. That just wasn't possible when Tony was prime minister. As Chancellor, with interest rates delegated to the Bank of England, he had only two big events a year: the Budget in the spring and the Pre-Budget Report in the autumn. For the rest of the year, the Chancellor was free to sit with his team and plot. The prime minister was not.

Many of Gordon's attacks on Tony, both directly and via surrogates, were left-wing in tone, designed to curry popularity in the party and with the unions. We faced a difficult decision in 2000 on where to locate the Synchroton, a huge scientific project that would generate jobs. The expert advice was that it should be built near Oxford, and the Wellcome Trust, the co-funders of the project, made it clear that that was their strong preference. There was an alternative site in the North-West, and a number of backbench Labour MPs from the region campaigned in favour of it. It generated enough strong feeling on North/South grounds that a whip from the North-West threatened to resign. We wrestled with the problem and eventually agreed with the expert advice and plumped for Oxford. Gordon let it be known in the Parliamentary Labour Party that he disagreed with Tony and favoured the North-West.

Gordon built up a team of henchmen on the Labour back benches to oppose Tony, centred around those ministers we had sacked from government, like Nick Brown and George Mudie. He eventually got one of them, Tony Lloyd, elected as chair of the PLP, having first considered and then ditched Joan Ruddock for the job. This group of Brownites was deployed in an attempt to thwart, in a semi-deniable way, Tony's efforts at public service reform in the Commons, including particularly foundation hospitals, top-up fees and education reform.

Gordon made a strategic mistake in positioning himself against public service reform, particularly schools reform, but it worked well tactically as a way of harrying Tony. In an unusually frank discussion, Gordon said to Tony that he didn't understand why we were trying to change state schools. His own state school had done well by him. When Tony pressed him, though, he admitted that his school had been selective, a form of Scottish grammar school.

Gordon was trying to ride two horses. He was anti-Europe in the right-wing press and anti-poverty in the left-wing press. He cultivated the *Guardian*, especially columnists Polly Toynbee and Jackie Ashley, and assured them that, if only Tony went, the Labour government would introduce more leftist policies and roll back New Labour's compromises. Having been a strong pro-European in Opposition, he became a Eurosceptic in government in the hope of attracting the support of Rupert Murdoch and the *Sun*, and he embarked on a campaign on the issues of middle-class morality close to the heart of Paul Dacre, the editor of the *Daily Mail*.

The trouble with riding two horses is that sooner or later you will fall off. Machiavelli describes how Appius, leader of the Decemvirate, deceived the Roman plebs by pretending that he was a man of the people but then changed his character so quickly on coming to power 'that no one had any excuse for failing to recognise the crookedness of his mind'. He advises a leader to make changes by appropriate stages 'before the change in character has robbed you of your old supporters . . . otherwise you will find yourself at large without friends, and so will be undone'. In Opposition, as Gordon was from 1997 to 2007, it is possible to fool both sides. Once he took over as prime minister, he was soon found out and abandoned by both left and right. It is far better to choose and at least have one side with you than to be deserted by all.

From the beginning, the real issue at stake between Tony and Gordon was not top-up fees or city academies but Gordon's demand that Tony set a date for his departure. Following the 2001 election, Gordon repeatedly tried to lever Tony into resigning. At one meeting, he said he would only agree to the euro if Tony stood down as leader, and at another he said he would only put money into the public services if Tony went. Tony tried to appease him by saying that he was not sure about standing for a third term if Gordon would only start cooperating. Gordon refused. At their first meeting after the summer break in September 2001, Gordon clearly thought Tony was going to name a date. He arrived in our office looking pleased, but left an hour later looking sour. He demanded that Tony agree to go, but Tony refused. Gordon began to shout that it was 'a moral question': Tony owed it to him. In the aftershock of the meeting, Tony told me that he had felt physically threatened when Gordon got up and leaned over his desk, and he told Richard Wilson, the Cabinet Secretary, that Chancellors did not last for ever.

The rows were out of all proportion to surrounding events. In the aftermath of 9/11, Tony rang Gordon to ask for his advice. Instead of responding, Gordon used the call to demand to know when Tony was going to resign. Tony slammed the phone down in a rage. The only time I saw him appear to cheer up during that period was when the War Cabinet was told there was a specific terrorist threat to Tony's life. Tony told me in 2001 that he believed that Gordon's strategy was to wear him down and to make his life so unbearable that he would finally quit. But he was not going to be worn down.

We thought that Gordon might return from his paternity leave in 2001 with some sense of perspective, given the personal tragedy that had overwhelmed him, but he didn't. He demanded a seat on the party's NEC and took on Tony over Europe. When he came to see

Tony in November, he demanded to know 'Why did you start this all off?' Tony threatened to walk out of the meeting, saying the argument was not about policies but all about personalities, adding, 'You are not the only person in this government.' In March 2004, Gordon threatened to bring down the government unless Tony agreed to leave immediately after the next election. Tony defied him to do so.

One of the interesting things about the relationship between the two was that the public manifestations of the fighting seemed to be out of sync with reality. Whenever there were press stories of rows, things had usually settled down temporarily and the two of them were working together, but when the media reported them as working in harmony I could hear the shouting spilling out under the door of the den and see the glowering looks on Gordon's face as he stormed out past my desk.

Gordon was convinced that he had secured a deal with Tony at a dinner hosted by John Prescott in November 2003. He expected Tony to leave in 2004 and to hand over to him. He appointed a transition team, including a new head of Number 10, and started a charm offensive on existing Number 10 staff to win them over to the new regime. His staff approached them individually and said that Gordon wanted to spend more time with them. He started to read up on foreign policy. But it didn't last. The war resumed in 2004 as a new election loomed. In December, Gordon lost his temper and called Tony a liar, a cheat and a fraud. He said, 'You can't talk about yourself as a Christian if you don't honour your word.' Tony threw him out of the office. Tony told me he was thinking of standing down and fighting a leadership election against Gordon, although only among Labour MPs rather than the whole Labour electoral college of unions and party members. I thought it was a very bad idea. It was much too much like John Major's shock resignation to take on 'the bastards' in the 1995 leadership election that had solved nothing.

The public manifestations of the rows were beginning to unsettle the Cabinet. Jack Straw told both sides to stop it in January 2005. The problem for us was that the Labour Party were tempted to believe that both Tony and Gordon were behaving as badly as each other. I was scarcely an impartial observer, but it seemed to me that the war was pretty one-sided. Alastair Campbell and Philip Gould were worried that the divisions would cause us to lose the 2005 election, and pressure from the Cabinet forced Gordon back from the brink. He emerged from the den after a meeting in March blinking back tears, having called a truce. He went out and briefed the papers that he had come back for the election and that his Budget had saved the day. Peter Mandelson subsequently accused Tony of having sold his birthright as a result of a temporary panic by Alastair and Philip, but it was hard to see what else he could do. The rapprochement in March and April was rather gruesome, and we dubbed Anthony Minghella's election film about Tony and Gordon working together *Love Story II*. In preparing for the press conference to launch the manifesto in April, Gordon tried to get Tony to say publicly he would hand over to him after the election and offered to say something in response about not challenging Tony. Tony declined the offer.

As I noted in my diary, the honeymoon lasted just twelve hours after polling day. Gordon was back pressing Tony to set a date for his departure the very next day. A week later, he said to Tony, 'So you are going to stand for a fourth term after all.' Tony laughed. Gordon kept coming back, and at the end of June he said to Tony, 'You completely shafted me last year by ratting on our deal. You have to set a date.' In October, he told Tony once again he had 'a moral duty to go' and demanded that Tony set a date, but added that, even if he did, he would not believe him. A few weeks later, Gordon came in and again demanded a date. Tony took him aback by saying he thought he would go at the end of 2007. Gordon went wild and threatened 'to spill the beans'. Tony asked what beans, but Gordon didn't reply. Tony suggested they have dinner together to discuss how to deal with the new Tory leader, David Cameron. Gordon blurted out 'But you are behind Cameron' and declined the invitation. The press began to publish stories about Gordon demanding a date for Tony's departure, but Gordon denied publicly that he was. When he next came to see Tony he demanded instead 'clarity'. Tony asked him if by clarity he meant a date. Gordon said no. In November 2005, Tony thought again about resigning and fighting a leadership election against Gordon, but again we prevailed on him not to.

The issue continued to dominate their relationship until in 2006 Tony finally agreed to stand down. The pressure was too much, and support in the party was fracturing. Tony told me he did not want to stay if he was not wanted.

Tony would often speculate about whether Gordon really wanted the top job, or whether in fact he was subconsciously happier just to nurse his grievances and be cheated at the last minute. He noted that Gordon had repeatedly backed off from the opportunity of taking the leadership in the past, and wondered whether perhaps he knew that he was not cut out to be a leader. Given his miserable period as prime minister, perhaps Gordon's subconscious was right. I sometimes thought of him as the dog that chased an airplane: what would he do with it if he caught it? Perhaps he preferred glorying in victimhood to taking the responsibility of being prime minister.

In retrospect Tony should have sacked Gordon early on. Machiavelli's advice was 'that to a person to whom offence has been given, no administrative post of importance should subsequently be assigned'. In the early years, Gordon gave us a number of opportunities to rid ourselves of him by threatening to resign, but Tony never took advantage of them. In December 1998, when Tony demanded that Charlie Whelan be sacked, Gordon, in tears, threatened to leave. In 1999, more seriously, Gordon put it about that he wanted to go off and become the head of the IMF. And in 2004 Tony told me that he had offered the presidency of the World Bank to Gordon, although it is hard to see how we could have secured what is traditionally an American job for him.

Tony first started talking about sacking Gordon in April 2001, even before that year's election. A pattern was established. After some new outrage over a weekend, Tony would tell me on Monday that he was going to have a showdown with Gordon on Friday and he would sack him if he didn't agree to cooperate. We ran through a range of possible alternatives as Chancellor. In November 2001 it was to be Charles Clarke; in January 2003 it was to be Jack Straw; and in November 2003 it was to be John Reid. The nearest it came to happening was in 2003. In July, after a very rough patch, Tony told me that he wanted to get politically strong again so he could solve the Gordon problem in November. It wasn't worth going on as prime minister with him still in place. He intended to have a mini reshuffle before the summer break so that he could then have a bigger one later in the year and make Gordon Foreign Secretary. If Gordon turned the job down, then he could be sacked without being able to win a big sympathy vote in the party. Gordon got wind of the plan and told people in the Treasury that he would resign before he could be offered the position. The prospect of resigning or being sacked seriously frightened him and he retreated. Unfortunately, the idea was prematurely leaked in October 2003, making it impossible to implement, and Gordon came into Tony's office the day the story appeared with a broad smile saying, 'No more nonsense about me being moved then?'

There were good reasons why Tony never did act. At one level, Gordon ranting and raving was absolutely impossible, but at another, in Tony's view, he was head and shoulders above the rest of the Cabinet. Would it be right to dispense with such a big political talent? Certainly putting him on the back benches would have created an important centre of opposition around which Old Labour forces could coalesce with the aim of ousting Tony. Better to have him inside the tent than out. And there had to be a reason for dispatching him or it would just look like jealousy on Tony's part, and since we had never made Gordon's behaviour public no one would under-stand the real reasons for getting rid of him. This intractable problem was what I termed the 'Gordonian knot', and we were never able to cut through it.

Partly the difficulty was that Tony had strung Gordon along for so long that it was hard for him to change that tactic for dealing with him. Tony was, however, aware he had missed an alternative route. He said to me rather pensively in July 2005, 'Do you think I have made a terrible mistake not dealing with this man earlier?' And of course he had.

John Prescott repeatedly tried to make peace between the two, and he relished the power their disagreement gave him. Tony was convinced that John's opposition to Gordon as leader would be a fatal black spot to his aspirations. Gordon clearly believed that too, given his frantic efforts to win John's support. Gordon would go to PMQs when John was standing in for Tony, even though he would rarely attend Tony's sessions. He gave money to John's department in 2004 even while he was reducing the budgets of other departments. In 2005, he told John he could stay on as deputy prime minister when he became leader, up to the subsequent election. Although totally unrealistic, this was attractive bait – John couldn't face the prospect of retirement. He hosted numerous armistice dinners at his official flat and even offered to host one at Dorneywood, which Gordon had given up as the Chancellor's official residence, but they never led to a lasting peace.

John told me in March 2005 that a deal had been struck between Tony and Gordon at a dinner at his flat in November 2003. Gordon certainly told everyone that there was such an understanding, dating back to Opposition days. Even Jim Callaghan told Tony in May 2002 that Gordon had told him that Tony had made him promises and said he had to be kept to them. Tony explained the reality to him. There was no deal because Gordon never lived up to his part of the bargain. Tony had clearly tried to mollify him when he ran for the leadership in 1994, suggesting that Gordon could be his successor and could play a big role in the government if they worked together. And in November 2003 Tony was under great pressure. He invited me up to the flat for a drink at the beginning of the month and said he felt beset on all sides, by Gordon, by Michael Howard, by the media and by Iraq. In that mood he clearly did give Gordon to understand that he could take over as leader after the election. But Gordon refused to hear the quid pro quo that Tony demanded: that he cooperate on the reform programme. Since Gordon never delivered on his part of the deal, it is not too surprising that Tony didn't hand over the leadership to him as he wanted. Tony had decided by June 2004 that Gordon was never going to cooperate on the reform programme and that he was therefore not going to hand over power to him straight away. If one part of a deal is not respected, then you can't expect the other half to be implemented, particularly when a promise has been extracted under duress. This is one of the lessons that Machiavelli repeats most often: 'forced agreements will be kept neither by a Prince nor by a republic', 'peace treaties can be relied on when they are made voluntarily' and 'promises extracted by force ought not to be kept'.

Deal or no deal, Tony handed over to Gordon in the end, but Gordon made a number of mistakes in the way in which he took the leadership that coloured his tenure in the job and ensured that it was a failure. The first was what I dubbed in 2004 the 'King Herod strategy' of killing off any rivals for the leadership at birth. Bizarrely he saw Ken Livingstone as a rival. In 1999, he told Tony that he knew he was positioning Livingstone as a counterweight to him in the Labour Party; and in 2001, Gordon was furious when he discovered that Tony had been secretly seeing Bob Kiley, an American executive whom Livingstone had brought over to run the Tube. A note of the meeting by a Number 10 civil servant had fallen into the hands of Ed Balls. Gordon lined up Nick Brown to attack Tony in Cabinet for even thinking about talking to Ken. Tony told Gordon after the Cabinet session that he would have to go if he carried on behaving like this, but it made no difference.

His treatment of Alan Milburn and Steve Byers as potential rivals for the crown was even more vicious. They were subjected to the full briefing bombardment, and their departments were sometimes financially starved. In 2005, Gordon demanded that Alan Milburn be sacked from his role as election coordinator and replaced with Douglas Alexander as his price for coming back to work in the campaign, and during the 2006 coup attempt, he insisted that Tony suppress Alan and Steve Byers. When he found out that Tony had made Charles Clarke party chair in 2002, he had a fit. And he reacted very badly when David Miliband, James Purnell and Pat McFadden were promoted in 2006, seeing them, correctly, as the next generation of potential Blairite challengers. The one colleague he seemed to be genuinely scared of was John Reid. When gradual attrition of the Cabinet led to John Reid moving up the table and sitting next to him, I loved watching the twitches and grimaces that would pass over Gordon's face whenever John spoke, and John would wink at me in mutual enjoyment. It was a mistake on Gordon's part to be so ruthless in seeing off potential rivals. It left him with no real friends or supporters in Cabinet. They all hated him personally and when given the opportunity to do him harm did so.

One of Gordon's weaknesses on becoming prime minister was that he had never been elected. He would have secured greater legitimacy if he had faced a challenger and won a debate of ideas within the party, but he was scared that, if people were allowed to vote, they would vote to stop him, and he took every possible step to ensure that there was no contest. He pursued a course that I called the 'inevitability strategy'. By deploying his three spin doctors – Charlie Whelan, Damian McBride and Ed Balls – to brief against his enemies within the Cabinet, he kept the Cabinet cowed and sullen. He wanted his colleagues to accept that he was the dauphin and the crown was his as of right. Charlie Falconer correctly said that 'ninety-five per cent of the Cabinet believed he would become prime minister but ninety-five per cent of them did not want him to do so'. Even Douglas Alexander, one of his supporters, told a colleague in October 2006 that, while Gordon would win the leadership, he would not win the election unless he changed.

Gordon's positioning as he manoeuvred to take over was paradoxical. Distancing himself from Tony and his record was understandable. The public were tired of ten years of a one-man show and wanted something different. But he chose to position himself by flagging up his own weaknesses. He set himself up as a long-term strategist when everyone who knew him well realised that he was a brilliant political tactician and street fighter but not a long-term thinker. He announced that he was against spin when he had employed some of the most vicious spin doctors ever known to British politics. He said that he was above politics – and made much of appointing a rather threadbare Government of All the Talents – when he was known as being a fiercely partisan politician. He said he would reduce the number of political appointees in Number 10 but actually increased them. Flagging up these negatives in such an obvious way came back to haunt him as his premiership went wrong. Because he had thrived for so long by asserting that black was white and white black, and getting away with it, he thought he could make his weaknesses vanish by an act of sheer will.

His biggest and most inexplicable mistake, though, was not to have thought about what he wanted to do with the job. If nothing else, a leadership election would have helped him define why he wanted to be prime minister and to set out his own agenda. It was odd to have coveted the job since his youth but not actually to have come up with things he wanted to change. He told Tony in 2005 that he had a plan for exactly what he was going to do as prime minister but wasn't going to tell him until he went. Douglas Alexander briefed Polly Toynbee of the *Guardian* in 2005 that

Gordon was 'fizzing with ideas'; but, when he was asked to come up with specific proposals, embarrassingly he could only suggest removing soft-drinks machines from schools. He really only had one idea, and that was to displace Tony. Tony predicted to me in 2003 that Gordon would be 'truly cautious' as prime minister and would do nothing other than introduce more tax credits, and he was proved right. The Conservatives were able to pivot their entire election campaign around Gordon as a block on reform. If he had been replaced as prime minister by any other Labour politician, the Tories would have been left without a campaign in 2010 and perhaps the Labour Party would have won the election.

When I look back at my diaries, two things leap out from every page. The first was our repeated efforts to deal with Northern Ireland, and the second was the endless references to some new unreasonable demand or action by Gordon Brown. In retrospect, it is hard to see how or why Tony put up with it. Tony should clearly have sacked him early on or at least threatened to do so in a sufficiently convincing way to make him behave. But I doubt whether Gordon was capable of behaving. He was consumed with ambition, and nothing was going to stop him. Machiavelli correctly observes that 'so powerful is the sway that ambition exercises over the human heart that it never relinquishes them, no matter how high they have risen'.

Leaders may actually be better off without dauphins. Certainly Princes of Wales have been a thorn in the side of British monarchs for centuries. It is true that Margaret Thatcher wasn't saved in 1990 by the lack of a clear successor, but to avoid becoming the victims of blackmail, leaders should make sure they have a choice of more than one possible successor and cultivate competition between the candidates. They should ensure that none of their colleagues becomes overmighty and should cut them down to size early on before it becomes too late to do so without paying too high a price. As Machiavelli says, you have to deal with threats like this early or it is 'too late to resort to severity; while any leniency you may use will be thrown away, for it will be seen to be compulsory and gain you no thanks'.

Potential successors should give thought in advance to what they would do in office. They should not fear contested elections but welcome them as a chance to put an argument and to win a mandate for what they want to do. They may want to distance themselves from their predecessors, but they should preserve those parts of their record that suit them and not make their predecessors so dissatisfied that they sit brooding in the Commons for decades to come, as Ted Heath did, making the lives of their successor miserable.

Tony won all the policy battles in the end. Gordon didn't stop him doing the things he wanted to do; he just made it more difficult and slowed him down, so that he was not able fully to reap the benefits of his reforms while we were still in government. All in all, it was a tragic waste of time and effort. It is true that Gordon was more of the old-fashioned 'soft left' than Tony, who was more in tune with the aspiring swing voters of Middle Britain, but that was not what Gordon's insurgency was really about. It was principally about who should be leader, a struggle that would have been readily recognisable to Machiavelli.

Machiavelli gives examples of other leaders who came to power 'by paths of wickedness', particularly Agathocles of Sicily. That individual's vices were conjoined with great vigour both of mind and body, and he came to power not by luck but as a result of his own efforts. In doing so, he had resort 'to slaughter fellow-citizens, to betray friends, to be devoid of honour, pity, and religion', and his skills 'cannot be counted as merits, for these are means which may lead to power, but which confer no glory'. As a result, 'his unbridled cruelty and inhumanity, together with his countless crimes, forbid us to number him with the greatest men'.

In the end, Gordon got his way. He became leader, but his crimes came back to haunt him. As Machiavelli says, 'For it is easy for force to acquire a title, but not for a title to acquire force.' For Tony, Gordon's behaviour just made the politics of governing much harder and more uncomfortable.

CHAPTER SIX

'Whether it is Better to be Loved or Feared'

Politics and Parliament

Machiavelli poses the question 'whether it is better to be loved rather than feared, or feared rather than loved. It might perhaps be answered that we should wish to be both; but since love and fear can hardly exist together, if we must choose between them, it is far safer to be feared than to be loved.'

Most people who go into politics have a craving to be loved, and being loved is a good route to becoming leader. Michael Foot and Neil Kinnock were far better loved by the Labour Party than Tony Blair ever was. Bruce Grocott, Tony's Parliamentary Private Secretary who had been part of Kinnock's team, used to describe to me the sinking feeling in every Labour MP's stomach as Mrs Thatcher flattened Neil at PMQs in the Commons week after week. They would rally to him out of affection as he got into difficulties, but he could never command their respect. Mrs Thatcher, on the contrary, was never much loved but she was certainly respected, both in her own party and more widely in the country.

When Tony first became leader of the Labour Party, he was dismissed by the Tories and the media as 'Bambi', a defenceless lightweight who would be quickly run over. It was extraordinary how rapidly he moved from being Bambi in the eyes of his critics to being Stalin, a dictator who trampled over the wishes of others. As a leader, if you have to choose, it is better to be Stalin than Bambi, for as Machiavelli observes, 'men are less careful how they offend him who makes himself loved than him who makes himself feared. For love is held by the tie of obligation, which, because men are a sorry breed, is broken on every whisper of private interest; but fear is bound by the apprehension of punishment which never relaxes its grasp.'

In the early years, Tony was seen as a politician who simply followed the focus groups and always wanted to be popular. Later, he came to be seen as someone who ignored public opinion and insisted he knew best. In fact, in both periods he was extremely solicitous of public opinion and followed the polls closely. Machiavelli wisely counselled that 'it is essential that the Prince be on a friendly footing with his people, since, otherwise, he will have no recourse in adversity'.

Interestingly for a writer in the sixteenth century, Machiavelli attached importance to public opinion. He writes in *The Discourses*: 'A wise man will not ignore public opinion in regard to particular matters, such as the distribution of offices and preferments; for here the populace, when left to itself, does not make mistakes, or, if sometimes it does, its mistakes are rare in comparison with those that would occur if the few had to make such a distribution'; and, 'Not without good reason is the voice of the people likened to that of God; for public opinion is remarkably accurate in its prognostications, so much so that it seems as if the populace by some hidden power discerned the evil and the good that was to befall it.'

A prime minister depends for his place on public opinion. If his popularity goes down, his party becomes restive. As long as it is high, he is unassailable. But prime ministers need to work at their popularity. Machiavelli observes that 'He who becomes a Prince through the favour of the people should always keep on good terms with them.' Prime ministers have to continue to campaign even while they govern, although it is sometimes hard to combine the two.

Polling is an essential tool of prime ministers, but polls, like secret intelligence, have to be handled carefully. Without them, a modern leader is driving blind. However, they are a snapshot of the past not a glimpse into the future, so if a leader uses them to govern it is like steering while peering over the stern of the boat. The numbers help locate your whereabouts in the ocean and tell you the state of the tides, but they do not tell you how to set your forward course. And sometimes polls can be misleading. In the course of the three-week election campaign in 1997, one poll popped up halfway through that showed our lead over the Tories closing suddenly to just a single figure. It threw Tony and the rest of the team into an immediate panic. Within days, it was clear that the poll was a rogue and the panic subsided, but it had distracted from the campaign in the meantime. It happened again in the 2005 campaign when one poll showed our lead going down to just 3 per cent. Again there was panic. A wise leader should use quantitative polling as a tool but not as a substitute for his own political instincts.

It is sensible to supplement opinion polls with qualitative research like focus groups. But focus groups are subjective and are often coloured by the views of those conducting them. They can be simply a tool of flattery. Gordon had a personal pollster, whose groups always seemed to show him in the most favourable light. Such polling can provide reassurance, but it also misleads. As with polls, a sudden turn in the focus groups can upset and distract a leader, particularly in the run-up to an election. In May 2001, there were terrible focus-group results in the middle of the campaign, and the same thing happened again in April 2005, with a group in Edgware showing all ten participants voting for the Tories because of immigration. On both occasions the results threw Tony into a depression. In both cases they were wrong, and we won the elections comfortably. Leaders should always be suspicious of sudden unexplained switches in poll findings. They probably mean that there is something wrong with the polling rather than that the public have suddenly gone mad and changed their views for no discernible reason.

We had a wonderful adviser in Philip Gould, who knew Tony as well as he knew the electorate and whose very familiarity helped Tony instinctively understand his advice. He would call Tony in the evening after one of his focus groups to give him the headlines and would be the first with the numbers when a quantitative poll was in the field. He was supported by two very different American pollsters during our time in Number 10. The first was Stan Greenberg, who had been President Clinton's pollster in 1992 and was mathematically focused; regression analysis was his best tool for understanding opinion. He regularly came in to brief Tony and the team in the Cabinet Room with stacks of figures and graphs. In July 2004, we switched to Mark Penn who had been President Clinton's pollster from 1994 onwards and who was working for Hillary Clinton as she geared up for her presidential campaign. We switched on the advice of Bill Clinton, but Philip had to break the news to Stan. It rubbed in his sense of grievance at being snubbed by Clinton, and he took it badly.

In fact, he refused to give up and in the 2005 election we ended up with two pollsters working at the campaign headquarters producing different results, often from the same polling. Mark's approach was completely different from Stan's. He tied his polling to specific policy and message questions and produced essays arguing for particular courses of action. The personal tensions between them were made worse by an ideological divide. Stan was more left-leaning, and his advice tended to push the need to win over downscale voters with more redistributive messages, while Mark was more centrist and his advice tended to point to being tough on security issues.

Wise leaders understand that pollsters are not strategists, even if they sometimes want to be. Their role should be gathering and explaining the evidence. Political strategy is a different skill, harder to define, but essential to a leader. Political strategists have to market themselves, and sometimes their reputations are overblown. It is the politicians who make the decisions and win elections, not the advisers. Philip Gould frightened Tony by telling us in 2004 that Maurice Saatchi was coming back to work for Michael Howard as leader of the Tory Party in the election campaign. His reputation as the person who brought the Labour Party down in 1979 and again in 1992 was deeply ingrained in the Labour psyche. I was, however, somewhat less worried than the others because Alistair McAlpine, a close confidant of Mrs Thatcher's and author of two Machiavelli-themed books, had told me a few months before that Saatchi had played no serious part in any Tory campaign until 1992. In 1979, he had had no strategic role at all.

As well as Philip, Tony's strategists were Peter Mandelson, Alastair Campbell and, above all, himself. The interesting thing about the three original figures of the New Labour troika is that their skills were almost the polar opposite of their public caricatures. Gordon wasn't a long-term thinker at all, but he was a brilliant day-to-day tactician, concentrating on how to turn each day's media battle to the party's advantage. Peter wasn't primarily a spin doctor but rather a long-term strategist who could translate our vision into the kinds of practical steps that delivered successful campaigns. And Tony was the one with the vision of where he wanted to take the party and the country, and whose instincts told him where public opinion was now and where it would be five years hence.

The key political skill of a leader is the ability to build a coalition of support. Those who try to do so by cobbling together a rainbow coalition of small groups with no natural common cause, as Al Gore did in 2000, tend to fail. A sustainable coalition needs to be united by a shared interest. Ronald Reagan understood this in 1980, when he detached skilled blue-collar workers from the traditional Democratic base and united them with the more upscale traditional Republican voters. Mrs Thatcher did a similar thing in 1979 when she convinced aspiring 'Essex man', known by advertisers as C1s and C2s, that they had more in common with the successful middle classes above them than with the poor below them, whose welfare bills, she said, they were paying. The insight of Bill Clinton and the New Democrats was that it was necessary for left-wing parties to move back to the centre, particularly on economic issues, if they were going to win back 'Macomb County man' whom Reagan had stolen from the Democrat coalition. Tony similarly saw that, if Labour were going to win again, it needed to convince aspiring 'Mondeo man' and 'Worcester woman' that they had more in common with the hard-working mass of people than they did with those who were already highly successful. Once you have built this coalition, it is essential that you govern to sustain it. If you run to the centre in an election campaign, you must govern from the centre after it. Tony remained fixated on the interests of Middle Britain exactly because that was the key part of the coalition that had elected him.

The popularity of a successful leader in government can follow one of two post-election trajectories. Mrs Thatcher's governments would start the Parliament popular, then go through a trough of unpopularity as she tried to undertake difficult reforms, and finally come back up the other side of the U to win a further term. Being at the bottom of the U was nerve-racking for Tory politicians, but they were able to hold on, at least until the 1990 trough. When we won in 1997, I thought we would have a similar trajectory, but instead the government's popularity actually rose in the course of 1997 and only slowly declined over the following decade. So from 1997 to 2007, instead of a series of deep Us, we experienced a long, slow but seemingly inexorable slide into unpopularity. That made it easier to maintain support for Tony in the party because we were not tested by slumps in the middle of a term. Unlike the Tory Party,

Labour does not regard itself as having the divine right to rule and it is therefore more inclined to lose its nerve when things get tough. There was even more of a premium on a leader's role in putting a brave face on every disaster and on instilling confidence however uncertain he may feel personally. Powers of endurance are essential for the leader but not always easy to maintain. Tony told me in the middle of the 2001 election campaign that he didn't know why he wanted to be re-elected: his life was a living hell. But he regained his nerve by the end of the campaign and kept going for six more years.

Leaders have a choice between being uniters or dividers. Mrs Thatcher opted from the beginning for a divide-and-rule approach, both in the country and in her party. Machiavelli observed that the Venetians 'fostered the factions of Guelf and Ghibeline in the cities subject to them; and though they did not suffer blood to be shed, fomented their feuds, in order that the citizens having their minds occupied with these disputes might not conspire against them'. Mrs Thatcher found it useful to divide the country over the miners' strike in order to galvanise her supporters and persuade them to concentrate on fighting the enemy instead of fighting each other. The strategy backfired on the Venetians because one of the factions eventually won and took all the territory that the Venetians had captured by their ruse, and in the end the strategy backfired on Mrs Thatcher too. She was brought down by her own side when the divisiveness over the poll tax became too much for them to stomach. Gordon Brown was another divider, obsessed with finding 'dividing lines' with the Tories to help define himself. It did him little good.

Tony, on the other hand, began deliberately as a 'one nation' leader, trying to bring people together after the Tory years, and that is why his popularity rose during his first years in office. As time wore on, he became a source of division in the country over Iraq and other issues. Perhaps it is impossible to remain a uniter over a long period as leader. Every time leaders make difficult choices they are bound to lose some part of their support base, and over the years that leads to division and eventually the polarisation of the electorate.

Political parties are the instruments with which leaders win power and stay in office in modern democracies, and any leader who forgets his party in Parliament will not last long. Gerald Kaufman writes about the importance of ensuring that leaders spend long hours in the tea room hobnobbing with their party's backbenchers, and Bruce Grocott tried to get Tony to do so, but without success. MPs are divided into Londoners, who go home in the evening, and forced bachelors or spinsters who hang out in the Commons tea room or bars. Tony was always a natural Londoner even though his constituency was in the North-East, and, if it is not your habit to spend time in the Commons, then a sudden appearance in the bar or tea room can actually alarm your troops rather than reassure them. It makes them think there must be a political crisis looming. Having a good Parliamentary Private Secretary and good political staff who spend their time talking to a wide cross section of MPs helps, but is not a substitute for a leader meeting the foot soldiers on a regular basis. We used to wheel backbenchers through Number 10 in groups of twenty, rebels as well as loyalists, so they could question Tony and let him know their worries. PLP meetings on Monday evenings open to all Labour MPs provided a safety valve for discontent and a chance for a pep talk. The elected parliamentary committee of the party used to meet in Tony's office in the House of Commons after PMQs and gave him a chance to take the temperature. But the key points of contact between the leader and his party in Parliament are ministers.

Machiavelli writes that 'the choice of Ministers is a matter of no small moment to a Prince. Whether they shall be good or no depends on his prudence, so that the readiest conjecture we can form of the character and sagacity of a Prince, is from seeing what sort of men he has about him. When they are at once capable and faithful, we may always account him wise, since he has known to recognise their merit and to retain their fidelity. But if they be otherwise, we must pronounce unfavourably of him, since he has committed a first fault in making this selection.'

This is even more true for a prime minister than a prince. The only power he has is the power of patronage, so for him the choice of ministers is the way he exercises his influence, and unlike the prince he depends on their continuing support for his survival. New prime ministers, however, have no management experience and, when we arrived in Number 10, there were no written rules on reshuffles, just lore handed down from one PPS to another over the generations. Alex Allan kindly prepared a rule book for us on the basis of his experience under John Major.

If prime ministers had their way, they would appoint all the MPs on their benches to ministerial office. The payroll vote is an essential parliamentary tool, and the bigger it is the better. The only thing that restrains prime ministers is the Ministerial Salaries Act. This piece of legislation limits the number of Cabinet and junior ministers in a complicated interlocking matrix of permitted totals. So far, no government since the 1970s has dared to change it, although at the margin successive governments have found increasingly imaginative ways round it.

The trouble with the Ministerial Salaries Act is precisely that it is so complex. You really need to check with lawyers whether you have exceeded any of the totals when you get to the end of a reshuffle, but there isn't time for that with the media waiting to report each and every appointment in rolling news, so you sometimes get to the end and realise you have appointed too many ministers. In that case, you have two choices: you can either dismiss those ministers you have just appointed, which they don't take very well, having told their families and constituents immediately on receipt of the phone call appointing them; or you can persuade them to take the job but without a salary. That was what I had to do with the unfortunate Meg Munn whom we had appointed as Minister for Women in 2005. We finished the reshuffle and only then realised we hadn't got enough salaries. As she was the last appointed, she had to do without. It was, however, slightly awkward to explain why we were not paying our new minister, among whose functions was ensuring equality of pay for men and women. We had to come up with even more elaborate arrangements in other cases, and in 2004 ended up giving one minister a whip's salary while not paying one of the whips. Of course, anyone who can afford to go without a salary – like Geoffrey Robinson and Shaun Woodward – does so.

One of the key rules is not to appoint anyone to a job until it is empty. But that is easier said than done. In 2005, we thought we had persuaded John Prescott to give up his department and remain simply as deputy prime minister, but he was furious when he discovered that the department was installing Braille machines for David Blunkett, his successor. He decided to stay on. Sometimes people want time to think about a job they have been offered, but you can't hold up a whole reshuffle while they do. When Tony moved Robin Cook from Foreign Secretary to Leader of the House, Robin quite understandably asked for time to consider whether he wouldn't rather resign from the government altogether. But we had to move on with filling the other jobs.

Demotions are among the hardest things to do. In the cases of both Robin Cook and Jack Straw, they had been assured by people outside Number 10, whom they believed, that they would not be moved. So when they were summoned in to see Tony and were told they had to give up the Foreign Secretaryship they were shocked. In neither case did they accept Tony's argument that they had had a long run in the job and room had to be made for others to have a chance, but on both occasions, after deliberation, they decided to take the Leader of the House slot with the minimum of drama. In the case of Jack Straw, the press speculated that he was dismissed because he had upset the Americans, but that was completely untrue.

Machiavelli favours the practice of demoting ministers, writing that 'Venice even makes the mistake of thinking that a citizen who has held office, should be ashamed to accept a lower; and the state is content that he should decline to accept it'. He thinks that while this may be honourable from the point of view of the individual, it is of no use whatever from the public standpoint, 'for a republic rightly places more hope and confidence in a citizen who from a high command moves to a lower, than in one who from a lower command rises to a higher because of their experience'. Of course, persuading the ministers concerned of the virtue of this particular course is a different matter.

It is best to get any sackings done the night before the reshuffle begins, to spare the ministers the humiliation of walking down Downing Street in the glare of the cameras only to be dismissed. If possible, it should be done in the prime minister's office in the Palace of Westminster so the media do not notice that the process has started. A minister should be allowed to resign with dignity, and an exchange of letters should be drafted that can be released to show they always intended to go at this point. Occasionally ministers tell you in advance of a reshuffle that they would like to leave the government but are happy to wait for a convenient moment.

Sometimes press stories revealing that a particular minister is about to be sacked in the run-up to a reshuffle convince the minister concerned that they are for the chop and they therefore decide to resign first. I would advise against this. Press stories in 2004 convinced Andrew Smith that he was about to be sacked, and he came to see Tony to ask to be allowed to resign in advance. Actually, Tony wasn't planning to sack him at all, but accepted his resignation anyway, once he came in, since we needed the headroom to promote others.

Sometimes ministers play 'hard to find' in the hope that, if they can't be reached, you will give up on the idea of sacking them. They have a good excuse since the date of the reshuffle is supposed to be secret, so there is no reason why they shouldn't be up a mountain in the Andes or on a fact-finding visit to Papua. Nigel Griffiths was a particular exponent of this survival tactic. When we couldn't find him in 2005, we decided to sack him anyway, but Gordon, as usual, came to his rescue at the last minute and persuaded Tony to re-appoint him. By that stage we had run out of jobs and salaries and had to make up a job for him in the Leader of the House's office and appoint him without a salary. He didn't appear to mind, although he resigned over Trident two years later. He announced that he was coming to Downing Street to hand in his letter of resignation, so I promptly put a ban on him entering the street. Jack Straw, his ministerial boss, called me and said it would be terrible to send him away. He would have his detective accompany him, and he could come in through the back gate. I agreed, but with no illusions about what would happen next. Predictably, Nigel got the TV cameras to film him handing his letter to the doorman and gave interviews in Downing Street with the Number 10 door behind him.

Some ministers refuse to be sacked. Tony phoned Geoff Hoon in 2005 anticipating a difficult conversation in removing him as Defence Secretary after six years, but he was taken aback when Geoff refused to accept dismissal and insisted on coming in to see him. Once in the room, he managed to persuade Tony to keep him in the government after all, and he became Europe Minister. Geoff decided to interpret his new job as having full Cabinet minister status and went out to tell the press, which left the new Foreign Secretary, Margaret Beckett, an MP for a neighbouring constituency and not a close friend, extremely unhappy. It took us months to unravel the problem.

People react in different ways to the unpleasant experience of being sacked. I used to sit with Tony as he imparted the bad news. He hated having to do it, and would cut to the chase rapidly. He would say, 'Look, X, there is no easy way of saying this but I'm afraid I'm going to need your job.' Some would threaten blood-curdling revenge, as Ivor Richard did when he was sacked as Leader of the Lords. Some are ominously reassuring, as Nick Brown was in 2003, telling Tony that he would continue to support him on the back benches as he had in government – exactly what we were afraid of. Chris Smith, when dismissed in 2001, said he would nurse his disappointment but was actually very decent after he left office. Some burst into tears on the news and have to be consoled, while others try to negotiate. Some arrive expecting to be promoted and are horrified when they are told they are out. Barbara Roche, who afterwards became a firm supporter of Gordon, was particularly outraged when she saw Tony. She told him she thought she had been summoned in to be elevated to the Cabinet, not to be sacked. But the majority are professional about it, although obviously disappointed. Jack Cunningham was a complete *mensch* when Tony finally let him go, and Harriet Harman in 1998 was sweet, taking the news well and simply asking if Tony would write a handwritten letter to her daughter assuring her that it was not because of incompetence.

In politics, sacking someone is even harder to do than it is in the private sector. You have to tell them that it is not about their lack of merit, just that you need to give everyone a chance. They don't believe you and it is hard for them not to be resentful. When someone is sacked in the private sector, they leave the firm and are no longer a problem. In politics, they are still there on the back benches and can now exact their revenge by making your life a misery, often in cahoots with a rival who is after the prime minister's job. Not many CEOs could manage a company if all the sacked directors remained in the boardroom. In politics, the weight of these people builds up over time until eventually there are more of them than there are supporters of the prime minister on the green benches. When you take into account those who are too old or too mad to be considered for a ministerial job, those who are ideologically opposed like the Campaign Group in the Labour Party or the 'bastards' in the Tory Party, and those who have been overlooked in the past, then there are simply too few left who hope for advancement from the prime minister. He no longer has anything to offer them. At that point the 'disappointed' outnumber the appointed, and the days of the prime minister are numbered. That simple equation was in the end what happened to Mrs Thatcher and later for Tony Blair.

Appointments, while more pleasant, are also difficult. They often come as a complete shock to the individual concerned. Jack Straw seemed knocked sideways when Tony told him he was to be Foreign Secretary in 2001. Sometimes the new appointee hesitates. David Miliband wasn't keen either time we appointed him to the Cabinet. The first time, when he was sent to John Prescott's Department of Communities and Local Government as deputy in 2005, he complained, but in fact he was given a huge opportunity as John stood back and gave him room to prove himself. When Tony made him Secretary of State for Environment, Food and Rural Affairs in 2006, he complained about being sent off to deal with 'cows farting'. I tried to persuade him that it was an unparalleled opportunity to take on David Cameron on environmental issues, which he then proceeded to do with distinction. Ruth Kelly worried that her Catholicism would be a problem in her appointment to Education, but Tony persuaded her that it would not.

Sometimes prime ministers back out of appointments at the last moment. In 2006, we had decided to replace Jack Straw as Foreign Secretary with the Home Secretary, Charles Clarke, but in the weeks preceding the reshuffle a series of disastrous crises at the Home Office over the release of foreign prisoners tarnished Charles's reputation. Charles started the crisis in blasé mood but by the end was badly rattled. Tony no longer thought he could promote him to the Foreign Office, although I continued to argue that he should be sent there. Tony saw Charles and offered him Defence or DTI instead, but he declined and decided he would rather go to the back benches. Our hopes of him as a counterweight to Gordon Brown were finished. We looked desperately for a replacement for the Foreign Office. We nearly opted for David Miliband, but we decided in the end that he was still too young and inexperienced. Putting him into that position at that moment would have made him a target for the Gordon Brown death machine. So instead we chose Margaret Beckett.

The appointment of junior ministers is a mass-production exercise. 'Switch' gets five or six about-to-be ministers stacked up on the phone, and then they are put through to the prime minister one after another. The private secretary's job is to stick the right bit of paper in front of the prime minister to make sure that he appoints the right person to the right job. There were frequent shouts from the den asking what on earth the job was that the next caller was supposed to be doing; and, if they asked questions, the stock reply from Tony was that we would get back to them with the details. The private secretary then calls the Permanent Secretary and Private Office in the department concerned to tell them which new minister is coming in and they send round the ministerial car. On one memorable occasion in an early reshuffle, switch put the wrong person through to Tony. We had been intending to appoint Bernard Donoughue, the former policy adviser to Harold Wilson, to an agriculture job. Instead, Brian Donohue, a Scottish MP whom there was no danger of us appointing to anything, came on the line by mistake. Luckily, Tony realised when he heard Donohue's voice and instead of offering him a job asked him what he thought about the political situation. Having stopped on the motorway hard shoulder, Brian gave him the benefit of his thoughts and Tony rang off. Later, we discovered that Brian had told his colleagues how impressed he was that Tony had found time to discuss politics with him in the midst of a reshuffle.

In the melee you can make mistakes. In May 2003, we appointed Chris Mullin as a junior minister to replace a minister who had resigned over Iraq. We had forgotten that Chris had voted against the war too, but by the time the chief whip reminded us it was too late as he had the job already. Judging by Chris's excellent memoir, he clearly didn't enjoy being a junior minister much anyway, so it was a suitable punishment.

To make reshuffles even more complicated, Cabinet ministers won't always accept the junior ministers whom the prime minister proposes, and there can be difficult negotiations. Robin Cook would not initially accept Keith Vaz and Kim Howells as junior ministers in the Foreign Office in 1999. We managed to persuade him to change his mind by offering him a place on the podium at the launch of the 'Britain in Europe' campaign alongside Tony and Gordon and the Lib Dem and Tory leaders. He had been very suspicious that we were trying to hive off Europe into the Cabinet Office, a perennial Foreign Office fear. Ruth Kelly refused to accept Andrew Adonis as a junior minister of education in 2005. As we had been thinking of making him Secretary of State instead of her, Tony insisted and in the end she agreed.

Of course negotiations with Gordon were always the most difficult. In pretty much every reshuffle from 2000 onwards, Tony would propose the removal of the Brownites Dawn Primarolo and Michael Wills, and pretty much every time Gordon would insist on their reinstatement, and Tony would agree. Negotiations would be more complex on other personalities. In 2001, we wanted to sack both Nick Brown and Andrew Smith, and after much agonising Gordon decided to sacrifice Nick in return for keeping Andrew. After the 2005 election, it was clear that Gordon wanted Tony to appoint Ed Balls, who had just become an MP, straight into government but Tony wasn't prepared to do that. In January 2006, Gordon sought to have Ed appointed as Chief Secretary to the Treasury, but he couldn't quite bring himself to ask, saying things like 'How can you appoint such useless people to the Cabinet when there are such talented people available?' Tony proposed John Hutton for the job. Gordon refused. He then proposed John Denham. Gordon rejected him too. Tony said Hutton and Denham were quality. He tried Des Browne, but he was initially rejected as well. Tony asked who Gordon did regard as quality, but Gordon was not prepared to say. Tony should just do what he wanted to do. He had not been consulted. Gordon had clearly made a promise to Ed Balls, and he was frightened of accepting any other candidate, but he could accept an appointment for which he was not responsible.

The process of ministerial appointment ought, of course, to be more rational, but it is politics and it never will be smooth. You start with the advice of the chief whip on who has done well in the chamber and who is supporting the government. Dennis Skinner was an even better source on who was doing well in the chamber as the most regular attender amongst MPs. You add to that the private advice of the civil servants about who is doing well in a department and who has less mastery of his brief. I sometimes thought it would be better to ask the government car service, as ministers' drivers usually had a far better assessment of them than their Permanent Secretaries. I remember being taken to a meeting by Paul Murphy's driver in 2005 shortly after he had stood down as Northern Ireland Secretary. The driver spoke very highly of Paul, but by then it was too late to reappoint him. The Civil Service also say how many jobs there should be in each ministry. In almost every case they want fewer ministers; in their view, ministers are nuisances who just get in the way of the department's efficient working (except for House of Lords ministers whom they always want more of to handle the department's business in that chamber). One of the things that always surprises an incoming government is the need to have new ministers security-cleared. The security service check their files and the Cabinet Secretary comes back saying there is 'no character defect or other circumstance that would endanger national security'. Only rarely do they raise a problem. In the end, you draw up a grid of the jobs in government with a space for those being sacked or moved and then a space for who should replace them.

Appointing the first government is relatively easy as all the jobs are empty, but when you are carrying out a major reshuffle of an existing government it becomes fiendishly complicated. One last-minute change in one department leaves you with havoc elsewhere. The prime minister has a tendency to suddenly come up with a left-field idea that throws everything else out of kilter. In 1999, Tony suddenly suggested that Peter Mandelson should come back into government as Mo's deputy in the Northern Ireland Office, an idea that I later discovered had been put to him by Mo.

Reshuffles are not an HR exercise and prime ministers have to consider the political balance of the resulting government. If you appoint only your own supporters, you build up resentment among others. If you pass over your supporters too readily, they grow resentful. You also have to be careful who you sack. If you sack too many of your enemies, you will find them organising opposition to you on the back benches. It is sometimes better to have them in than out. That was one of the reasons why Tony decided not to sack Nick Brown in 1999. But equally you don't want perversely to reward people for plotting, or that will convince more of them that attacking the leadership is a safe way to secure a job. You also have to achieve generational balance. If we had promoted too many of the 2001 or

2005 intakes too quickly, those left behind from previous generations, who had soldiered through the years of Opposition, would have assumed that they would never get a job and would have become permanent critics of the government. Equally, you cannot leave older ministers too long in place or the younger MPs will grow restive.

The problems are compounded when your rival for the leadership phones all those you have dismissed on the day of the reshuffle, sympathising and saying that he simply does not understand why they have been let go, the clear implication being that if he were prime minister they would once again be in the government. Even the most unlikely people fell for this blandishment in their moment of vulnerability. Gordon always wanted to insist on a say in the appointments and then to deny that he had been consulted. It was difficult to balance the two. In 2005, following the election campaign love-in, we suspected Gordon's team of briefing the media on all the names Tony had given him as his draft list for government. Gordon was furious when he subsequently discovered that Tony had changed the list. In an attempt to restore harmony, Tony offered Gordon a briefing on all the jobs, but Gordon declined and the journalists reported that he had not been consulted.

When William Hague stood down as Tory leader, there was one criticism that he made of Tony that struck me as well judged, and that was his suggestion that Tony had not been sufficiently ruthless in his reshuffles. Tony had a ruthless streak, which made him a good leader, and he even sacked his old mentor Derry Irvine in 2003. Generally speaking, however, when it came to reshuffles he was too nice to want to inflict pain on his colleagues and he was too inclined to listen to the pleas of those trying to save ministers who belonged to their respective political camps in the party. Sally Morgan, the political secretary, was always urging Tony to be more ruthless. In response, he called her 'Madame Defarge', carrying on with her knitting as the tumbrels rolled. But she was right. The myth that 'the night of the long knives' finished off Harold Macmillan politically is just that, a myth, despite the bad reviews for his dramatic reshuffle the next day. A prime minister should always err on the side of sacking more people and bringing on more young talent faster, even if in doing so he is taking a political risk by building up resentment on the back benches. If he lacks talent in his government, he will lose anyway, and, if the government succeeds, his popularity will discourage those on the back benches from trying to remove him.

Commentators argue that it would be better to leave ministers in their departments longer rather than moving them around, so that they can gain expertise and see reforms through. In most cases that would be true, with of course the exception of those ministers whom you have to keep in the government for political reasons but whose damage you can limit if you keep moving them on. In fact, though, the length of tenure of an average minister in a department is not very different from that of the average CEO in a large corporation, and in politics ministers are suddenly felled by scandals and you have to replace them immediately. When that happens, other ministers have to move jobs too. Most mini-reshuffles are the result of resignations. In those cases, you have to act fast and replace the person who is departing within hours to demonstrate the government is not unravelling.

Unexpected resignations are generally the result of scandals, but sometimes it can be the pressure of the job. Estelle Morris came to see Tony in March 2002 to tell him she did not feel she was up to the job of Education Secretary. Tony encouraged her to continue. Her confession was rather touching because lack of confidence is not usually something politicians suffer from. She came back in October to say she really did want to go and suggested that she should swap with her deputy, David Miliband, so that she could continue as a junior minister. Tony gave her a chance to think again, but she was clear she wanted to go and he replaced her with Charles Clarke. Once a minister has lost confidence in themselves it is hard for the prime minister to maintain confidence in them.

Sometimes the process can go badly wrong. In 2004, when David Blunkett was Home Secretary, he became embroiled in a controversy over a passport application and was fighting for his political life. The first calls indicating trouble started coming in in mid-morning. Andrew Turnbull came to see Tony and said that Alan Budd, who was conducting the inquiry into the passport affair, had turned up something unexpected. David came in through the back door to see Tony and made an emotional plea to be given a chance to survive. Tony agreed to give him more time, and David left to attend a previously arranged meeting of a select committee. Unfortunately the committee's chairman announced that David had resigned and abandoned the meeting. The news was running on Sky, and David had to come back to Number 10 with no choice but to resign.

Whenever Tony sacked a minister, he would suggest they come and see him after the reshuffle to discuss what else they could do for him. He did it to soften the bitterness of the blow and to give them some hope for the future, but he always overdid it and made it sound as if he had some crucial role that he really wanted them to take on. Even Charles Kennedy fell into this trap. Tony phoned him to commiserate about his resignation as leader of the Lib Dems and suggested he had a role in mind for him. Charles then called me up but soon realised there wasn't a real job for him. Before Tony would see those he had sacked for these second meetings, we would have to scrabble around to create a new job in charge of a task force or as an envoy. The Cabinet Secretary, however, objected strongly to this ruse and would refuse to provide staff or funding for such roles, seeing it as a back-door attempt to create yet more ministers. Many of those sacked wanted to be ambassadors, and we did appoint some former ministers to overseas posts, but the Foreign Office was very keen not to go the way of the US State Department, where most of the plum ambassadorships are filled by party donors and supporters, and the FCO Permanent Secretary sensibly refused to agree to more than two political appointments in total.

With the media, prime ministers are in a catch-22 situation on reshuffles. For journalists, reshuffle speculation is an extraordinarily easy way to fill pages, only surpassed by writing about the SAS or the secret services. In both cases, they know nothing will be confirmed or denied so that nothing they write can be shown to be wrong. They can advance the zaniest of ideas, confident that all Number 10 will do is say they never comment on reshuffle stories, for the good reason that if Number 10 denied the story then the journalists would keep throwing out possible moves until one was right. So journalists speculate like mad, almost always without foundation, and when it comes to the actual reshuffle and the moves the prime minister makes are not the ones that the journalists predicted, they say it is a bungled reshuffle. As far as they are concerned, the only explanation for the fact that they are not the appointments they predicted is that a series of last-minute changes have been forced on the prime minister. It is irrelevant that the prime minister never intended to do what the newspapers had suggested and that the moves that actually happened had been planned for months. It is impossible to convince the papers that they got it wrong. So the newspaper-manufactured story becomes the reality and the reality is a lie. A prudent prime minister wouldn't worry about what the newspapers write about the reshuffles on the day after, since they can never win. They should concentrate instead on the substance. They can have the last laugh if the government they appoint is successful.

Prime ministers are in a similar bind when they introduce changes in the machinery of government. We twice tried to dismember the Home Office to create a Ministry of Justice and were only partially successful on the third attempt. The first time we planned to divide the Home Office in two, crime and the rest. David Blunkett got wind of the idea and saw it off in the press. The second time we proposed to put the courts into the Home Office, and David Blunkett was in favour, but when we got the four senior judges into Downing Street in June 2001, they were adamantly opposed and insisted that it would compromise their independence to be managed by a department that was also responsible for other parts of law enforcement, even though that is the case in many other democratic countries. When we finally introduced changes to the antiquated Lord Chancellor's Department in 2005, we were denounced in the media for not having prepared them properly in advance, and the House of Lords eventually voted down part of the reform. Again we were in a catch-22. If we had discussed the changes with the departments in advance, the plans would once more have leaked and opposition would again have been given a chance to coalesce and prevent the reform taking place. If we did not discuss the proposed changes with the department till after the announcement, we would be accused of a bungled reform because we couldn't work through all the details in advance. The best course for prudent prime ministers is to concentrate on the substance of the reforms they want to make, which will pay off in the long term, rather than on the bad press reviews for their precipitate action, which will soon pass.

It is true that there are opportunity costs in making changes to the machinery of government, and a leader should only undertake them if there are genuine advantages that justify the disruption. It is amazing how much time a department can take thinking about its new name or headed paper and how many resources are required to merge two different cultures and pay scales, as when we merged MAFF and Environment into DEFRA, where pay in the former was half what it was in the latter. That, however, is an argument against making any change, and sometimes change is necessary. There is no right way in which the tasks of government should be divided up. One change we planned but never had the opportunity to put into effect was to merge Northern Ireland, Scotland and Wales into a Department of Constitutional Affairs. A prudent prime minister would put this rationalisation into practice when he is strong enough to do so – but probably won't because of the special pleading of the nationalist parties even though the separate secretaries of state have very little to do.

We struggled with a lack of talent when forming the government in 1997, not surprisingly because becoming a Labour MP was not an obvious career path for any ambitious young person during our eighteen years of Opposition. The Conservatives now have a similar dearth of talent after thirteen years in the wilderness. With the prospect of victory, talented people are willing to stand, but even then the way in which the party systems work makes it hard for them to be parachuted into Parliament straight away. Once they are there, they are expected to serve their apprenticeship on the back benches before they can become ministers. If they advance too quickly, they become the object of their colleagues' envy and their political careers do not prosper. The most sensible solution to this lack of talent would be to remove the requirement that most ministers be drawn from the ranks of MPs. Limiting yourself to the three hundred or so MPs on the government benches leaves a prime minister with a very small talent pool. Most countries are able to draw their ministers from any citizen of the country, regardless of whether or not they are an elected representative. In France deputies have to resign from the Assembly in order to be able to become ministers at all. Of course it is essential in the UK that ministers should be answerable to the democratically elected chamber, but that would only require a change to the rules of the Commons so that outsiders could answer questions, participate in debates and manage the passage of legislation. Making outsiders into ministers in the Lords does not resolve the problem because they are still not answerable to the democratically elected house, and ministers there should not be charged with important and serious functions of the state.

Of course MPs, the last remaining closed shop, will resist such changes fiercely. But they would be far better off with a different career path of their own rather than aspiring to be junior ministers. Their objective should be to become prestigious and well-paid chairs of select committees, ones with real power to hold ministers and officials to account, for example holding hearings to ratify appointments as the Senate does in the US. If this alternative career path existed, MPs might be more willing to allow outsiders to serve as ministers.

Those who oppose this change point to the fact that ministers who have come to the job from outside politics have not been a great success. There have been some exceptions, but in general the gulf between the culture of business and politics is so wide that it is hard to bridge it in either direction. I remember David Simon, the former head of BP, commenting to me after a year of working with Margaret Beckett in the Department of Trade, that he couldn't work out what she spent her time doing. Many outsiders soon drown in the job because they have not had an apprenticeship in the world of politics and Parliament. This, however, is an argument against technocratic ministers rather than outsiders as such. There is no reason why you should not have partisan and political outsiders rather than experts as ministers. They should be able to master the secrets of success in Westminster as well as any MP. They might even change the culture of an otherwise closed House of Commons.

We perhaps learned the lessons of Labour indiscipline in the 1970s and 80s too well. Sometimes in government we tried to be too controlling. It obviously matters who chairs a select committee, but it doesn't matter that much in the current system. Our attempt to prevent Gwyneth Dunwoody and Donald Anderson being re-elected as chairs of the Transport and Foreign Affairs committees after the 2001 election was a mistake. Even more mistaken was our attempt to prevent Ken Livingstone running as Labour candidate for mayor in 1999. He was bound to win and presented no threat to the national party in the new circumstances. We may have paid a price if he had done daft things as mayor, but in fact most of the things he did were sensible. Our attempts to bring him back into the party were equally stumbling. A wise leader should be reluctant to throw people out of the party and would only try to control those things that really matter rather than having zero tolerance of any opposition.

Heavy-handed measures of discipline in the Commons usually backfire. Physical threats and blackmail of the sort favoured by Michael Dobbs's fictional chief whip are largely counterproductive, although a certain amount of it still goes on. Withdrawing the whip is a useful threat, but a threat that should almost never be implemented. We were urged to withdraw the whip from particularly recalcitrant MPs from time to time, but we didn't want to make the mistake that John Major had made in turning his Eurosceptic rebels into martyrs. In 2004, we considered expelling Clare Short for making public the details of the sensitive intelligence she had had access to as a minister, but rightly we decided that to do so would give her the publicity she craved. It didn't help our attempts at discipline that at the time Gordon was telling her that he would make her Education Secretary when he became prime minister.

The real test for a leader comes with rebellions. The Labour Party has a contingent of more than twenty permanent rebels from the left-wing Campaign Group and associated eccentrics. Luckily we had large majorities so we didn't have to worry too much about them, but as time goes on and you tackle difficult issues you inevitably face rebellions in the House. On foundation hospitals in 2003 the situation looked bad with eighty rebels. Alan Milburn said he would resign as Health Secretary if we lost the vote, but we won in the end. On top-up fees and on ninety-day detention we faced really serious rebellions. Tony spent hours sitting in his office in the Commons speaking one by one to rebels who might be persuaded to support the party. The flattery of individual attention and the power of argument, or just an appeal to party loyalty, would sometimes work. In all three of these cases, we were facing a shadow whipping organisation headed by Nick Brown and George Mudie under Gordon Brown's patronage. They were effective at organising the recalcitrant elements in the PLP, and no amount of Tony's individual attention could break through their net. Gordon could usually bring them round when he wanted to, but sometimes he let them go so far that it was too late for even his last-minute change of heart to bring them back.

Occasionally even a strong leader just has to give in to his parliamentary party. The Labour Party had long supported a ban on hunting as a symbolic blow in the class war. Tony had no wish to do anything so illiberal, but in the end all he could do was delay the ban rather than prevent it. By luck, none of the private members' bills on hunting got through in our first years in government, but by September 1999 it was becoming clear that we had to do something. Tony suggested in July that we look at proposing a county-by-county referendum on a ban, but the idea attracted no support on either side. That same month there was a large and rather aggressive demonstration against the ban in Parliament Square. I was walking back from a meeting in the Commons and decided to walk right through it. Just as I got to the rowdiest part by St Stephen's Church, surrounded by well-refreshed Welsh farmers, I was spotted by Elinor Goodman, the Channel 4 correspondent, with her TV crew filming the demonstration. She was a hunter herself and a strong opponent of the ban, and she started shouting at me to ask how much it was worth not to tell the crowd who I was. The farmers began to take an unhealthy interest in me, and I speeded up my pace to get out of the crowd and back to the safety of Number 10.

Finally, in June 2003, the whips made it clear to Tony that the PLP wouldn't accept further delay and we had to accept a government bill. When the bill came to the vote in 2004, Tony decided we would insist on a two-year delay in implementing it. He said that if MPs refused to agree to the delay we would drop the bill altogether. By this stage, Alun Michael was the minister in charge of the issue and he was coming up with all sorts of imaginative ideas for a solution, including allowing ratting with dogs but banning hunting. My favourite was Tony's own idea. He suggested that the hounds be equipped with electronic collars so that once they closed on the fox they could be administered with a shock by radio control to prevent them from killing it and one of the huntsmen riding on a quad bike should then shoot the fox.

Tony was constantly preoccupied with finding a way out. When we were negotiating on the future of Northern Ireland at Leeds

Castle in 2004, Tony spent his time between meetings pacing the grounds with me worrying away at the issue. He sent me off to see the head of the Countryside Alliance, John Jackson, offering a compromise. But Hilary Armstrong, the chief whip, was clear that we could not deliver foundation hospitals and simultaneously block a ban on hunting. Labour MPs would insist on a ban. Our final hope lay in the courts' preventing the police prosecuting hunters, but even that was disappointed in February 2005. We ended up with a very British compromise. We pretended to ban hunting by passing a bill, but the legislation was ineffective. The huntsmen pretended to stop, but actually carried on.

One of the main ways of offering leadership to the parliamentary party is through PMQs. Presidents Clinton and Bush both used to tell Tony how much they enjoyed watching it on the US cable channel C-SPAN and would comment on particular sessions. When I was in Washington in the early 1990s, I recommended to the Clinton White House introducing presidential questions before Congress, modelled on PMQs. I said it would change the nature of the presidency. You could not have someone like Reagan as president if you had to think on your feet in a debating chamber. When they explored the idea with Tom Foley, the Speaker of the House of Representatives, however, he was clear that it was not compatible with the separation of powers in the American Constitution and the idea fell by the wayside.

For Bush and Clinton, their enjoyment was, to a large degree, derived from the fact that they didn't actually have to do it themselves. For prime ministers, PMQs is an ordeal, and they never get used to it. Harold Macmillan regularly used to throw up before going into the chamber. Tony would start preparations the evening before with a giant folder, and first thing the next morning a mixed team of civil servants and political appointees would gather in the living room of the Number 11 flat, perching on the arms of sofas or sitting on the floor, to run through what we thought the Leader of the Opposition would ask, what the other questions of the day would be, and to start rehearsing answers. About eight times out of ten we would get it right. Tony worked away at the briefing all morning and summoned officials from departments to explain whatever disaster was dominating the news that day, or asked for more written briefing. He had a barrister's capacity to absorb huge amounts of material and PMQs was a useful tool to probe what departments were up to.

At about eleven thirty we would leave Number 10 for the House of Commons, and that is where things could go wrong. On one occasion the police decided to take us the long way round via the South Bank to avoid a demonstration, and Tony got increasingly nervous as we got stuck in a traffic jam. The minutes ticked by and it appeared we would be late. I am not sure what happens if the prime minister fails to turn up for PMQs. Later, the police used to drop us at the back door of one of the House of Commons office buildings and Tony would stride at full speed through the kitchens and an underground tunnel into the Commons, with us keeping up with him as best we could. He would do his last bit of preparation in his cavernous office with us squatting outside in the outer office. If bad news came in, I would keep it back from Tony till afterwards so it did not upset his concentration. He was appropriately superstitious and we were not allowed to say good luck as he left the office and went into the Chamber and as we scurried along behind to watch the duel from the officials' box next to the Speaker's chair.

The session, which is watched on TV by about a million people, does nothing for any prime minister's standing in the country. The public hate the Punch and Judy sight of politicians slagging each other off. It is, however, an essential tool for rallying your troops on the back benches. Their mood for the week is determined by the leader's performance. If the prime minister has been able to put down the Leader of the Opposition with a telling one-liner, they rise to their feet cheering and waving their order papers; but if the prime minister has been caught by some cutting jibe from the Opposition, they slink away silently. It is like gladiatorial combat in the Roman circus, with the crowd putting their thumbs up or down at the end. A wise leader acquires the ability to laugh at himself, apparently genuinely, when he is the butt of jokes. And a thick skin – or at least enough make-up to hide a blush – is an essential requisite for a prime minister in the television age.

Unless you have been there, it is hard to appreciate the barrage of noise that is thrown at a prime minister from the Opposition benches as he gets to his feet, and you would be embarrassed at the things MPs yell to try to put a prime minister off his stride. About halfway through our time in office, Tony had to start wearing reading glasses to be able to decipher the briefing notes in his folder. It took him a long time to accept the need, and when he did Alastair Campbell arranged a special event to unveil the glasses in public. Once he did start wearing them, they were a useful tool in the Commons. As he stood up to answer questions, he would put them on to read his notes and they made it impossible for him to see the snarling faces opposite. The other useful trick for a prime minister is to listen out for mad things yelled by the Opposition, or even *in extremis* to mishear what has been yelled, so that he can turn them back on the other side. Tony did this particularly effectively on Europe. On one occasion, he rhetorically asked the Tories which other country supported their position. The Opposition front benches remained with lips firmly sealed, but one unfortunate Tory backbencher yelled, or appeared to yell, 'Norway.' Tony was able to turn on him with scorn and point out that Norway wasn't even a member of the EU.

When David Cameron became Tory leader, he announced that he was going to adopt a new approach and instead of the usual political pantomime he would ask serious questions. At his first session in December 2005, we correctly identified the questions he would ask and Tony answered them. Cameron seemed unable to think on his feet. He read out the second question written on the typed sheet in front of him despite the fact that Tony had just answered it. He sat down without asking his third question. Gordon, sitting next to Tony, kept jabbing him in the stomach when he was sitting down and pulling on his jacket when he was standing and demanding that Tony attack Cameron on cuts. Eventually Tony succumbed and did so. I noted in my diary that I did not expect Cameron's new consensual approach to last long, and it didn't. He soon reverted to the traditional shrieking Punch and Judy performance demanded of him by his audience.

I used to feel sorry for Opposition leaders. Having worked for Tony in Opposition, I knew how hard it was to stand up and ask questions. Their hands used to shake as they put their questions on the dispatch box in front of them. David Cameron even seemed to blush when caught out in the first few weeks. He had reversed many of his party's policies and made the mistake in 2006 of talking in one of his questions about 'flip-flops', which we had just made our line of attack on the Tories. When you make that kind of blunder all you can do is rock back on your heels and smile as the Chamber collapses in laughter. Cameron turned puce and looked miserable. Sometimes Opposition leaders avoid the political issue of the day and opt for safe questions on a bipartisan topic to avoid giving the prime minister an easy opportunity to give them a verbal thumping. From 2001 onwards, the Tory leaders effectively stopped asking questions about Europe because they knew that it simply made the public think they were obsessed and they managed, fairly successfully, to close down the issue.

Occasionally the session can provide some unexpected drama. In May 2004, protesters threw condoms filled with purple flour from the gallery. The bulbous Tory chief whip rose to his feet and shouted at everyone to get out, and the Speaker, instead of locking down the Chamber until it was established whether or not the substance was harmful, cleared the House. Tony went back to his office but wanted to continue with the session regardless of the threat. The Speaker wouldn't allow it.

There were repeated demands that Tony make more statements and take part in more debates in the House of Commons. In fact, he made more statements and participated in more debates than Mrs Thatcher ever did, but he was reluctant to do even more. He saw them as mostly downside with only a very limited upside. In his view, all a parliamentary occasion like that achieved was to get the Leader of the Opposition on to the evening news. The annual debate on the Queen's Speech, in particular, proved the point. They were good occasions for after-dinner speakers, but not for substance. They start with comic speeches by two backbenchers followed by the Leader of the Opposition in much the same vein. By the time the prime minister gets to his feet, the parliamentary audience is already beginning to wilt. If he tries to put across a serious message about what the government is trying to do, the Chamber is resentful and bored, and, if he just tries to join in by cracking jokes, it is hard to compete with the warm-up acts. In the end it was usually a waste of time. Tony's staff remained keen that he participate in more set-piece debates. He was very good at them, particularly the parliamentary technique of waiting for a daft Opposition MP to try to intervene in your speech so that in response you can score a particularly vivid political point, to cheers from your own side. And parliamentary events intended by the opposition to challenge the government can in fact serve as a moment of catharsis that draws a line under some political drama.

Prime ministers expend a great deal of effort getting the measure of new Leaders of the Opposition, so much so that they even obsess about people who aren't yet leaders. Tony was mesmerised by Michael Portillo in 1999, who he thought would become Tory leader 'and change everything'. But he didn't. Tony was studying him and told me in July 2000 that Portillo had lost the fire in his belly. When I asked him how he knew, he said because he recognised it in himself. We were blessed with William Hague as Leader of the Opposition in the first term. His fundamental flaw was that, while he was a brilliant debater and had a good line in jokes, he didn't seem to spend any time thinking about substance. Jokes will only take you so far in politics. You have to stand for something. Alistair McAlpine told me that the Tories had discovered Hague in 1977 when they had had a bad conference. It needed lifting and, when they found someone with a regional accent, they seized on him. They wrote him a speech and when he was finished they packed him off, never expecting to see him again.

We were rooting for Iain Duncan Smith as Hague's successor and did everything we could to keep him in place once he was elected. He was very much in awe of Tony and I couldn't help noticing that he would stand to attention virtually saluting when brought in to see the prime minister. I was transfixed by the metal plates nailed to the tips of his shoes. IDS, as the 'quiet man', had terrible trouble with PMQs, which had been Hague's strong suit. In November 2001, I observed from the officials' box that he was so nervous in the Chamber that he virtually couldn't stand up to ask his question, and in January the next year I couldn't help thinking of a beached fish with his mouth opening and closing and nothing coming out. In 2003, when the plotting started, we were desperately worried that he might go and were enormously reassured when he appeared to get a reprieve at the party conference in October. His subsequent agonising political death gave us no pleasure. Once he was gone, Tory MPs heaped praise on him. He, on the other hand, appeared to feel a huge sense of relief on being out of the job, as though a weight had been lifted off his shoulders. At last he seemed happy.

Tony was worried about Michael Howard as the next Tory leader. They had sparred before when Tony was Shadow Home Secretary, and he was extremely nervous before their first clash in November 2003. I thought Howard would be an effective Leader of the Opposition but would not be capable of being elected prime minister; the public remembered him, he was too old, too right wing, and his character too much that of the pantomime baddy. His histrionic manner got on people's nerves. I assumed the Tories had the same focus groups as we did and would register these points too. His hallmark was crass political opportunism. At a difficult time, Howard served a useful purpose in uniting the Labour Party. He was much given to political tricks, for example taunting Tony at PMQs about the differences inside the Labour Party on tuition fees; but, instead of worsening the divisions, his attacks caused the party to close ranks. If instead he had supported the reforms, he would have caused us real difficulties and our MPs would have started thinking they were being asked to adopt Tory policies. By calling for Tony's resignation at the most inappropriate times he made himself look foolish. Opposition leaders should only call for a resignation when there is a real chance that one will happen. At the time of Michael Howard's last PMQs in November 2005, I noted that while he had made the Tories feel better about themselves, he had failed to reform the party, prepare them for the future or move them to a more electable position. His had been two wasted years.

I met David Cameron before he had been fully discovered by the media, and told Tony in January 2005 that I thought he would become leader rather than David Davis. Tony was sceptical. I didn't think at the time that Cameron had thought through what to do with his party, but it turned out that he and his team had a plan to reposition it and to imitate many of the things we had done with the Labour Party between 1994 and 1997. The Tories themselves were not certain what to expect. The Tory leadership candidate Liam Fox told a friend of mine that they would now have a leader who was *primus inter pares* and that the Shadow Cabinet would to a large extent be able to do their own thing.

Gordon was extremely unhappy about Cameron's election.

He complained that Tony had promised him in July 2005 that David Davis would win, and he even accused Tony of backing Cameron. Tony suggested that we would probably now be behind in the polls for two years. Gordon's response was that that was 'unacceptable'. He said Tony should leave straight away so that he had more time in the ring with Cameron – probably the subconscious source of Tony's reference to Gordon as 'the big clunking fist'. Gordon wanted to pound Cameron as an Old Etonian in favour of cuts. Tony was unwilling and thought we should give Cameron enough rope to hang himself.

I thought it sensible to handle the Opposition in terms of process as fairly as you could. We tried whenever possible to give them Tony's statements in advance so that they had time to study them and formulate a response, and we arranged official briefings for them on matters of national importance even though they would sometimes abuse them. Not all ministers agreed. Some were so fiercely partisan that they would deliberately produce statements at the last minute and find other procedural ways of making the Opposition's life even more difficult. Ed Llewellyn, Cameron's chief of staff, complained to me in 2007 that Gordon had briefed the Sunday papers on counterterrorism. Did we want bipartisanship, as Tony had said to David Cameron, or not? I rang Tony who called Gordon who said he had just been answering a few questions. I called Ed back and said we wanted to continue bipartisanship. He was pretty sniffy, pointing out that Gordon had issued a written statement and complained that this was not the way to do business. I said that we were going, and that with the new regime he had better get used to it.

Governing parties love the symbolism of political defections from the Opposition. It helps maintain their morale. Peter Temple Morris was a very decent pro-European Tory who was simply left behind by his party as it galloped to the right. He no longer felt comfortable in it. I first met him in a restaurant in Chinatown with Clive Soley, one of our sanest MPs, and he wanted to talk about defection. We agreed a framework and I went back to tell Tony. Over several months we worked out the game plan and finally were ready to execute it in October 1997, but the Tory pro-Europeans persuaded him not to jump ship at the last moment. To our surprise, William

Hague withdrew the whip from him in November and I persuaded him to come and sit on our benches the next day. The Tories' vengeance was brutal both in his constituency and in turfing him out of his office in the House of Commons.

Later, we were surprised when we were approached in 1999 by an ambitious young Tory MP, Shaun Woodward, who had helped run John Major's election campaign in 1992. He was particularly upset, having been dismissed from the front bench over his opposition to the old-fashioned Tory attitude to gay issues. The mating dance in this case was particularly delicate because he was keen to secure assurances about a seat and a job. Some of the negotiations were carried on through a mutual friend of ours, Sidney Blumenthal, who was working in the White House. He would convey messages back and forth. I persuaded Tony to see Shaun. Once we had an agreement, we handed him over to the embrace of Alastair Campbell and his deputy Lance Price for the public stage. The defection went beautifully, but Shaun overplayed his hand by talking publicly about 'Neil and me' as if they had been the two protagonists of the 1992 election. Parties are very suspicious of defectors who join their ranks, and it takes time for them to be accepted.

A prudent prime minister will try to keep the Opposition on the back foot the whole time, not just with defections but by dividing their ranks whenever possible. One of our most successful attempts at doing so was our deal with Cranborne, the Tory leader in the Lords, on the removal of nearly all the hereditary peers. One afternoon a year after our election, I got a call from Tristan Garel Jones, the former Tory minister. He said he was sitting in St Tropez on the sixth biggest yacht in the world and that he thought that, if we played our cards right, we could come to an agreement with Cranborne on what to do about the hereditaries. We linked up Derry Irvine and Cranborne, and by the end of the year they were close to an understanding.

Towards the end of November, Alistair Goodlad, a former Tory chief whip and Tony's former 'pair' in the House of Commons, came into Number 10 together with Cranborne to negotiate the final points. Sitting in the Number 11 flat with Tony and Derry Irvine, they came to an agreement. I was afraid Cranborne would renege on the deal; I noted that history showed there were centuries of treachery in his blood. The following day Alastair and I were to talk to Cranborne to discuss the details of how we would announce the reforms. I didn't have his number so I called Alistair Goodlad, who turned out to be shooting on a grouse moor, which seemed appropriate to the matter at hand. We got hold of Cranborne, and he seemed ready to go ahead despite Conservative opposition. He would brief Hague on the morning of the announcement and had arranged for three cross-bench peers to make the statement after PMQs. On the day itself, I suggested to Tony that he prepare an answer for PMQs just in case Hague raised it, although that day we expected him to concentrate on European tax harmonisation. We assumed that, if he did raise the Lords issue, he would welcome the deal and claim credit for it.

When he got to his feet and opposed the deal in the Chamber, our jaws dropped. Tony was flabbergasted. Hague clearly believed that, by attacking the arrangement, he could provoke our backbench MPs into rising up against it. But he had badly miscalculated. In response, Tony set out the whole deal with Cranborne in detail and Hague visibly wilted. During the rest of the day, his position gradually crumbled. When he opposed the deal, his front bench in the Lords resigned en masse and by the end of the day he had to reverse himself on the substance and ended up in support.

It is not, however, just the party in Parliament that should concern the prime minister. He is also the leader of his party in the country. The Labour Party has a tradition of the two parts of the party, the PLP and the National Executive Committee (NEC), going in different directions once in government. We were determined to do our best to avoid this traditional split and adopted an elaborate approach entitled 'the party into power' before the 1997 election to reduce the ability of the NEC to undermine the leadership. As long as Tony remained popular in the country, we were able to maintain a majority on the NEC, but as time wore on more opponents were elected to it and we lost the unions bit by bit, despite the efforts of our Number 10 union organiser, Jon Cruddas. Even so, we managed to keep on winning policy motions at conference, partly by changing the rules to make it harder to raise last-minute emergency resolutions at conference, partly by hard work in smoke-filled rooms at 'compositing' exercises by Pat McFadden and Jon Cruddas and their successors, but mainly because even if we lost votes on the floor of the conference we could demonstrate that we had the support of the overwhelming majority of individual party members and had only lost the votes because of the union barons. One innovation that helped was the creation of the position of party chair in the Cabinet that brought together the two elements of the party.

It used to be conventional wisdom that one of the key weapons in a prime minister's armoury in Britain was the ability to choose the date of an election. Now we are moving to fixed-term Parliaments, but it was in any case not such a useful tool as it at first appeared. In December 1999, we discussed going for an early election on the back of good poll numbers but wisely decided not to. In fact, it is almost never sensible to go for early elections unless there is some good public-spirited reason. If you call elections just for party advantage, there is a good chance the public will punish you for calling an unnecessary vote when you already have a mandate.

In reality, prime ministers have almost always called elections in the fourth year of the Parliament if they could. If they leave it longer, they are trapped at the end of their mandate with no flexibility, and when prime ministers comes to look at specific dates they are even more constrained. Prime ministers tend to believe it is best to avoid the autumn because people are gloomy then, and in spring the later you go the more advantage governments gain as the weather gets warmer. But they can't wait till July because the Midlands traditionally goes on holiday then. Then they have to bear in mind the local and European elections, which are on fixed dates. If they wait till after those elections, they face going to the country just after suffering a stinging defeat, and if they go before, their local councillors – on whom they depend for door-to-door canvassing – will not thank them because then no one will turn out for their elections. None of these arguments is insuperable, but they have tended to push prime ministers to the date of local elections in the Spring of the fourth year of their mandate.

Of course, external events can complicate this, as with foot-and-mouth in 2001. Hague called on us to postpone the elections in some areas in February. Charles Moore, the editor of the *Daily Telegraph*, called the Palace to find out if the Queen still had the prerogative to refuse a request for a general election. Gordon was strongly against postponement, and Tony was instructing us to resist any attempt to put the elections off, right up to the middle of March. If we did, he asked, how would we know it would be safe to have elections even in June? At the end of March, however, he decided that there was no alternative and opted for a delay until June. Alastair and Gordon were furious, although all Tony was doing was recognising the inevitable. It would have been physically and politically impossible to manage foot-and-mouth and run an election campaign at the same time. Tony said he just did not feel right pressing ahead.

Three-week election campaigns themselves can be dull and rarely shift voting intentions much, and will be even more so now that all the oxygen is absorbed by the television debates. The highlight of the 2001 campaign was John Prescott. I was at the campaign headquarters when we got a call saying that John had punched a protester and was now holed up in the village hall of Rhyl besieged by the media. His assistant Joan Hammell called me. John was upset and shaken and wished he hadn't done it. I came up with a plan to ex-filtrate him rapidly. The campaign staff at Millbank were in shock as Sky began to broadcast pictures of the event. Tony was unfazed until he saw the pictures. Alastair, Anji and Sally wanted John to apologise. It didn't seem such a big deal to me. At least someone had enlivened the campaign. Tony, correctly, decided that he would just dismiss the incident as 'John being John', which appeared to me to be unanswerable.

Much of my time during campaigns was spent preparing speeches for Tony and getting them rejected. Tony had inherited a trick from his old pupil master, Derry Irvine, of rejecting speeches without ever reading them, in the hope that the new version would be the drafter's best work. In March 2001, Tony rejected my draft speech on foreign policy, and I declined to redo it. In desperation he asked Derry to prepare an alternative for him. Two days later, just before he had to deliver it, he was faced with a 100,000-word draft. The scene in the hotel on the campaign trail as he tried using scissors and paste to reduce it to something he could deliver was apparently very amusing.

Elections are won not by the party leader who has the best campaign but by the leader who has been thinking about the public for the previous four years. Politicians sometimes think they can bamboozle the public, but the public are too smart for them. In an election, en masse, they usually make the right decision. Machiavelli observed that in hundreds of years of elections of consuls and tribunes in the Roman Republic the Roman people only repented the results of four elections. He felt that 'it is found, too, that in the election of magistrates the populace makes a far better choice than does the Prince'. For Machiavelli, the two greatest threats to a prince are the public's contempt and the public's hatred. A prince 'should consider how he may avoid such courses as would make him hated or despised; and that whenever he succeeds in keeping clear of these, he has performed his part, and runs no risk though he incur other infamies'. He thinks that 'Not to be hated or despised by the body of his subjects, is one of the surest safeguards that a Prince can have against conspiracy', and he describes the fate of the Roman Emperor Commodus who, by descending into the arena to fight with gladiators, 'became contemptible in the eyes of the soldiery; and being on the one hand hated, on the other despised, was at last conspired against and murdered'. It is when the voters say they almost feel sorry for a prime minister that he is at the greatest risk. If he has become the subject of pity, he is probably beyond salvation. Machiavelli is right that a leader should think about 'always maintaining the dignity of his state, which must under no circumstances be compromised'.

Machiavelli gives an example of how to avoid hatred in describing the fate of Remiro d'Orco, a 'stern and prompt ruler', whom Cesare Borgia put in charge of Romagna once he had conquered it, to restore order there. Once d'Orco had succeeded in brutally settling the province, Borgia, realising that 'the past severities had generated ill-feeling against himself, in order to purge the minds of the people and gain their good-will . . . sought to show them that any cruelty which had been done had not originated with him, but in the harsh disposition of his minister. Availing himself of the pretext which this afforded, he one morning caused Remiro to be beheaded, and exposed in the market place of Cessna with a block and bloody axe by his side. The barbarity of which spectacle at once astounded and satisfied the populace.' It is difficult to have recourse to this particular approach in modern politics, but prime ministers should be more willing than they are to sacrifice their ministers and let them take the blame when things go wrong. After all, this is part of the point of them. As Machiavelli says: 'Wherefore, a wise Prince should devise means whereby his subjects may at all times, whether favourable or adverse, feel the need of the State and of him, and then they will always be faithful to him.'

At the end of his chapter on the subject, Machiavelli writes: 'Returning to the question of being loved or feared, I sum up by saying, that since being loved depends upon his subjects, while being feared depends on himself, a wise Prince should build on what is his own, and not on what rests with others. Only, as I have said, he must do his utmost to escape hatred.' In the end, from the point of view of the leader that is a good part of what politics is about. But, if he is to be successful at avoiding contempt and hatred and ensuring that people respect him, he cannot be content to operate from day to day. He needs to think ahead. He needs to have a strategy.

CHAPTER SEVEN

'Sundry Reflections on Strategy, Tactics, New Devices and Discipline'

The Importance of Being Strategic

Prime ministers find it is all too easy to be driven by their inbox. Harold Macmillan famously talked of 'events, dear boy, events' forcing themselves on a government, and there are always plenty of events to keep a prime minister occupied, many of them real crises demanding their attention. But unless they want their time in office to be entirely driven by reacting to those events, a wise leader learns to distinguish between the urgent and the important and sometimes leave others to deal with the urgent while focusing on those decisions that will make a difference in the long term.

To leave a lasting mark, prime ministers need to be proactive rather than purely reactive, which in turn requires that they have a long-term vision of where they want to take the country and a plan to implement that vision. Machiavelli's advice was this: 'The wise man should always follow the roads that have been trodden by the great, and imitate those who have most excelled, so that if he cannot reach their perfection, he may at least acquire something of its savour. Acting in this like the skilful archer, who seeing that the object he would hit is distant, and knowing the range of his bow, takes aim much above the destined mark; not designing that his arrow should strike so high, but that flying high it may alight at the point intended.'

Leaders should therefore have an overall plan, choose their target and aim high. Machiavelli quoted Philip of Macedon and certain Roman leaders as examples who demonstrated the importance of a strategic approach in classical times: 'The Romans did as all wise rulers should, who have to consider not only present difficulties but also future, against which they must use all diligence to provide; for, these, if they be foreseen while yet remote, admit of easy remedy, but if their approach be awaited, are already past cure, the disorder having become hopeless; realising what the physicians tell us of hectic fever, that in its beginning it is easy to cure, but hard to recognise; whereas, after a time, not having been detected and treated at the first, it becomes easy to recognise but impossible to cure.' A prudent leader needs to prepare in the good times for the bad times that will follow: 'Hence every government, whether it be republican or of the princely type, should consider beforehand what adverse times may befall him and on what people it may have to rely in time of adversity, and should in its dealings with them act in a way in which it judges that it will be compelled to act should misfortune befall.' A great leader is strategic, not merely tactical.

This advice does not mean that leaders should be inflexible. They also need to be ready to change as circumstances change. If they become too entrapped in their own strategy, they will fail. In Machiavelli's view, 'a man who is accustomed to act in one particular way, never changes . . . However, when times change and no longer suit his ways, he is inevitably ruined.'

There are some simple, practical steps that can be taken to make it easier for a leader to stand back and think strategically and to plan for the long term rather than just living day to day. Prime ministers are always in demand and can easily fill their diaries, but, if they do so, it leaves no time to think. John Major's diary was so filled that he had back-to-back meetings from nine in the morning till eight in the evening every day, with official dinners or events most nights. There were no breaks. We made it clear when we came into Number 10 that we would not be accepting outside requests for meetings unless they were absolutely necessary, and we told the Foreign Office that we would not be encouraging foreign visitors to come to Britain if they expected a meeting with the prime minister. From time to time foreign leaders would threaten to cancel their visits to the UK unless they could be guaranteed a meeting with the prime minister. Our response would be to suggest that in that case they might want to consider cancelling their visit. It was not a great way to make friends in the short term, but as long as such a rule is uniformly applied foreign leaders get used to it. President Obama adopted a similar approach to foreign visitors in his first year, and it seems to have worked in freeing up time in his diary to deal with pressing domestic issues.

Tony was absolutely clear that he wanted time to stand back and think about the big picture and would throw a fit if his diary became too congested. We would ensure that most days he had at least an hour or two free in the middle of the day. Unlike a president, a prime minister is a chief executive and has to run the government day to day. Creating empty space in the diary puts a huge strain on the diary secretary, who has to say no to demands for essential meetings on specific policy problems and crises. To make life easier, we started putting bogus meetings into the diary to ensure that time was kept free. Tony didn't always understand the code we had built in and would ask for these non-existent meetings to be cancelled.

Tony often used the time we had so carefully protected to go to the gym, to talk about football or gossip with his staff, but that was preferable to his not having time to think. We arranged regular political strategy meetings with polling and advice from the party, but most of his strategic thinking was carried out in what Alastair Campbell described as a never-ending, circular discussion. For those of us with a more operational cast of mind, the never-endingness and the circularity could be frustrating, but it was the way Tony's mind worked, to try and get himself comfortable with the strategy he was formulating. We would sit in the den watching him eat his lunch or drinking mugs of tea while he ruminated and we argued over a particular point. Eventually, the process would give birth to a lengthy strategy paper, usually produced at a weekend or over holidays, setting out where we should go next. The paper would be distributed around the key staff and outsiders like Philip Gould and Peter Mandelson, and would serve as the start of yet another round of the same conversation.

In the context of conference speeches or other major set-piece events, we would find ourselves groping for grand concepts and big phrases, what Peter Mandelson used to call a 'washing line' on which to hang specific policy ideas. In doing so, caution is necessary regarding suggestions from outside for the organising idea. In 2004, a consultant suggested we use the phrase 'opportunity society' as the organising idea of the conference speech. It was an attractive phrase with a ring to it, but when I Googled it, I discovered that it had already been used by, among others, JFK, Ronald Reagan and George W. Bush. So we didn't use that phrase, but we worked our way through a good many others, starting with 'stakeholder democracy' in a major speech in Singapore in 1996, on to 'young country' and then the 'battle against the forces of conservatism'. Generally, the catchphrases lasted so short a time before we moved on to the next that they had little impact other than providing a headline for the day of the conference speech itself, when Alastair would brief the phrase as a way of putting the journalists in the mood.

'Forces of conservatism' is an example of why it is a mistake to seize on a resonant phrase without thinking it through. The phrase sounded good and was well received on the day, but the politics of it were all wrong. Tony had been a 'one nation' leader building a big tent, with support from Conservative as well as Labour and Liberal supporters. By using the word 'conservative' pejoratively, we alienated that strand of support. And it is absolutely essential to avoid setting deadlines in pursuit of a well-rounded phrase as we did with 'Year of Delivery' in 1999. By the time we reached 2000, we really regretted it. We started talking to each other about being caught in the pre-delivery and post-euphoria period, and a very long and uncomfortable period it was too.

Leaders do, however, need big, bold policies or big ideas to define their approach for voters. People can't make much sense of lots of little disconnected policy initiatives. Mrs Thatcher was defined by her emblematic policies like the sale of council houses. Gordon Brown produced a blizzard of almost daily micro-policy initiatives which failed to leave any impression on the public. For most of the ten years in government, Tony was searching for a conceptual framework that captured his two big aims of modernising the party and the country in a way that ensured greater fairness in society. Sometimes he came up with terrible ways of expressing it like the need to combine 'good manners and casual clothing' (which he had been thinking of for his notorious Women's Institute speech but, thank goodness, didn't use).

Tony wanted the country to modernise to keep up with, and take advantage of, the rapidly changing world around us, in contrast with the Conservatives who wanted to maintain things as they were. Before every conference, he would demand a list of new technological developments to refer to in his speech and we had to send someone off every September to identify the latest gee-whiz inventions. Tony's fascination with technology was reminiscent of the great progressives of the nineteenth century who built Victorian Britain. At the same time, he wanted to ensure that, in modernising the country, we increased fairness within society rather than building in new inequalities. He came closest to capturing the idea in his conference speech in 1999 when he talked about our goal being 'equal worth'. This was classic third way, positioned between the extremes of the Conservatives on one side and Old Labour on the other. Conservatives talked about equality of opportunity, by which they meant that everyone could compete on the basis of what they had at the moment. That is not fairness because all it does is entrench existing privilege; those with wealth ensure that their children inherit their privileged position through private education, private health care and other advantages that can be bought with money. Old Labour was wedded to equality of outcome, which was unattainable and in any case did not allow for people to be rewarded for their skills and their efforts. We were looking for something in between that allowed people a genuine equality of opportunity rather than an artificial one that handicapped them according to their family's starting place on the social ladder.

Eventually, this belief led Tony to an attempt to rehabilitate the concept of meritocracy that had effectively been mocked to death by Michael Young in his satire of that name in 1958. Young, a Labour intellectual and one of the drafters of the 1945 Labour manifesto, argued that the notion that people should be rewarded by their merit would lead to a brave new world in which some people would not only be better off than others but would be able to justify their relative prosperity by saying that the outcome was fair because they actually were better than others. People, on that view, should be equal rather than being rewarded according to their skills and efforts. His little book had made the term 'meritocracy' toxic for succeeding generations of the left and in the process skewed the policy debate away from trying to achieve greater social mobility in which people could go both up and down the social ladder.

As we tried to reclaim this ground, I had some stormy arguments with Bruce Grocott, a friend and of the traditional left, who maintained that we should insist on equal outcomes as the goal rather than giving people genuinely equal opportunities. He disapproved of people leaving working-class areas to go to university to better themselves and moving away to middle-class areas. He wanted them to stay with their own kind. This seemed to me a remarkably conservative view with a small 'c', with the working class remaining working class and the middle class remaining middle class, entrenched in their positions, just as the Conservatives wanted them to for their own reasons. It seemed to me that progressives should want social mobility so that anyone could succeed according to their skills and their efforts, without being hobbled by the social position or wealth of their parents.

Tony's focus on meritocracy led us to pursue different policy priorities from those of Gordon Brown. Gordon was a traditional redistributionist. He thought that greater equality could be achieved largely through the tax code, and his priority was introducing and extending tax credits. The original idea was a good one: to remove the huge cliff that discourages people from moving from benefit into work. Tax credits, however, function far better in the US where the tax system is different and where a great bureaucracy to make the calculations on how much should be paid back to, or taken away from, recipients at the end of each year is not required. As tax credits were extended into more and more abstruse areas, they incurred more and more dead-weight cost without producing any obvious benefits. Tony's focus was on health and education, with the aim of having excellent provision in the public sector so that those who could not afford to pay for schooling or treatment were not disadvantaged. This tension between the two approaches continued throughout our time in government without being resolved, and at every Budget, as I have described, there was a competition between the two of them to put the funds available into tax credits or into health and education spending.

When I came to work for Tony in Opposition, I discovered we were operating more or less blind. We had no system of ensuring we were aware of forthcoming events, and we reacted ad hoc as we were confronted with developments rather than being able to plan ahead. We started a media monitoring service which gave us some sense of what was about to happen in the world around us, and in government we overlaid this with a grid of external events and policy announcements, day by day, over the coming six months. This gave us an invaluable tool to ensure discipline over the government so that departments did not compete with each other by making policy announcements on the same day. Ministers were only allowed to take a major initiative if it had been agreed for inclusion in the grid on a particular date. This iron rule was enforced by a quiet, self-effacing fifty-something-year-old civil servant in Number 10 who unexpectedly became the terror of Whitehall. No one would dare to plan an announcement without his agreement, and people would mention his name in hushed tones when seeking clearance.

The process also forced Number 10 and ministries to think ahead about what they wanted to achieve with a particular policy announcement, how they would prepare for it and how they would relate it to what others were doing. The staff from all the sections in Number 10 used to meet monthly in the Cabinet Room to look at the grid for the next six months in parallel with Tony's long-term diary to try and make the two mesh together. We tried many different approaches to impose a pattern on events, from themes for particular weeks, such as education or crime, to alternating the key public services day by day during the course of the week, so that we had a health announcement followed by a transport announcement followed by an education announcement and so on. None of these stratagems really worked, but the grid itself did provide a framework that forced us to think about what we were trying to achieve in the longer term, rather than simply wrestling with events as they hit us.

We had prepared a hundred-day plan on coming into government, but not an overall strategy for what we were trying to achieve, and in the early days there was a certain amount of scrabbling around for policy content on the eve of major events like the conference speech. We were determined, however, to make the approach to policy more strategic as we went on, and we tried a number of different structures. First, we put Geoff Mulgan, a wide-ranging and fertile thinker, in the Policy Unit with a couple of other people dedicated to the strategic policy challenges, but that didn't really work. All too often they found themselves dragged into day-to-day policy issues just because they were working alongside the rest of the Policy Unit. We therefore decided to set up a Strategy Unit, housed not in Number 10 but in Admiralty Arch, a few hundred yards away. In doing so, we were haunted by the experience of the Central Policy Review Staff, which had been set up under Ted Heath with the aim of being the government's strategic think tank. It did some good work in its time and had an impressive cast of alumni, but every time it ventured into sensitive policy areas its work seemed to leak, causing embarrassment for the government, and Mrs Thatcher closed it down in the early 1980s. We were afraid we might be creating the same rod for our own backs.

The challenge of finding the right way to deal with strategy is a common problem for governments around the world. The US State Department Policy Planning Staff is one of the oldest strategic units in the world, set up after the Second World War, and first headed by George Kennan, the author of the 'long telegram' from Moscow in 1946, which set out the basis for the policy of containment that the West followed from then on throughout the Cold War. The Planning Staff swung back and forth during its existence, between being an academic ivory tower of no relevance to the Secretary of State and being dragged into day-to-day policymaking, as it was when its head, Dennis Ross, was used by Jim Baker as his principal negotiator on the Middle East.

We finally managed to resolve this problem by leaving the Strategy Unit as a free-standing entity outside Number 10, but by making sure at the same time its agenda was set by the head of the prime minister's Policy Unit, so that we could be certain it would work only on projects that were of direct relevance to the prime minister. It made itself unthreatening to departments by being clear that it would only address cross-cutting issues rather than core issues belonging to individual departments, and it was staffed by teams drawn from the departments and outside experts, each team headed by a junior minister.

It is the cross-cutting issues, like drugs or energy policy, that are the most difficult to deal with in government, precisely because they fall between departments and no one feels they own them. We tried appointing 'tsars' to take responsibility for them at the centre, in the Cabinet Office, but the system rarely worked well. On drugs, neither the Department of Health nor the Home Office would surrender their budgets for treatment and eradication, so the tsar was left largely powerless. The Strategy Unit could bridge that gap, and, for example, on energy policy came up with a far-reaching and practical policy for returning to nuclear power as well as developing renewable sources, so that Britain has a chance of achieving its targets for reducing greenhouse gases without the threat of the lights going out. It is crucially important for the centre of government to have a strategic capacity. Otherwise you will deal with problems as they arise rather than thinking about them in advance.

Most governments nowadays come in with a hundred-day plan. But they frequently don't have a 'Second Act', in the Shakespearian sense, prepared. They rush to deliver their hundred-day plan in the gap between the May election and the summer break and then collapse exhausted. No one has thought about what is to follow in September and when they get back from their holidays, prime ministers discover their strategy has run out. That is why they need a unit that is preparing the second act while they are busy performing the first.

For really radical strategic thinking, you need to go to an individual rather than a bureaucracy. John Birt has been much mocked over the years, but he has a remarkable mind. When we asked him to look at an issue, he would go back to first principles and come up with a radically different approach, although it is true that his answers tended to focus more on new processes rather than new policies as such. We used to joke that the solution to every policy problem was not a new policy but an 'organogram'. When he did come up with a policy it was certainly radical. When we asked him to look at drugs policy, he proposed that possession of heroin should result in a mandatory jail sentence with release only possible when the addict could prove that he had undergone a treatment programme and was genuinely free of the addiction. Given the huge recidivism rate in heroin addiction, this would have led to very full jails, and we didn't implement the proposals, but no one could accuse John of being bland. Unfortunately, his people-handling skills were not perfect, and he seemed to rub the Secretaries of State he worked with up the wrong way so that they were often adamantly opposed to his plans, regardless of how good they were.

Tony used to complain that all the new ideas came from Number 10 rather than the departments. This was to some extent our fault for dominating the system in the way we did, but it was also

extraordinary how little capacity for original thought the departments seemed to have. Departments were almost as weak in
policymaking as they were in terms of delivery, in part because that
capacity had been effectively hollowed out during the Thatcher
period. We encouraged ministers to set up mini Strategy Units in
their departments, and even if they didn't do much strategic thinking
at least they helped act as ginger groups within the departments to
stimulate them into being more creative.

Tony's lament also reflected a disagreement between him and senior
civil servants. The mandarins did not think that new legislation was
necessary. They thought Tony was clogging up the system by
demanding more and more of it, particularly on crime. His
argument, however, was that you needed new legislation to send the
signals that forced the system to change. Just issuing edicts from departments or instituting new measurements of progress didn't do the trick.
Machiavelli sides with Tony in this disagreement: 'There is no need
of legislation so long as things work well without it, but, when such
good customs break down, legislation forthwith becomes necessary.'

Our main strategic focus in government was reform of the public
services. We started off timidly because of a lack of money and
partly because we were scared of opposition within the Labour Party.
We then put in the investment and we tried to impose change by
central fiat. But it didn't produce the improvements we wanted, and
we were held back from being more adventurous by opposition inside
government and from our back benches. In May 2003, Tony decided
to up the pace in the drive for reform. He said to me he had been
'driving with the handbrake on for too long' and was now going to
be truly radical. We could look at the abolition of Local Education
Authorities, giving schools independence, the creation of charter
schools set up by parents and the involvement of the private sector
in NHS delivery. I was delighted. Since 1999, I had been writing
notes to Tony and pressing at Policy Unit awaydays – to a certain
amount of ridicule – for a more radical approach. This approach
was intended to promote competition and create a mixed market of
private, voluntary and public provision. Instead of letting consultants build up waiting lists so that they could divert patients into
their lucrative private practices if they wanted prompt treatment,
we provided private sector 'factories' for hip and knee replacements

that wiped out waiting lists more or less overnight. We changed doctors' contracts so that they were better paid but had to work more hours for the NHS.

Taking on such powerful vested interests caused a counter-reaction. As Machiavelli observes:

> Let it be noted that there is no more delicate matter to take in hand, nor more dangerous to conduct, nor more doubtful in its success, than to set up as a leader in the introduction of changes. For he who innovates will have as his enemies all those who are well off under the existing order of things, and only lukewarm supporters in those who might be better off under the new. This lukewarm temper arises partly from the fear of adversaries who have the laws on their side and partly from the incredulity of mankind, who will never admit the merit of anything new, until they have seen it proved by events. The result, however, is that whenever the enemies of change make an attack, they do so with all the zeal of partisans, while the others defend themselves as feebly as to endanger both themselves and their cause.

This was exactly the problem we faced. When we proposed new performance-based pay for teachers in 2000, head teachers weren't prepared to choose between good and bad performers and simply wanted everyone to be paid more. Doctors fought back against the reforms by arguing that they should make the decisions on health care, not politicians. The lesson is that in the public service you have to carry the vested interests with you because you need them to deliver your reforms, and you cannot afford just to fight them in a head-on conflict. We didn't make it easy for ourselves by piling new bureaucratic requirements on staff, with endless form filling, but equally it is difficult to justify pumping masses of public money into reformed services without some form of accountability and some way of measuring results. In future, those taking on a major reform process that needs to be delivered by the very professionals being confronted, would be well advised to adopt a more Machiavellian approach in winning their support for the reforms, while at the same time pressing ahead with radical measures that they may not like.

Only a strong leader can bring about such changes. Machiavelli notes that 'we must look at whether these innovators can stand alone, or whether they depend for aid upon others; in other words, whether to carry out their ends they must resort to entreaty, or can prevail by force. In the former case they always fare badly and bring nothing to a successful issue; but when they depend upon their own resources and can employ force, they seldom fail.' He argued that the great reformers in history were strong leaders like Moses, Cyrus, Theseus and Romulus, who could force through change even if, when they did, the public wavered in its support. Thatcher and Blair were strong enough to bring about radical reform. Major and Brown were too weak.

Machiavelli believed that 'Nothing confers such honour on the reformer of a State, as do the new laws and institutions which he devises; for these when they stand on a solid basis and have a greatness in their scope, make him admired and venerated.' Tony Blair hasn't received much veneration yet for the reforms he introduced, but they will show real benefits over time, even if the full effect of many won't be apparent for some years yet. Changes in health and education take a long time to work through the system. 'Teach First', for example, is bringing bright graduates into teaching in state schools in unprecedented numbers, but those young students will not become head teachers or heads of departments for decades yet, and only then will we feel the full benefit of having raised the calibre of teachers in the country. The cumulative effect of pumping more money into the health service so that we match spending elsewhere in Europe, and the increased pay for doctors, will mean that we have better doctors in future, but again the impact will take time to work through. It is all too easy to forget how bad the public services were in the 1980s and 90s. It is striking that there are no longer winter health crises as there were every winter from 1979 to 1997; average NHS waiting lists were reduced in just three years from eighteen months to eighteen weeks; teaching went from being one of the least popular choices of those starting a second career to the second most popular. In the long term, the combination of increased spending on the public services and introducing competition into the sector with a mixed economy will give consumers choice, and by exercising that choice they, rather than the government, will drive the improvement of free health and education provision, and that will make society in Britain fairer. Gordon tried arguing in Cabinet in 2006 that we should treat people as citizens rather than as consumers. It sounded plausible and got heads nodding round the table. And it is of course true in general, but when it comes to driving change in health and education you want the public to act precisely as consumers, able to walk away and go somewhere else if provision is not satisfactory.

We did not secure these reforms without a battle. Gordon did his best to undermine them, and they were strongly opposed by many Labour backbenchers. John Prescott instinctively opposed the very ideas of using the private sector in the public services and intro- ducing choice, and he argued against them in Cabinet. The Conservatives opposed many of them, but Tony persevered at consid- erable political cost and got them through, even if we had to water some of them down along the way and were too slow in introducing them. In an ideal world, long-term reforms would be carried out on a bipartisan basis with the support of all the main parties, particu- larly on issues like pensions and long-term care, where it is coun- terproductive to have systems that change every time the government changes. As it turns out, we seem now to have reached a period of political consensus on at least some of Tony Blair's reforms. There appears to be a new form of 'Butskellism', the consensus that appeared in the 1940s and 50s on the welfare state in Britain named after Rab Butler on the Tory side and Hugh Gaitskell, the centrist Labour leader. Now, again, both major political parties support the Blair reforms, and the Conservatives have promised more of what Tony did rather than threatening to reverse it in education and health. If this consensus were maintained for another decade, there would be a period of stability in which public services really would benefit from the reforms and improve in a sustainable manner.

There are of course cases where you come up with a strategy and it turns out to be completely counterproductive. John Prescott had long been committed to the idea of regional devolution in England to balance devolution in Scotland and Wales. When I came to work for Tony and I was negotiating with John about his job in government, he gave me a pile of pamphlets he had produced in the 1970s and 80s on the subject. Once in government he pursued the idea relentlessly, despite the apparent lack of interest of people in the regions or in the government. Finally, Tony gave way in 2004 and allowed John to hold a referendum in the North-East, the region most likely to want devolved power. He campaigned manfully and pretty much single-handedly in the region for months.

In November, towards the end of the campaign, he came to Cabinet, shamefaced, to tell us that he had been deploying the latest campaigning technology to win over the people of the North-East to the idea but unfortunately it had gone wrong. He had personally recorded phone messages saying, 'This is John Prescott, I am ringing to urge you to vote yes in next week's referendum.' They were to go out to households across the region in three bursts around teatime, in a technique known as push polling. Unfortunately, the technician programming the machinery had got the timing wrong so that thousands of sleepy households across the North-East answered the phone at four thirty, five and five thirty in the morning to hear John Prescott's voice urging them to vote yes. There was never much chance that the people were going to vote for regional devolution anyway, but those phone calls pretty much finished off any slim chance that remained.

During the course of our ten years in government, we gradually learned how to handle radical reform plans. We started in 1997 with a plan for welfare reform, but it foundered on personality. In Opposition, Tony had intended to make a bold gesture by appointing the radical Frank Field as Shadow Welfare Secretary, but when it came to the moment he stepped back from what was just too dangerous a move politically and instead appointed Harriet Harman to the job, with Frank as her deputy. The partnership did not work and the two spent most of their time fighting. Harriet was inclined to phone Tony and complain interminably. I noted in my diary in December 1997 that after ten minutes of listening to her Tony handed the receiver to Peter Mandelson who was with him in the den and walked out, leaving her continuing to complain without realising that he had left.

On top of that, we had a major problem with Gordon Brown, who thought welfare reform was part of his bailiwick. When Tony announced that he was going to chair a committee on the subject, Gordon immediately set up a committee of his own, telling Tony that Tony's committee was not allowed to decide on any issues being considered by Gordon's. When eventually Gordon agreed to come to Tony's committee, Ed Balls, who came with him, spent the whole meeting whispering in Gordon's ear, driving Tony absolutely crazy.

Towards the end of our time in government, we had worked out better how to manage such reform. We used outsiders like Adair Turner and David Freud to draw up ideas, and then we would put forward a series of strategic five-year plans. Even then, however, it wasn't plain sailing. When Tony wrote to ministers explaining the concept of the five-year plans in January 2004, Gordon followed the next day with a letter trying to impose his own agenda on the exercise. Even if politics of this style persisted, by putting the plans in a strategic context, by basing them on a proper analysis of the problems that were being tackled and by driving them from the centre, we gave ourselves a much greater chance of success.

By mid-2005, however, Tony's power was waning, civil servants were looking to a new leader, and Tony was no longer, in Machiavelli's words, 'an armed Prophet'. The political dominance to overcome the opposition and drive through the implementation of the reforms had gone. John Hutton even told us in 2007 that his Permanent Secretary had advised him not to publish his White Paper on welfare reform because Gordon might not like it. A prudent prime minister would learn from our mistakes and implement reforms early while still politically strong, and anchor them in a strategic framework like the five-year plans, to maximise their chances of success.

Even the wisest of leaders finds it difficult to choose between conflicting priorities. There is some truth to the old saying that if a politician comes to a fork in the road they pick it up. There is, though, no way any prime minister, however good, can advance far across a broad front even in ten years of power. He or she has to choose certain areas of policy where they want to make radical change and prioritise those above all else. It is not possible to choose more than two or three top priorities and still be effective.

I made my one contribution to Tony's catalogue of sound bites when I suggested a catchy phrase for inclusion in his 1995 conference speech. It had come to me when, earlier that year, I went to see an old friend in Washington, Mary McGrory, the liberal *Washington Post* columnist. She asked me what our top three priorities would be in government, and after thinking a moment I replied, 'Education, education, education.' My play on the estate agent's mantra of 'location, location, location' was deliberate. I thought we would be able to change only a few areas of policy in a fundamental way during our time in government, and the most important – as well as the most likely to make Britain more equal – was education. When Tony came to that point in his speech, the conference erupted in applause, in part because so many of the delegates were teachers, but also because so many recognised that that was what we needed to focus on in government. A good sound bite has to resonate with people; it is no good trying to force something counter-intuitive down their throats. It only works if they nod with it and say, 'Yes, that's right.' It became such a popular phrase that we even managed to work it into a radio soap opera in Russia in which Tony made a guest appearance later that year when we were on a visit to Moscow.

When I would discuss the need to prioritise with Tony, he would say that prime ministers have to be able to walk and chew gum at the same time. He simply could not afford to ignore health or transport or welfare reform or even agriculture. That is undoubtedly true. Prime ministers cannot say they are ignoring any area of policy. But a prudent leader who wants to leave a lasting mark should privately narrow down priorities to no more than three and spend as much time on them as possible, leaving other issues to the departments to manage. For Britain, the first three priorities, in my opinion, should still be education, education, education.

Prime ministers in office don't have time to think about 'isms'. They are too busy governing. Mrs Thatcher managed to establish Thatcherism while in government in part because she had had a longer run-up in developing its intellectual underpinnings. The economist Milton Friedman had been refining his ideas in the Chicago School since the 1940s, and provided her with the basis for her reform programme. We didn't have the same sort of prior intellectual ferment to build on, and to a large degree we had to make up our philosophy as we went along.

It was, however, striking at the time how much interest there was around the world in what we were trying to do. The third-way agenda, although now largely forgotten, was the principal progressive agenda in the world at the time. Gerhard Schroeder was keen to work with us when he was first elected. David Miliband and I went to meet Frank Walter Steinmeier and the rest of Schroeder's team in Hanover during the German election campaign and diverted to Stuttgart to meet Bodo Hombach, one of his key political supporters, at the same time. I went to see Bodo again a few days after their victory when he was ensconced in the Chancellery in Bonn. He produced an excellent bottle of German red wine which he said he had liberated from Kohl's cellars, and I proposed to him the idea of a joint paper on a reformed social democracy. Unfortunately, the resulting 'Hombach Mandelson' paper was a political disaster for Schroeder inside the SPD and turned him against further direct political cooperation with us, although he continued as a regular participant in the third-way international circus, and it is interesting how many of the ideas in that paper were eventually put into practice in his subsequent economic reforms as Chancellor of Germany. The third way has now run its course, but in time it will reappear, called something else, among a new generation of progressive politicians. The same challenges remain, and the centre left will need to find new answers in the same political space.

Blairism has been defined since Tony left office and in part by contrast with what followed. His brand of economic stability, radical public service reform and strong foreign policy may be temporarily unfashionable, but it is an unmistakable political philosophy and will reappear in the future. Tony shifted the centre of gravity in British politics in a lasting way. No one in British politics will reverse Mrs Thatcher's liberal economic reforms, and no one will reverse Tony Blair's public service reforms. At the moment the Blair government is more remembered for spin than for strategy. But when history comes to be written I think it will be the other way round because in truth we succeeded in strategy but failed in spin, and it was spin that contributed in a major way to our downfall.

CHAPTER EIGHT

'Calumnies are as Injurious to Republics as Public Indictments are Useful'
Spin Doctors and Media Moguls

Machiavelli did not have to deal with the British tabloid press or twenty-four-hour news, but he was well aware of the importance of presentation. He advises a wise prince, even in the sixteenth century, 'that it is necessary, indeed, to put a good colour on this nature, and to be skilful in simulating and dissembling'.

He says, 'It is not essential, then, that a Prince should have all the good qualities I have enumerated above, but it is most essential that he should seem to have them.' He goes on to argue, 'A Prince should . . . be very careful that nothing ever escapes his lips which is not replete with the five qualities above, so that to see and hear him, one would think him the embodiment of mercy, good faith, integrity, humanity and religion . . . because men in general judge rather by the eye than by the hand, for everyone can see but few can touch. Everyone sees what you seem, but few know what you are, and these few dare not oppose themselves to the opinion of the many who have the majesty of the State to back them up.'

This advice applies every bit as much to leaders today. People see what is in front of their eyes rather than what lies behind, and they judge largely on the basis of what they see. The best advice I ever heard about televised leaders' debates, whether in the United States or Britain, is that the way to watch them is with the sound turned down. One can judge the winner by assessing who looked into the TV camera most sincerely and whose demeanour was best rather than by assessing who made the most telling points in any argument. It is for this reason that politicians devote so much of their attention to presentation and particularly to the media, which are the mirrors through which their image is refracted to the public.

The Labour Party learned bitter lessons about handling the media from its eighteen years in Opposition. Above all, it learned that it could not win elections without a professional approach to presentation and without finding some way of winning over the traditionally Tory-supporting tabloids. The picture of Neil Kinnock's head inside a light bulb on the front page of the *Sun* on the eve of the 1992 election symbolised the problem. It may not in fact have been 'the *Sun* wot won it', but it was sufficiently true for the New Labour team to be determined to avoid the risk of anything like that happening again. We consciously devised a strategy of winning over the Tory tabloids prior to the 1997 election and then of endeavouring to keep them with us.

Our primary target was Rupert Murdoch, and Tony went out of his way to woo him. I had been told by the *Sunday Times* correspondent in Washington that the American economist and columnist Irwin Stelzer was a confidant of Murdoch's and the best way in to him. Tony struck up a friendship with Irwin that lasted through his time in government, and he helped Tony win over Murdoch. We were thrilled when Tony was invited to be the keynote speaker at the 1995 Newscorp annual gathering on Hayman Island in the Great Barrier Reef off Australia. Murdoch likes to back the winning side, and he could read the opinion polls as well as anyone else, and so in the course of that year and into 1996 a number of his titles shifted in favour of New Labour. Tony put great efforts into maintaining the relationship right through his time in government and thereafter. It paid off.

But Tony's ambitions went further than that, and he tried to advance into the very heart of the enemy camp. He cultivated Viscount Rothermere, owner of the *Daily Mail*, and his brilliant editor, David English, as well as dyed-in-the-wool Conservative columnists like Simon Heffer and Paul Johnson. Many of Tony's staff thought this cultivation distasteful and a waste of time, but I could see the point of it. Even if he could not stop them being Tories, a bit of flattery and attention made it harder for them to attack him with the same venom as they had his predecessors.

Sometimes cultivating the enemy can go too far. Gordon Brown, convinced that that tactic lay at the root of Tony's success, became obsessed with winning over Murdoch and the *Mail*. He appeared to think that passing the Murdoch test was effectively the primary election that he had to win to become leader of the Labour Party and even that he could use Murdoch's support to lever Tony out prematurely. Gordon adopted the mantle of a Eurosceptic to win Murdoch's support. The tactic backfired, however, when a new generation of Murdoch took over the British operation in 2009. Rupert's son James had more in common with a young David Cameron than with the old grouch in Downing Street as well as hoping that a Tory victory would provide greater opportunities for Sky TV. He shifted his titles back to the Tories. Gordon was so keen to woo Paul Dacre, David English's successor as editor of the *Mail*, that he lavished time on him and even stayed the weekend with him at one of his country estates. Their shared interest in a hair-shirt approach to life, and an addiction to old-fashioned moralising, helped build a personal rapport and secured the support of the *Mail* in his battle to unseat Tony but it didn't do Gordon much good in the long term. Once in Downing Street and as things got difficult, the *Mail* abandoned him. Gordon would have been better off saving his dignity and not looking too desperate in his pursuit of such untrustworthy allies.

Tony had made his career in the Labour Party by attracting favourable press comment, and he continued to make a point of seeing journalists regularly once in government. Whenever things were getting difficult, we would go through another round of inviting in the editors and their key staff for lunch, one after another, and the relaxed chats in the small dining room in Number 10 delivered results in terms of coverage.

Intimate contact between a leader and journalists is not, however, always advisable. Tony had a habit of putting his foot in it when-ever he would go to the back of the plane while we were travelling to meet the accompanying press pack. The journalists insisted on such visits and thought they were included in the price of their ticket, but they would usually go wrong. On his trip to Australia in 2006, Tony had made a slip by admitting in an Australian TV inter-view that it had been a mistake to say he was leaving office, thereby trampling all over the coverage of an excellent speech to the Australian Parliament. The following day, when he went to speak to the journalists on the plane, they pressed him hard on his comments, and he told them that he had decided on a date for his departure but was not going to tell them what it was. His announcement set off a frenzy of speculation, as such visits to the rear of the plane had done every time I could remember, right back to the first time he did it on a trip to the US in Opposition in 1995. It is invariably a mistake to respond to the travelling press packs' questions without checking the premise of their question first. When we were in Moscow in 2003, the accompanying press told us that Mrs Thatcher had died and asked Tony for a comment. I checked with my brother who asked one of her staff to go and look. He reported back a few minutes later that it was true that she was a bit sleepy but she was definitely not dead.

Very occasionally Tony phoned journalists directly to try to head off particularly damaging stories. For example when Gordon rubbished the government's proposals on asylum and welfare reform to journalists as not being radical enough, Tony had to call Andy Marr, the BBC's political editor, just before he went live on the evening news to opine on the subject. Gordon, on the other hand, rang up journalists regularly to rage about their stories or to try to apply the spin himself. Making yourself too familiar to the press can lead to your being held in contempt, Machiavelli's cardinal sin. Machiavelli advises that 'a Prince should consider how he may avoid such courses as make him hated or despised'. Prudent prime ministers would keep a certain distance from the media and see them rarely so that encounters with them feel special.

Tony was so scarred by the way in which the media had dealt with the Labour Party in the previous decade that, when he started building his team as party leader, he began with a professional press operation led by the brilliant and mercurial Alastair Campbell, a tabloid journalist. Alastair understood the language and the mindset of the tabloids, could see a story before they could and knew how they needed it served up. He made it his mission to win them over to Tony and New Labour.

Alastair also managed to impose some message discipline on both the historically anarchic Labour front bench and on their press people by a remarkable act of will, subsequently lightly caricatured in *The Thick of It*. He made the Labour Party better able to defend itself. In the past, the party had always been too passive and too slow to deal with damaging attacks. Too often it just stood there and took the punishment. The mud that was flung, however unjustified, tended to stick. Under Alastair, our response became much more robust.

We established a rebuttal unit that jumped on false stories as fast as possible to kill them off. In the US, it was John Kerry's failure to respond robustly and quickly enough to the attack on him by the Vietnam 'swift boat veterans' that contributed to his defeat in the 2004 presidential campaign. Politicians too often think that people won't really believe these sort of attacks, particularly in the case of John Kerry, who unlike George Bush, was a genuine Vietnam hero. This, however, was a clever new tactic of Karl Rove, Bush's political adviser: to launch an attack on the strengths of an opponent rather than on his weaknesses. Unless such attacks are firmly rebutted they hang around and, however outlandish and however unfair they are, they acquire credibility. There is a good reason why politicians and newspapers resort to such tactics: they work.

When we arrived in Number 10 we inherited a run-down and ineffective press team. They were civil servants and, under constant attack, they had developed a purely defensive stance. The number two who remained behind in Downing Street when Alastair arrived would invariably come up with a way of killing off any story. In the kind of cricketing metaphor that was compulsory under John Major, he was not interested in scoring sixes but only in preventing the loss of wickets. As a new and popular government, we needed a proactive media operation which did not just respond to stories but created them, and we needed a political press secretary who could range over the Labour Party's interests as well as those of the government. John Major had had Civil Service press spokesmen, and, whenever the journalists asked them about anything at all political, they had to stop and say they could not talk about such issues, referring them to the party press secretary. As almost all the issues you might raise with Number 10 have both a political and a governmental aspect, this led to fractured communications, with journalists playing off one side against the other. In addition, a Civil Service spokesman can all too easily find himself dragged into partisan politics, as Bernard Ingham did working for Margaret Thatcher. A prime minister is therefore wise to appoint a political spokesman who can cover both spheres and who will leave Downing Street when the prime minister does.

Alastair was unfairly criticised for politicising the government press service. Actually, what he did was to professionalise and modernise it. When we arrived it was in a parlous state, and by the time we left it had regained its confidence and become far better at what it did. The seamier side of political press briefing is the domain of ministers' special advisers and, of course, of ministers themselves. It is the special advisers like the Damian McBrides, Charlie Whelans and Ed Ballses, not departmental spokesmen, who specialise in character assassination through the pages of the newspapers. What always surprised me was that the assassins managed to persuade the press to keep quiet about their activities, however many incriminating emails or texts they sent. They succeeded in building up a dependency among the political correspondents by feeding them a constant supply of stories, so that the journalists were reluctant to endanger that supply by revealing their methods.

A wise prime minister would try to bring this behaviour under control in his own ranks. More than anything else, it saps the morale of ministers who spend their time speculating about who has been briefing against them and why and then responding in kind. It is, however, only possible to solve the problem if you can stamp out the divisions between the politicians themselves, who use their special advisers to engage in this subterranean warfare.

In 2000, Mo Mowlam clearly came to suspect me of engaging in this sort of behaviour. A series of stories had appeared about the prospects of her running for the London mayoralty instead of Frank Dobson, and she had been speaking to Tony about whether she might. I imagine she thought the press stories were attempts to force her arm. They were followed by a very unpleasant story in the *New Statesman* saying that Number 10 thought her brain tumour affected her judgement. Presumably she was convinced that I was behind the briefing, although I was not, and the response was a story in the *Daily Mail* accusing me of being the 'poisoner of Downing Street', who was briefing the press against both her and Frank Dobson. The story was picked up in other papers. I threatened to sue, and one paper agreed to an apology and a donation to charity, but the *Mail*, of course, held out. I told Mo that I had not been behind the stories and made a point of not briefing the press at all. Mo insisted on a public kiss-and-make-up drink on the terrace of the House of Commons in front of political correspondents and MPs. I didn't feel at all comfortable, being convinced that everyone was staring at me, but I was left with little choice.

In government we had our share of leaks. One newspaper actually went to the lengths of taking on a young woman to arrange to be hired as a temporary clerk in the Cabinet Office. Other leaks were more politically targeted. Someone managed to scoop up a large number of the sensitive documents given to the Butler Inquiry into the Iraq War and then released them, one by one, during the 2005 election campaign with the aim of doing the maximum possible damage to the Labour Party. Virtually on the eve of that election, Channel 4 was given a copy of a summary of Attorney General Peter Goldsmith's legal advice on the war. We were operating out of the election headquarters on Victoria Street, and we needed to get a copy of the full advice so that we could work out how to respond. Peter Goldsmith's house in Queen Anne's Gate was besieged by TV cameras, and we couldn't send over anyone who would be recognised to collect it, so we sent one of the Number 10 messengers and watched on television as she pushed past the cameras, got into the house unnoticed by the assembled journalists and returned with the document.

During our decade in government, we commissioned plenty of leak inquiries, usually conducted by former security officials, but they seldom achieved results. On the few occasions when they managed to close in on the perpetrator, he or she turned out to be a minister and the inquiry had to be abandoned to avoid embarrassment. Leaks make foreign relations difficult to manage. After a series of official letters recording conversations with George W. Bush had appeared in the press, Bush joked in a videoconference with Tony that the private secretary should write down what he said carefully so that it would appear accurately when it was leaked. If your allies lose faith in your ability to keep a secret, they are loath in the future to trust you with confidential information. It is all too easy, however, to become obsessed with worrying about who has been responsible for a leak and even to lose faith in your own staff. While it is hard to make government work when you are subject to a campaign of leaks, freezing up the system with a pall of suspicion is even worse.

We made a sustained attempt to open up government and remove some of the secrecy that had obscured it in the past, but we got scant credit for doing so, and most of the steps made our life harder rather than easier.

Immediately after the 1997 election, we brought the parliamentary lobby, which had long existed in quasi-Masonic secrecy, into the open with the transcripts of the twice-daily Number 10 briefings released online. Later we invited other journalists, including specialist and foreign correspondents, to the briefings. Part of our reasoning was to try, unsuccessfully, to embarrass the political lobby correspondents into abandoning their more juvenile lines of questioning, as well as dispelling some of the myths that had long hung over the lobby itself. We even considered televising the lobby briefings so that there would be a government spokesman on the record every day, as in the US and many other countries. Gordon, however, made a huge fuss, and other Cabinet ministers, who didn't want their thunder stolen by a non-MP, objected on the ground that it would lead to greater 'prime ministerialism', with the Number 10 spokesman speaking for the whole government, so we abandoned the idea.

Our most important innovation, unlikely to be reversed, was the monthly prime ministerial press conference, which began in 2002. It gives the prime minister the opportunity to communicate directly with the people so that they can see and hear him. Tony didn't have an opportunity to do much preparation for his first appearance and, as often happened when he had done little in advance, he sailed through. Over-rehearsal can often be a mistake for a politician. Tony was good at the kind of self-deprecating jokes and one-liners that the media love, and initially the journalists liked the exposure that the press conference gave them on television. As they came to realise, however, that they were no better than MPs at catching Tony out, they found the conferences boring and ceased to broadcast them on the evening news bulletins.

Press conferences with visiting foreign leaders can be disconcerting, and because of their unpredictability we tried to avoid them wherever possible. If we did have one, we usually had to apologise for the British press who would insist on asking domestic questions and showed no interest in the visiting leader at all. Very occasionally we had to apologise when they did show an interest. President Nazarbayev of Kazakhstan visited in November 2006 at the moment when the film *Borat*, which purported to be about Kazakhstan although filmed in Romania, was released in the UK. We had to rehearse with the president in advance how he would respond to the inevitable question. He did very well, saying that 'We have a saying in my country that all news is good news.' President Bush was not the best of performers, but we noticed a remarkable improvement in his performance when Tony did a press conference with him in Washington in 2002. He told us afterwards that he had been asking the former president, Bill Clinton, for tips on how to do it.

Finally, we introduced the Freedom of Information Act. In retrospect, this was a mistake, not because secrecy is a virtue, but because policymaking, like producing sausages, is not something that should be carried out in public. It was designed to help the public by giving them access to their own records and illuminating the work of government. Unfortunately, the number of requests lodged by the public was dwarfed by those from journalists, and their aim was not illumination but harassment. They sought the names on guest lists for dinners and on Christmas card lists and attendees at meetings and anything trivial that could cause trouble. The real damage came when the Information Commissioner attempted to spread the net to capture advice to ministers as well. This had been deliberately excluded from the initial rules.

Civil servants and others will not give ministers honest but uncomfortable advice if they know that soon afterwards it will be made public. In 2005, the Commissioner decided that the Attorney General's advice on Iraq should be released. We did not mind releasing it by that stage, since its content was already well known, but doing so would establish a principle that confidential advice to ministers could be made public. If we resisted, the Commissioner threatened to publish damaging comments about the government and the way in which it had handled the issue. In the end, we decided to protect the principle and suffer the damage, but it didn't stop the Commissioner later pushing out the boundary even further. The institutional problem is that the Information Commissioner is, through a mistake in the initial legislation, at the same time both the judge on what should and shouldn't be released and also an advocate for extending the boundaries of what should be released, so that, when he sits as a judge, he naturally always favours extending the boundaries.

The rules required the addition of large numbers of staff in Number 10 and elsewhere in government to sift the requests for information, gather the papers and make judgements according to the rules about what should be released and what should not. In 2004, the whole business almost brought work in Downing Street to a halt. The extra bureaucracy is wasteful, but the really damaging impact is the reduction in the amount of confidential work conducted on paper for fear that its release will be demanded later on. In the end, this will lead not to any greater openness but to inefficiency in the way government works. In Germany, all finalised official papers are required by freedom of information laws to be released to the Bundestag. As a result, no paper in the Kanzleramt ever reaches final status but remains in draft so that it doesn't have to be released. In the most extreme example, in the US no White House official is willing to commit anything sensitive to his computer since the hard disks can be subjected to interrogation. All such work is carried out on yellow Post-it notes which can be destroyed subsequently. A wise prime minister would reverse the counterproductive elements of the Act and think of other ways of giving the public greater insight to the workings of government. Sadly, it is unlikely that anyone will, because they will not want to face the opprobrium of being presented in the press as reversing freedom of information.

As well as trying to make the work of government more open, we also managed, over time, to make the government's approach to the media more long-term and strategic.

In the world of modern politics, the government needs to have a proactive media strategy. It needs to go out to explain what it is doing and why. This requires government to think ahead, and we set up a strategic communications unit alongside the press office in Number 10, charged with thinking about the longer term. Those in the unit would decide when and how policy announcements should be made and could, for example, help TV channels make thoughtful packages about, say, a new education reform, explaining its impact on the real world in film rather than news programmes having no advance warning and simply having to broadcast a lot of talking heads commenting on the reform.

The unit was also in charge of the new media, including the Internet, as well as correspondence. The government has a huge opportunity to communicate with the people by replying to their emails and letters; but, when we arrived in Number 10, most of the letters addressed to the prime minister would be shipped off to departments and never get a reply. In the first few months of office, a letter arrived addressed to Tony congratulating him on his election and signed 'Your loving pa'. It never got to Tony but Leo, Tony's father, received a reply a month later addressed to 'Dear Mr Loving Pa', thanking him for his letter and saying that his views had been noted, with an illegible signature underneath.

We tried to learn some of the lessons from the way in which the Internet had been used in the US presidential campaign by the Democrat politician, Howard Dean. Our team came up with the idea of petitions on the website, which generated some real enthusiasm. When some bright spark posted a petition on the controversial issue of road charging, the Brownites responded by denouncing the member of the Number 10 staff who had come up with the idea of e-petitions as 'a prat'. The website nevertheless became a huge success as a way for the public to access information about the government. We started releasing bits of news and statements on the website first, and in a moment of weakness Tony agreed to record a regular TV podcast to attract more attention to the site, a bit like the US president's radio broadcast. It was a mistake. You should never agree to anything regular unless it has a huge and immediate benefit, because it always turns into an unwanted burden and, once you have started it, you can never stop it without an excellent reason.

Politicians need constantly to explain what they are doing, and they have to repeat their message again and again until they are heartily sick of it before there is any chance of its being heard by the public. Sometimes they feel that the media have turned against them, and they just can't get their message through at all. In the second half of his first term Bill Clinton felt that he could no longer communicate his message through the national networks. His staff devised a method whereby he could speak directly to the people through the far less hostile local TV stations. They would line up a satellite truck beside the Old Executive Office Building, and Clinton would go there and do ten short interviews back to back for local TV stations from Nebraska to Texas. We tried a similar local media strategy designed to bypass a cynical national media. Tony would go on regular regional visits and get far more positive coverage on local TV news and in the local press than he would nationally. It is certainly true that local media have a greater penetration rate and are far more likely to be believed than the national media, but politicians kid themselves if they think this is an alternative to fighting the battle at the national level. They have to win both.

It took me time to get used to the lengths the press would go to in order to obtain a story. I was surprised in November 2000 to read some of my own handwritten notes on the front page of the *Sunday Times*. It was an aide-memoire listing a series of pretty sensitive issues that I had to raise with Tony. I had left them at home by mistake, and the cleaner had thrown them in the bin. When I went to work on Wednesday morning, I noticed that the bags of rubbish I had put outside just before midnight the night before had been opened and garbage strewn down the street. A couple of bags had disappeared completely. It appears that an investigator who specialised in raiding people's rubbish for sensitive documents had taken them and passed them on to the *Sunday Times*. Given that we had a one-year-old baby and the bags were full of soiled nappies, he had probably earned his fee in this case. Luckily for me, the *Sunday Times* were unable to read my crablike handwriting, and all their guesses were completely wrong, so although they published the notes on the front page, they had been forced to show them to a handwriting expert who had concluded that I was very 'devious and secretive'. Unfortunately, some of those referred to in the notes could work out what they said, and Chris Smith complained to me about the note of our conversation in which he, the MP for Islington, had suggested moving the new Arsenal stadium into the Dome.

On another occasion, I was caught out by the duplicity of journalists. I was cycling home from Number 10 in 2004 when I noticed Boris Johnson, whom I knew vaguely, on his bike stopped at the traffic lights at the top of the Mall. I came to a halt for a bit of banter. He started asking me about the well-publicised rows at the time between Gordon and Tony. I replied with a few jokes and said that it was a Shakespearean tragedy and that I doubted Gordon would ever be prime minister. He went into a spiel about the Scots and Macbeth. I thought nothing more about it until I was waiting in the British Midland lounge for a plane from Heathrow to Dublin a few days later, and the Number 10 press office called me to say Boris Johnson had given an account of the conversation to one of his colleagues at the *Spectator*, and it had appeared in that week's edition. Predictably, given Boris Johnson's history as a journalist, he had attributed to me not just my part of the conversation but also his own, describing Gordon as Macbeth. In fact, I had been reflecting on a conversation with one of Gordon's Cabinet colleagues who had described him to me as a classic Aristotelian tragic hero, brilliant but undermined by his fundamental character flaws: he combined the overweening ambition of Macbeth with the indecision of Hamlet and the appalling judgement of Lear, all rolled into one. Gordon was naturally furious, and it gave him one more stick with which to beat Tony.

Our relationship with the media started off well in government. We were a breath of fresh air, and we still managed to surprise in the early days. Above all, we provided the journalists with a new narrative after years of the same old stories about the Tories. The arts of spin worked. In 1998, Peter Mandelson cleverly briefed the papers that John Prescott had won concessions in internal government negotiations on trade union recognition, and the positive coverage helped to persuade John to sign up to the eventual compromise. But it began to go wrong pretty quickly, for example over the demise of the Royal Yacht *Britannia*. Gordon raised the issue of its future with Tony in September 1997. Tony begged him not to brief that it was going to be mothballed before the decision had been made. Two hours later, the *Independent* were on the phone to the Number 10 press office about the decision and the story was launched. Gordon hadn't, however, told the MoD, and George Robertson publicly denied that there was any such decision, leaving the government looking in total disarray.

The most irritating case of such briefing warfare was the running story of 'Blair Force One'. Throughout our time in Number 10, we tried to deal with the relatively minor problem of what to do when the ancient VC10s went out of service in the Royal Flight. We were left with no official planes and needed to find new ones to ferry the Queen and government ministers around the world on official trips. At EU meetings we would be the only country without an official plane. Even Ireland, Latvia and Luxembourg had planes. We, on the other hand, had to charter private jets specially for such journeys at far greater cost, leaving us without communications or defensive measures. Every time we even thought of buying or leasing a plane for the government, the Treasury would brief the papers, and a story would appear saying that Tony was looking for an extravagant Blair Force One complete with shower and gold-plated jacuzzi. We would then back off. In the end, we asked Peter Gershon, a distinguished businessman who had run the Office of Government Commerce for the Treasury, to conduct an independent study of the best solution. When he recommended the leasing of a number of planes and helicopters to save the government money, a new rash of stories appeared about Blair Force One and we had to give up the idea for good. I once had the embarrassing duty of standing next to King Abdullah at the royal terminal in Riyadh as Tony boarded a plane bound for Singapore to lobby for the Olympics in 2005. The British company BAE had just sold the Saudi air force £5 billion-worth of Typhoon fighter planes. The King asked me in a puzzled way why Tony's plane, which was chartered, had a Swiss flag on its tail fin. I had to think fast. I couldn't tell him it was because we had no plane of our own, given what we had just sold them, so I said it was for security reasons. He seemed satisfied with that explanation.

All too soon, however, the relationship with the media soured irretrievably. Partly this was our fault. We had learned the lessons of Opposition too well. Having realised that we should not let negative stories go unchallenged, we had become overly aggressive and started to fight every report. We got carried away in boosting stories, as Alastair did in suggesting that Tony's 2000 speech in Tubingen meant that the police would be able to march offenders straight to cashpoints to make them pay fines. We also tried to be too clever in playing one paper off against another, giving a story exclusively to the *Sun* and thereby making a permanent enemy of the *Mirror*. And we became entrapped by our adherence to the less famous of the two maxims written over James Carville's desk in Little Rock during the Clinton campaign: 'Speed kills' (the more famous one being 'It's the economy, stupid'). We felt we had to respond immediately to any story. The speed addiction led to Peter Mandelson's second departure from the government in January 2001 over allegations surrounding a passport application made by one of the wealthy Hinduja brothers. We were so mesmerised by the press that we believed we had to respond to journalists' questions by the time of the 11 a.m. press lobby or we would bleed to death. As a result, we rushed into dismissing Peter precipitately, before making a decision, rather than waiting for the outcome of Sir 'Wally' Hammond's inquiry into the whole affair.

In the end, it was our very success at becoming professional that brought about our undoing. Once spin and the spin doctor became the story, we had lost the battle. You cannot communicate your message if the communicating of it itself gets in the way.

Of course, the most spectacular manifestation of New Labour's fall from grace with the media was Alastair's war with the BBC and his departure from Number 10. Even before Gilligan's appalling behaviour, Alastair was no longer enjoying his job. He was always better at offence than defence, and he was increasingly miserable as the government was put more and more on the back foot. We were all outraged by what we perceived to be the biased way in which the BBC reported the wars in both Kosovo and Iraq, but unlike the rest of us he took it personally and would not let go. In the row over Gilligan, I told Alastair we needed to find a ladder for the BBC to climb down rather than try to bludgeon them to death, but he would only settle for a knockout. Tony himself tried to reach out to the BBC, sending a conciliatory message to the chairman Gavyn Davies, a Labour supporter married to Sue Nye, via John Birt, but Gavyn did not respond. When Tony toned down Alastair's letter to the BBC, Alastair complained it was a climbdown because Tony had removed the demand for an apology. When the BBC's response came from their Director of News, Richard Sambrook, it made no concessions. Alastair was at Wimbledon, and he called me at six forty-five asking whether he should go on *Channel 4 News* at seven to rebut it. I urged him not to, saying that if he lost his temper he would become the story, not the BBC. But he went anyway. The whole thing was an unnecessary tragedy, and I missed Alastair terribly in Number 10.

But the fault for the end of our good relationship with the media was not entirely ours. The media appear to have acquired a form of attention deficit disorder and get bored quickly. The news cycle has speeded up. Celebrities are built up, lauded and then trashed and spat out in months rather than years. The same is true of politicians. Journalists want to move on and find a new narrative. They no longer report the event as it happens but only the anticipation of the event. It got to the ridiculous state that a BBC correspondent would appear on the TV news standing in front of Tony delivering a speech and would give his view of it without broadcasting any of the speech itself. We had made a mistake in habitually briefing speeches in advance so that they were no longer news when they were actually delivered, but when we stopped doing that the media didn't report the speeches at all. Comment and reporting, which used to be kept separate, have now merged into one. In response to perceived government spin, journalists have taken it upon themselves to add their own spin to stories.

The competition between newspapers with fewer readers and the demand for twenty-four-hour news has led to an inexorable decline in quality as the media grasps for shock as a way of attracting attention. The aim is impact rather than nuance and to generate heat rather than light. Interviews seem to be no longer about illuminating politicians' arguments but about the promotion of the celebrity interviewer who cross-questions and constantly interrupts. A type of 'gotcha' journalism has developed where the only aim appears to be to catch the politician out in a mistake and thereby generate a headline. Not surprisingly, politicians become risk-averse and determined to avoid putting their foot in it. They try to be extraordinarily bland and mechanical in their responses, which in turn alienates the public.

There is a lack of accountability by the media. We would sometimes ask journalists why they had run a story that was untrue, and they would reply that it was a great story. We would insist, yes . . . but it is untrue, and they would cheerfully respond, yes of course it is untrue but it is a great story. Some of the Sunday papers are the prime exponents of the 'news as entertainment' approach to journalism. Their stories are no longer followed up by papers on Monday even within the same stable, because it is so obvious that what they write is fiction.

Paul Dacre has publicly justified the lack of formal accountability by saying that he, as a newspaper editor, is held to account every day by his readers who can choose whether or not to buy his paper. But of course he isn't. If a politician made the argument he would say he is held to account because he has to face election by the people and therefore can't be questioned about his veracity between elections. Dacre remains in charge as long as the paper is a commercial success and its owner wants him there. No one holds him to account on the accuracy or truthfulness of his stories – certainly not the pusillanimous Press Complaints Commission (PCC) which is paid for by the newspapers and on whose board he sits.

The fault was therefore on both sides and it was a disastrous combination: a government trying to be too controlling in its efforts to manage the press on the one side, and an unaccountable and hysterical media on the other. It led to a collapse in political dialogue and growing public cynicism. People felt powerless to bring about change because they were mere observers at an elaborate and rather unpleasant game played between the media and politicians.

All governments have problems with the BBC, and as a general rule that is to the BBC's credit. Our problem was rather unusual. We would have preferred a Conservative chairman and a Conservative Director General of the BBC so that the incumbents would not feel the need to lean over backwards to prove their independence of the government. The Conservative BBC chairman we inherited from the previous government, Christopher Bland, insisted on appointing Greg Dyke, a Labour Party supporter, as Director General in June 1999. Tony could see that the decision would spell trouble for us but went along with it. In 2001 we faced the same problem when Gavyn Davies was proposed as chairman in the middle of an election campaign. Tony was inclined to turn down the appointment, but Gavyn had been very helpful to us in Opposition in writing economic speeches and offering advice, and we did not want to appear churlish. So we ended up, against our wishes, with a Labour chairman and a Labour Director General. Once the Gilligan nonsense broke, they naturally felt they could not back down and admit that the story was wrong without looking as if they were giving in to a government of their own political stripe.

The other lesson we had learned too well in Opposition was the importance of staying on the right side of the media moguls. The moguls have no problem with their papers attacking politicians, but they have an unwritten rule not to attack each other. The *Mail* broke this understanding by constantly referring to Richard Desmond, the owner of the *Express*, as a pornographer. He eventually hit back with stories about the personal life of Jonathan Rothermere, the proprietor of the *Mail*. When Jonathan and his wife Claudia came to dinner with Tony and Cherie in April 2004, they complained bitterly about their treatment in the *Express*. When Claudia said, 'I can't believe they print that stuff,' Tony said Cherie was literally speechless. When she had recovered she asked mildly, 'Have you seen what they put in your paper about me?' The Rothermeres just laughed and said, 'Oh, that was just a little fun.' I have noticed that journalists tend to view such stories in a different light when they are themselves subject to the attack.

We should have been braver in confronting Murdoch and the other newspaper owners on the subject of Europe. Tony hoped in 1999 that Murdoch's growing business interests in Europe, when he was trying to buy Berlusconi's Mediaset empire, would change his attitude. In the end, Murdoch didn't invest in Italy, Schroeder kept him out of Germany, and his attitude to Europe didn't change. The minuscule group of British pro-European newspapers were worse than useless. Instead of giving the government support in its life-and-death battle with the Eurosceptics, they spent their time criticising the government for being insufficiently pro-European. There was simply no public space in which to have a sensible dialogue with the British people on the subject.

We first started discussing how we could remedy the failed relationship between the media and politics in 2002, and we even considered putting the PCC on a statutory basis and creating a right of reply that exists in other countries. In 2003, I commissioned Ed Richards in the Policy Unit to start working on a Royal Commission, limits on ownership and a privacy law. We discussed the issue back and forth for the next three years, but Tony never felt the moment was right to speak out, in part because the press would always have the last word, as it was they who would report and interpret what he said. In 2006, he told me he would consider putting surprise legislation in the Queen's Speech on the subject, but he didn't. When he finally did make a speech on the media in 2007, it was too late. His power was waning, he could not get any measures through before he left, and Gordon, who was courting the press, had no intention of agreeing to anything that might upset them. Tony was rightly nervous about the likely reaction to his speech, and predictably the press picked out one unfortunate phrase describing the press as 'the feral beast', rubbished the speech and moved on. They had no interest in having a serious debate on the subject, and since they have the last word on such matters no reform has happened and no politician has been brave enough to take the issue on.

A prudent prime minister should try to put the relationship between the media and politicians on a new footing before their honeymoon is over. But I doubt they will, and anyway, technology will probably resolve the problem. As newspaper circulations decline and the Internet becomes the medium of choice for news and comment, content from TV and the press will merge and it will make less and less sense to have two different regulatory systems for television and the press. Either the Ofcom rules for impartiality will have to be extended to the press, or the requirement of impartiality will have to be relaxed on TV news, or there will need to be a new framework covering both. So in the end, Paul Dacre's desire to be held accountable by his paying public will come to pass as the readership of the *Mail* dies out. The media will become yet more fragmented, and it will be harder still for the politicians to communicate directly with the public.

In Britain, the relationship between the media and the politicians has become a battle for power. Journalists run down the reputation of politicians because it strengthens their hand. As Machiavelli observes, calumnies are 'very effective when employed against powerful citizens who stand in the way of one's plans, because by playing up to the populace and confirming the poor view it takes of such men, one can make it one's friend'. He says: 'there is no need of any corroboration of the facts to set calumnies going . . . But one cannot in this way be indicted, for indictments must be corroborated and circumstances be adduced to prove the truth of the indictment. Indictments are made before the magistrates, before the people, and before courts. Calumnies are circulated in the squares and in the arcades.' Calumnies cause hatred, 'whence come divisions; from divisions factions, and from factions ruin'.

Machiavelli gives an example of the way in which such a poisoned relationship can damage a state, telling the story of Messer Giovanni Guicciardini who commanded the Florentine army in its siege of the neighbouring town of Lucca. When the siege failed, rumours were spread in Florence that Guicciardini had been suborned by the Lucchese. This calumny drove him to despair and, try as he might to rebut it, he could not. This gave rise to considerable indignation among his friends who comprised most people of standing and especially among the party who wanted to introduce innovations in Florence. The affair grew to such dimensions that it led to the downfall of the republic. Machiavelli believes that 'if in Florence provision had been made for the accusing of citizens and for the punishment of calumniators, there would not have ensued the innumerable scandals that did ensue'. He points to the solution, saying 'in what detestation calumnies should be held in free cities and in all other forms of society, and how with a view to checking them no institution which serves this end should be neglected'. In Britain, if politicians and journalists cannot agree on such institutions to remove the effect of calumnies that cannot be answered, then the judges will do it by means of the common law. They are already on the way to doing so.

Our biggest failing, though, was to take the media too seriously. While they cannot be ignored and the battles of politics are fought out through the media, they are not as important as politicians often think they are. I am always reassured by the fact that about one third of the readers of the *Mail* vote Labour, whatever the paper throws at the party. The innate good sense of people will work through.

In fact, leaders should not read the press at all if they can avoid it. John Major had a very thin skin and yet could not resist doing so even as it said increasingly vile things about him. When he visited the embassy in Washington, he would take all of the papers, including the tabloids, into the bedroom with him and pore over them. In Downing Street, he apparently used to pop out of the office to get each new edition of the *Evening Standard* as it arrived. Its reporting rankled with him and made him miserable. Mrs Thatcher and Tony Blair did not read the papers or watch the TV news. Tony would always demand that I turn off the TV if he came into the room and I was watching him being interviewed. Mrs Thatcher had a press digest prepared for her by Bernard Ingham. Tony had the papers spread out in the hall in his flat upstairs but generally would only glance at the front pages in the morning. We would draw his attention to any key stories the night before, and on the day of PMQs or a big debate he would read them. By keeping a distance and developing a thick skin, he managed to avoid becoming obsessed with the media, however much vitriol they poured over him and his family.

Even so, I noted in my diary in July 2001 that there was still a danger that we spent too much time thinking about speeches and managing presentation and again in 2005 that Tony spent too much of his time occupied with seeing the media. Machiavelli argues in *The Discourses* that 'It seems to me to be of the utmost importance in this business that you should consider what is to be done rather than what is to be said. It will be easy when you have arrived at a decision, to accommodate words to acts.' A prudent prime minister should not read the newspapers and should see journalists only rarely, deliberately creating distance. Above all a leader should not spend as much time thinking about the press as about policy.

CHAPTER NINE

'How Necessary Public Indictments are for the Maintenance of Liberty in a Republic'

Scandals, Inquiries and the Police

For Machiavelli, the threat that unjustified calumnies pose to the state can only be addressed by an agreed system to indict those who have engaged in wrongdoing. He advises that:

> No authority more useful and necessary can be granted to those appointed to look after the liberties of a state than that of being able to indict before the people or some magistrate or court such citizens as have committed any offence prejudicial to the freedom of the state. Such an institution has two consequences most useful in a republic. First, for fear of being prosecuted, its citizens attempt nothing prejudicial to the state, and, if they do attempt anything, are suppressed forthwith without respect to persons. Secondly, an outlet is provided for that ill feeling which is apt to grow up in cities against some particular citizen, however it comes about; and, when for such ill feeling there is no normal outlet, recourse is had to abnormal methods likely to bring disaster on the republic as a whole. Hence nothing does as much to stabilise and strengthen a republic as some institution whereby the changeful humours which agitate it are afforded a proper outlet by way of the laws.

Machiavelli gives the example of Coriolanus who was hostile to the plebs and their power in Rome and, when the city ran out of corn, suggested the time had come to punish them and take away their power. In response the plebs wanted to rip him limb from limb as he left the Senate, but the tribunes instead summoned him to answer before the tribunal and so he received due process. If he had been tumultuously put to death, 'this would have given rise to private feuding, which would have aroused fear; and fear would have led to defensive action; this to the procuring of partisans; partisans would have meant the formation of factions in the city; and factions would have brought about its downfall'.

In our system the same rules apply. It is fundamental that the rule of law is the same for everyone, including those in power. There are no exemptions to prosecution, such as the French president enjoys for example, and that basic rule is essential if we are to maintain our liberties. Scandals and allegations of wrongdoing, including unfounded accusations, are a staple part of our politics and there needs to be a system of investigating such accusations, in part to deflect the heat they engender and avoid the fate that Machiavelli describes. But the system needs to be agreed, and if the results of inquiries aren't accepted, or those conducting them feel under pressure to reach the conclusions that the mob demands, or if the investigations are abused or run out of control, then they no longer serve their purpose as a safety valve, with the result that, in the long term, the system itself is threatened.

We certainly had plenty of scandals, ersatz and real, to test whether our system works. And it doesn't. Calumniators get away with their calumnies unchecked, as discussed in the previous chapter, and the system of inquiries and investigations is unable, as presently constituted, to satisfy either the accuser or the accused.

I gave evidence to six different inquiries and came eventually to feel like a professional witness. We had our first experience of firefighting even before we came into government when the press launched an attack on how the office of the Leader of the Opposition was funded. Once the office had been set up, we established, on legal advice, a blind fund so that Tony and his staff would not know who the donors were, and they in turn could not hope to derive advantage from their donations. We formed a committee of Merlyn Rees, Brenda Dean and Margaret Jay to supervise the fund at arm's length. Unfortunately, the *Sunday Times* managed to hack into the fund's bank account. Their investigator convinced a young bank clerk over the phone that he was calling from the fund, and the clerk handed over the donors' details. When the bank realised the mistake and called back, the 'contact' turned out to be a serviced office used by one of the seedier sort of private investigator. The *Sunday Times* published the names of the donors. The fund was no longer blind.

The appropriate response in these circumstances is complete transparency. Blind funds appear to be impossible to operate in modern politics because no one believes they are really blind, whatever safeguards you build in. Even transparency, however, does not satisfy the critics and, when we introduced it in party funding, the press immediately moved on to suggesting that anyone who gives money to a party is after something. No country has yet come up with a system that satisfies the critics, and I doubt any ever will.

Our first fully fledged controversy in government was the Bernie Ecclestone affair. It hit us just after the birth of my eldest daughter, and I had to go back to the office taking her with me. She and Sarah sat upstairs with Cherie while I was downstairs wrestling with how to respond. My paternity leave lasted all of one and a half days.

Our sin in this case was largely one of naivety. Bernie Ecclestone, the Formula One racing impresario, had been a donor to the Conservative Party. William Hague even wrote to Tony asking for a knighthood for him. In the run-up to the 1997 election, Ecclestone gave £1 million to the Labour Party and we hoped he would become as regular a donor to Labour as he had been to the Tories. Once we were in government, he came in to Number 10 to see the prime minister to talk about Formula One and its issues and concerns. High among them was the pending EU ban on tobacco advertising, a major source of funding for motor racing. Ecclestone warned Tony that a ban, if suddenly introduced, might drive Formula One out of Europe. Tony was convinced that the very popular sport of motor racing in Britain was under threat, and he asked us to contact the Department of Health to ask whether there was a case for delay. We did so.

There was nothing corrupt with any of this, but we hadn't thought about how it would look if it became public. Inevitably, given that some in the Department of Health opposed a delay, the meeting with Ecclestone did become public. The mistake we then made was to think that the story was so embarrassing that we should admit to only as little of it as possible in the hope that it wouldn't come out in its entirety. Initially, we held back the amount of Ecclestone's donation and the fact that we hoped he might give more money to the party in future, partly because Ecclestone himself didn't want the facts to become public. The first question was whether we should give the money back. Derry Irvine and Gordon Brown thought we should not. Peter Mandelson and Robin Butler thought we should. Tony consulted Gordon in the margins of the Anglo-French summit, and he suggested that we get the General Secretary of the Labour Party to write to Patrick Neill, the chair of the Committee on Standards in Public Life, to ask whether we should repay the money. We hoped the answer would be no. This we did, and to our surprise Neill said we should give it back.

The full story didn't come out straight away, and before it did I wrote that it 'felt like waiting for a punch in the chops and being unable to do anything about it'. Inevitably, the partial answers we gave the media did not satisfy them, and our strategy of dribbling out the facts made it look as if we were trying to hide a much bigger scandal. We were protected a bit because, for obvious reasons, William Hague did not want to ask about the issue at PMQs; but the damage was serious, and we only escaped in the end when the full story was out and Tony gave his 'I'm a pretty straight sort of guy' TV interview to John Humphrys.

The lesson was clear: the full facts will always come out in the end. It may seem ghastly to confess to some foolishness, and you may hope you can dribble out the details slowly, but actually doing so is counterproductive and makes you look as if you have something to hide. It is far better to opt for full transparency and get the whole story out straight away. The controversy lasted only two weeks, but it was our first scandal and we felt it would never end. It was also my first experience of the sensation of being under attack personally over something like this. My father called saying he supposed it was my Westland – my brother had been in the frame over the Westland helicopter controversy under Thatcher and had had a couple of difficult weeks. The *Independent* ran a story claiming I had been involved as a keen Formula One fan. I had to write to them pointing out I wouldn't know a Ferrari from a Fiat.

At the time the whole affair felt like a sticking plaster that we just could not get off our fingers. Tony was not sleeping. I told him, with more foresight than I realised, that it would end eventually and that we would have to deal with worse scandals in the future.

Robin Butler suggested to Tony that the real problem was that he was depending too much on political advisers like me. Robin himself would never have agreed to Tony meeting Ecclestone, although he would not have known then that Ecclestone was a donor. He was quite right, however, that in such circumstances the chief of staff should take the blame.

Sometimes scandals are the result of cock-ups that are impossible to explain convincingly. The Mittal controversy over a letter to the Romanian prime minister in support of the acquisition of a steel-works in Romania in 2002 was a case in point. I knew that Lakshmi Mittal was a donor to the Labour Party; and, given what had happened over Ecclestone, I would have stopped Tony sending a letter if I had known about the proposal. But the junior foreign policy private secretary in Number 10 didn't know Mittal was a donor, nor did our Ambassador in Bucharest, and they thought it would be a good idea for the prime minister to write, as did the Department of Trade and Industry. When the fact that Tony had written became public we simply could not convince people that a letter could be drafted in one part of Downing Street without anyone in another part of the building knowing anything about it. As a result, we had to spend another couple of weeks saddled with alle-gations of sleaze, and a picture of us was building up in people's minds that would prove hard to erase. Again I was awarded a walk-on part since people were convinced that I must have approved the letter and that I must have discussed the matter with our ambas-sador in Bucharest, Richard Ralph, who had been with me in the embassy in Washington a decade earlier but whom I hadn't seen or talked to since. The *World at One* programme broadcast an artfully clipped quote from my former ambassador in Washington, Robin Renwick, appearing to suggest that I had changed the offending letter, which I had not.

Historically, the Labour Party suffered from money scandals and the Tories from sex scandals. At first, it looked as if we would conform to the traditional pattern, but we soon demonstrated that we could be as good at sex as any Tory administration. At ten in the morning of 27 October 1998, I got a breathless call from Jack Straw, then the Home Secretary, to tell me that the deputy commissioner of the Metropolitan Police had just rung him to say that Ron Davies, the Secretary of State for Wales, had made a statement in a police station in south London about being robbed by a black male prostitute. The real story, however, was more complicated. Jack called back a few minutes later with the deputy commissioner on the line who said Ron had been cruising Clapham Common and had picked up a male prostitute, taken him to his flat for sex and then been jumped by him and some mates and robbed. I pressed him on the details of this bizarre tale but he assured me it was true (as it happens, not all of it was quite right). I found Tony, who was doing a photo shoot upstairs in the state rooms, gave him an account of what the police had said, and he told me to summon Ron in. I called Ron on his mobile, and he came straight to Downing Street having just left the police station. At the best of times, Ron appeared shifty, but he was badly shaken and in these circumstances it was very hard to believe anything he said. He came into Tony's den and declined to sit down but insisted instead on pacing round and round the room as he spoke. He kept asking questions to see if he could find out what the police had told us. He denied gay sex was involved but his account seemed implausible. Tony kept returning to why Ron had dismissed his official driver and fallen into conversation with a Rastafarian on Clapham Common, who Ron said had invited him out for a curry and a beer. The story got more and more bizarre as he went on, and he kept trying to redefine what had happened.

It was clear that Ron would have to go. We sent him off with Alastair to draft a resignation statement and do a TV interview. It was awkward to come up with a coherent explanation of why he was resigning, since Ron wouldn't admit to the real reason. After the interview, we rushed him off to hide out in an off-season Centre Parcs holiday camp at Longleat. Hilary Coffman, one of our press aides, went along as a minder to protect him from the journalists. Ron tried to hang on to his position as leader of the Welsh Party, but by the weekend he realised that he had to give that up, too.

It can be difficult to explain why some ministers are brought down by a scandal and others are not, even when the scandal in question is very similar. The Ron Davies crisis was followed a few weeks later by a Nick Brown scandal when the *News of the World* was sold a story by a former researcher alleging sex with S&M rent boys. Tony thought there had always been something a bit odd about

Nick's choice of researcher, but somehow Nick weathered the scandal whereas Ron was taken down by his 'moment of madness'. Nick may have been saved in part because, under Alastair's advice, he cooperated with the *News of the World* in the production of the story.

The 'Cheriegate' saga of 2002 about the purchase of two flats in Bristol has been told many times by people closer to the heart of it than me and I won't retell it. But it is an interesting example of the pathology of such stories. It started for me with a phone call from the press office at two o'clock on a Saturday afternoon in November. At that moment I was in a toy shop with my children in Helmsley in North Yorkshire. The *Mail on Sunday* were putting twenty allegations to Number 10 and demanding answers by five o'clock. I eventually lost count of how many such calls ruined Saturday afternoons with the children in the playgrounds of west London. I always had a sinking feeling in my stomach when my mobile would ring after lunch on a Saturday. You are immediately in the grip of yet another catch-22 situation. The newspaper says that, unless we can give them detailed answers to all their questions within hours, they will run the story as true. The events in question may have occurred years ago, the files are two hundred miles away, and trying to piece together the truth in the time available is impossible. The temptation is to deny it all so they either don't run the story or run it with your denial. But if you do, it is always liable to come back and bite you. There will be some inconsistency in your answer or some loose thread that they can pull at. It is better instead to absorb the pain of the initial story and take your time to get the information before you answer and then to do so fully and with all the facts, holding nothing back. It is nearly always the politician's response to the story and the accusation of misleading the press that catches them out rather than the initial story itself.

It is, nevertheless, surprising how difficult it can be to establish the facts. Everyone has a different recollection, the papers are incomplete, and people's memories play tricks on then. In December 1997, Jeremy Heywood and I were sent over to the Treasury to interview Geoffrey Robinson, a Treasury minister, who had come back from watching his wife in an opera in Poland to see us, with the aim of establishing exactly what the facts were about an overseas trust of his which had been revealed by the media during the preceding days. After several hours, and with Geoffrey constantly popping out of the room, and with us spending most of our time talking to his lawyer and his accountant, we went back to Number 10 none the wiser. We thought he had done nothing wrong but there were enough loose threads to keep the newspapers going for weeks. When he threatened them with a libel suit, that propelled the story back into the headlines. Richard Wilson, the Cabinet Secretary, was given the same task later, but with little more success. It takes time to arrive at even a semblance of the facts.

Experience also suggests that it is best not to let a scandal drag on. If the person at the centre of it will have to be sacrificed in due course, it is no kindness to them, and a major problem for the government, to allow the limb to suppurate rather than cutting it off straight away. Jo Moore was a decent person and a loyal party member, but she had a serious lapse of judgement, as she herself admitted, in sending an email inside the department on 9/11 suggesting it was a good day to bury bad news. We realised how serious the gaffe was a few weeks later, as soon as we saw it when it was leaked to the newspapers. Tony decided that we would keep her on, only issuing a reprimand and requiring her to apologise publicly. It was a mistake. The poisonous ongoing battle between the special advisers and the civil servants in the department that lay behind the leak carried on and broke surface early the next year. We then had to let go both Jo and Martin Sixsmith, the former journalist who served as the department's spokesman. Even then the double resignation became fraught when Sixsmith changed his mind and decided not to resign after all. Eventually the whole affair cost the Permanent Secretary, Richard Mottram, and Steve Byers, the minister, their jobs as well. Steve went before Parliament to defend himself, but it was clear he was not going to survive. He had a good resignation, and, paraphrasing the well-known contemporary description of Charles I's execution, I noted in my diary that 'nothing became him like the leaving of it'. We had subjected the government entirely unnecessarily to nearly six months of damage, which would have been avoided if Jo had just gone in October, however unfair that might have been. As Machiavelli says, injuries 'should be inflicted all at once, that their ill savour being less lasting may the less offend; whereas benefits should be conferred little by little, that so they may be more fully relished'.

In politics it is almost always a mistake to issue an injunction or a libel writ with the aim of killing off a damaging story; it almost always has the opposite effect. Michael Levy issued an injunction in June 2000 to head off a story about to appear in the *Sunday Times* on his tax affairs. The judge turned Michael's request down on the grounds that he was a public figure, so instead of closing the story down, the threatened injunction boosted it to the top of the news.

Peter Goldsmith, the Attorney General, nearly made the same mistake a few years later. He had been told that the *Observer* was about to publish a leaked version of his full legal advice on Iraq and he started the process of seeking an injunction. He told me, and I had David Hill check the story out. David came back to say that in fact all that the paper had were a few comments from a former senior military officer suggesting that Goldsmith had changed his mind in the lead-up to the war. Peter pulled the injunction just in time. It would have turned a small story into a huge one.

The same rule applies to libel suits. However badly you feel you have been treated by the press, it is almost always a mistake to sue. I felt particularly sore about a story on the ITV news during the 'loans for peerages' investigation in our final year that suggested I had sent an email to Michael Levy about 'Ps and Ks' (peerages and knighthoods) and that there was a second secret email system within Number 10. Both suggestions were untrue. We asked the police to make it clear the story was wrong, but they would not.

I had to deal with the matter while on my way to Davos for the annual World Economic Forum, where Tony was making a speech, and I made the mistake of letting myself be rushed into consulting an expensive QC. He came back to tell me that I had no case even though the story was completely untrue and very damaging, the reason being that a recent House of Lords judgement meant that ITV could successfully plead that it was in the public interest. He advised me to hold a press conference on the subject instead of suing for libel. Luckily I abandoned the matter at that point, only £3,000 worse off. However hurtful and untrue a calumny, a politician would do better to avoid a libel suit and concentrate instead on firmly rebutting the story. A libel case just keeps the story going for longer and indeed pours petrol on the flames. It would, of course, be better if there were a legal right of reply, but that does not exist in this country.

One of the less attractive features of the British press is the feeding frenzy that develops when journalists smell blood. If politicians have been wounded politically by scandals, the press gather in a pack and savage them until either they have brought them to the ground and finished them off or the politicians in question have managed to limp away to safety. Sometimes, as a leader, you have to let accused politicians defend themselves in Parliament, a bit like a Roman gladiator in the circus, and if they survive they can have their freedom. Such parliamentary occasions can have a cathartic effect, and if they do not bring a politician down they draw a line under the story. Steve Byers did not survive his gladiatorial combat, but a few years later Tessa Jowell did survive hers.

The scandal about an alleged payment to her husband, David Mills, from Silvio Berlusconi blew up like a whirlwind. Tessa simply couldn't get the facts straight in time. She was afraid that Tony would throw her overboard, and sent Margaret McDonagh and Waheed Alli, two Labour Party stalwarts, to see me to plead for her political life. Fortunately, I was able to reassure them we had no intention of sacrificing her. I tried to encourage Tessa at the height of the controversy by telling her that such frenzies never last for ever. If you hold your nerve, you will come out on the other side in one piece. Tessa eventually managed to get the facts out and answer the questions that were being thrown at her about the Italian payment to her husband and his row with the Inland Revenue. The press felt cheated of their prey and remained determined to get her. Tessa called me to ask me if I really thought her husband had done wrong, and I did my best to evade the question. She obviously began to question herself what had gone on, and a few days later Alastair called me to say that he had Tessa and David in his house and that they were going to split up. I was sad for her and her family, but I could see why she had come to that conclusion. The media immediately suggested that the separation was a heartless act of political convenience, but clearly Tessa had come to see her husband in a new light in the course of the scandal. The final test was her appearance in the House of Commons for parliamentary questions on 4 March. She passed it with flying colours. She was home and free.

When you are under siege in government, you take a certain amount of pleasure in seeing the opposition embroiled in a scandal of their own. We were amazed when William Hague kept pressing for a peerage for Michael Ashcroft, given his chequered history, but we left it to the Political Honours Scrutiny Committee to sort out the problem under the chairmanship of a Lib Dem peer rather than trying to make it into an issue between the parties. When some of the correspondence about the peerage was leaked, William Hague demanded that we hold a leak inquiry. I replied that we would be happy to cooperate so long as the Tories also allowed themselves to be subject to questioning, since it was pretty clear the leak had come from the Tory side. They really were concerned about Ashcroft; and when a story appeared in the papers that one of the Tory nominees was to be turned down, the Tory chief whip called me in a panic. When I assured him that it wasn't about Ashcroft but about a peerage they had proposed for Conrad Black, the owner of the *Telegraph*, he was patently relieved. We had no objection to Black having a peerage, but it was hard to see how he was going to be allowed to have one: he was a Canadian citizen and under the existing rules Canadians couldn't even accept knighthoods.

The latter episode led to a long-running saga, when the Canadian Prime Minister, Jean Chrétien, who had been the subject of attack in Black's newspapers in Canada, vetoed the peerage. The Cabinet Secretary pointed out that the Queen could not be put in the position of receiving conflicting advice from her two prime ministers, one saying that he should have a peerage, the other that he should not. Conrad would call me every few weeks to update me on his struggle, announcing himself in his booming voice: 'Jonathan, it's the Great Commoner here.' Eventually he renounced his Canadian citizenship so that he could take the peerage. For the Prime Minister, however, there is little pleasure to be gained from the Opposition party suffering a bout of sleaze stories. Such stories seldom advantage one party over the other. They simply reinforce the public's prejudice that all politicians are as bad as each other.

When prime ministers come under real pressure over a scandal, and it rolls on and on and there appears to be no way out, they often reach for an independent inquiry. It seems an easy way to release pressure and buy time, but inquiries almost never settle anything.

In July 2003, I was staying at the beach in Virginia with my sons when, as I drove into town early in the morning to buy croissants at the bakery, I heard the news of the tragic suicide of David Kelly. I felt physically sick. I spoke to Alastair in London and Tony in Korea. Tony felt that he had little choice but to set up an inquiry. I was opposed, having been through enough inquiries already, and having promised myself that we wouldn't have any more. To head this new inquiry, the Lord Chancellor recommended Brian Hutton, a former Lord Chief Justice of Northern Ireland. Hutton got straight down to work, holding hearings in August.

I was on holiday, but Catherine Rimmer and Clare Sumner from Number 10, who were responsible for putting together the preparatory material for the inquiry, sent down a huge box of papers that I had to read at our rented cottage in Cornwall. When I opened it, it included a whole series of emails. I was horrified. I have always been appallingly indiscreet in emails, seeing them as a form of telephone conversation rather than the sort of formal document that you prepare with the aid of a lawyer. But they are in writing and they do not disappear. When read in the cold light of the day after, rather than in the heat of the day on which they were written, they look quite different. I have often been told that I should simply stop sending emails, but you cannot do that if you are running a place like Number 10. You have to issue instructions to tens of people at once and phoning each of them separately would take for ever. There is no time to check every email in detail before you send it, so there are always infelicities.

I pored over my own infelicities at the kitchen table in Cornwall. Luckily my comments were all over the place, and when they were published, they even led my ex-wife to conclude generously that I was opposed to the Iraq war after all, to her evident relief. When I went up to London to give evidence my brother called me. He knew Hutton, and he said the two things that the judge hated most were long hair and beards. But I was not going to shave my summer beard or get a haircut in August for any judge. I was pretty nervous before giving evidence and managed to put my foot in it at one point when the inquiry lawyer asked me who had told Alastair that Richard Sambrook at the BBC had said that David Kelly was the source of Gilligan's story. Without thinking, I replied Tom Baldwin of *The*

Times. There was an audible intake of breath in the room, and I realised at once that I had boobed by unthinkingly breaching the code of 'omerta' that is supposed to protect sources.

I noted in my diary how impressed I was by the sharpness of the judge's mind and by his ability to cut to the quick of the issue in the few questions that he asked me. The press, on the other hand, built up their case by reporting day by day what they wanted to hear from the evidence to prove that the BBC was right and the government was wrong. (The same thing happened all over again in 2010 with the latest Iraq Inquiry, where the actual evidence bore no resemblance to the media reporting of it.) Hutton clearly thought he was supposed to do the job of a judge: to hear the evidence and to draw conclusions from the facts without fear or favour. And his report was a model of how such a document should be written, providing absolute clarity about what had happened. It is a shame how few people have read it. Having praised Hutton all the way through the inquiry for his fearlessness, the media were furious when he reached a conclusion different from theirs. They asserted that the report was a whitewash without, as far as I could see, making any attempt to challenge Hutton's facts or his reasoning, only his conclusion. Hutton, quite rightly, felt unfairly treated.

Ahead of the Hutton report, Michael Howard made a fuss about the Tories' access to it when it was laid before Parliament. Entirely reasonably, he wanted a gap between PMQs and the Prime Minister's statement on the report so that he could read it and then respond. We agreed. He also asked that instead of Michael Ancram, the Shadow Foreign Secretary, he be accompanied in reading the report by David Cameron, a young MP who was working as his aide. But Howard misjudged the mood of the House and launched a vicious attack on Tony demanding his resignation. Given that the report had exonerated Tony, that felt a bit odd and had the effect, once again, of uniting our parliamentary troops.

The lesson from Hutton is that, no matter how clean a bill of health a prime minister is given, an inquiry is not going to vindicate them in the eyes of the media and therefore of the people.

When Tony felt he had to agree to yet another inquiry on Iraq, this time on the intelligence, we at first favoured Peter Inge, a retired Chief of the Defence Staff, to chair it. We got Peter into Number

10, and while he was willing to serve on an inquiry he did not want to be in the chair. I suggested Robin Butler and then had to get hold of him on holiday in Mexico. The phone line to the volcano where he was staying wasn't good, but once he grasped what I was proposing I got him to agree. The committee held their hearings in private and asked perfectly sensible questions about the nature and use of intelligence. I discovered once again that when I appear before an inquiry I find it very hard to remember what happened years before when so many other things are by now overlaid on top of it. In order to avoid saying 'I can't remember' in response to every question, I had to reread the files. It was clear from the beginning that, since it was obvious that the government hadn't made up the intelligence on Iraq – which was the original charge against it – the inquiry would make a lot of process recommendations, focusing on the fact that the caveats in the original Joint Intelligence Committee reporting had not been repeated word for word in the published dossier and on 'sofa government', which Robin had never liked in his brief time with us as Cabinet Secretary.

When Robin came to present the report to Tony in the den, he told us that he had enjoyed doing it. We did not enjoy the result. The report itself was a blow for Tony politically, and Gordon Brown was able to use it to mount yet another attempt to dislodge him. Howard again misjudged his pantomime-style response, and Tony was able to read back to him his fulsome support of the Iraq War at the time in his local paper, the *East Kent News*. Howard was floored.

The lesson from the Butler Report for a prudent prime minister is that the onslaught of the press will terrorise anyone you appoint to conduct an independent inquiry after what happened to Hutton, and they will bow to that pressure and find something to criticise rather than risk having their own reputations besmirched by being accused of conducting a whitewash. Inquiries therefore may buy a prime minister time, but they will rarely if ever completely vindicate the government or resolve the problem, whatever the facts.

The other reason prime ministers establish inquiries is in response to public demands to know the truth allegedly hidden behind some tragedy. Increasingly, those affected by such events are not content with the obvious. As the influence of religion declines, together with the solace it offered to those left behind, the families of victims search for more complicated explanations to relieve their distress and are easily seduced by conspiracy theories. They demand inquiries to expose the reality hidden behind the random deaths of their loved ones. But usually there aren't conspiracies to be exposed and they are disappointed by the outcome.

In our early years, we agreed to inquiries on BSE, the mass murderer Dr Harold Shipman, a series of train crashes and foot-and-mouth. None of them resolved anything. In 1998, in Northern Ireland, we agreed to the Bloody Sunday Inquiry. We were told by Mo Mowlam, by the Irish government and by Gerry Adams and Martin McGuinness that it was essential to reassure Nationalists and Republicans that the new government was even-handed. We succumbed, but we regretted it almost at once. I regretted it even more when Martin McGuinness told me subsequently, in a throw-away comment, that he didn't know why we had done it and that a simple apology would have sufficed. The eventual detailed report and David Cameron's well-judged response helped, in this case, to draw a line under the killings, but at a cost of nearly £200 million and after twelve years.

We also agreed to inquiries into the deaths of Rosemary Nelson, Robert Hammill and Billy Wright in Northern Ireland, although no one expects them really to shed any new light on events. We did not, however, have an inquiry into the murder of the Republican lawyer Patrick Finucane. I had a haunting meeting with his very dignified widow and family in October 2004. They asked for an inquiry yet again and I arranged for them to meet Tony. It was perfectly clear that something murky had happened, although almost certainly not involving the security service, and that an inquiry was merited to illuminate the facts. But the security services said that an inquiry under the existing rules would endanger the lives of former and serving agents, so we could not just press ahead. Instead we changed the legislation on inquiries which dated back to the 1920s to allow a more flexible approach. Unfortunately the family were not prepared to go ahead with an inquiry on that basis and there has still not been one.

Prime ministers often rush into such more general inquiries but nearly always repent at leisure. They rarely throw new light on to the subject under investigation and almost never satisfy anyone. You may have bought yourself time but publication of the report brings the whole gory detail up again when you thought it had died down and there are always loose ends for people to follow up. A prudent prime minister would think twice before calling for an inquiry as an apparently easy answer to a thorny political problem.

There has always been a tendency in British politics to imitate American politics with a few years' delay, and that is what we seem to be doing now by increasingly involving the police and public prosecutors in politics.

My own first experience was an investigation by the North Wales Constabulary. I was amazed to receive a letter from them in January 2006 saying that they were investigating complaints about a book by Lance Price, the former press officer at Number 10, which alleged that Tony had made some disparaging comments about the Welsh. I thought the letter was a spoof, but it was real and the Cabinet Office offered to hire a QC to advise me. When the policeman from the North Wales Constabulary came in to see me, he said the Director of Public Prosecutions had already made it clear that there would be no prosecution but that his chief constable wanted to pursue the matter anyway. He said his chief constable was like that. I pointed out that he, (the policeman), was English and that I was Welsh, at least by origin, so if anyone should feel offended it was me. It never went further.

I spent most of early 2006 on inquiries. The Welsh investigation in January was closely followed by the Tessa Jowell affair, and then I was catapulted straight into the 'loans for peerages' investigation. It started for me with a call from Dennis Stevenson, the head of the House of Lords Appointments Commission which nominates cross-bench peers and vets party 'working peers', those appointed by the two party leaders to vote with their party in the House of Lords. He told me the Commission was going to reject the names of three Labour nominees and one Conservative from the latest lists. I thought at the time it was another pain-in-the-neck issue that I was going to have to deal with, but I had no idea that I was about to waste nearly a year of my life dealing with the police.

The matter would probably have remained a familiar political row if the Labour Party honorary Treasurer, Jack Dromey, had not called for an investigation. It is interesting to consider how this came about. It happened at Tony's moment of maximum political vulnerability, with a difficult vote on education reform coming up. Gordon came to see Tony on 15 March demanding that Tony allow him to publish his paper on pensions, debunking Adair Turner's proposed reforms, at the time of the Budget. Tony told me afterwards that it was his ugliest ever encounter with Gordon. Gordon said that unless Tony let him publish his paper he would demand an inquiry by the Labour Party's NEC into the loans for peerages. Tony said he would not agree to blackmail and accused Gordon of 'mafia-style politics'.

Gordon stormed out of the room, and a few hours later Jack, Harriet Harman's husband, made a public statement saying that he had been kept in the dark about the loans and demanding an inquiry. Just the day before, Harriet had been moved out of the ministerial job with responsibility for supervising the rules on party funding. She was planning to run for the deputy leadership of the party and was hoping for Gordon's support. Not surprisingly, in the light of such a statement from the Labour Treasurer, the police thought they had to take seriously demands for an investigation.

The next day John Prescott told Tony that Jack Dromey had said he had been told to make the statement by Number 11. John added that Gordon had tried to persuade him to join the call for an inquiry as well, but he had refused. Tony Woodley, General Secretary of the Transport and General Workers' Union and Dromey's boss, called Tony to apologise and said he had never been so angry and embarrassed in his life. Tony did well at his press conference the next day and took it upon himself to take responsibility for the whole thing and to say that he had known all about the loans. We weren't at all sure that he had, but he thought it was better to confess to things he hadn't done than to fail to confess to things that might turn out to be true. Afterwards he asked me plaintively, 'Jonathan, will we get through this?'

We managed, with some effort, to convince the individuals who had loaned money to the Labour Party to make their names public, even though the Tories refused to publish their equivalent list. Gordon came to see Tony again. He said that Tony had clearly misunderstood what he had been saying at their previous meeting.

He was just trying to be helpful. Tony asked if he remembered Tony accusing him of 'mafia-style politics'. Gordon said, 'No, you didn't say that.' He had an extraordinary ability to call black white.

I received a call from John Yates of the Metropolitan Police on 24 March saying that he was sending an email instructing me to ensure that no one in Number 10 destroyed any documents or emails. He said he did not want to alarm me. I asked if this was a private or a public call. He said it was private, but of course it almost immediately became public – in the Sunday papers. I asked Yates if it would be quick, and he said it would be very speedy. The investigation was only dropped over a year later.

The main problem we had throughout the investigation was the constant stream of stories in the media. Some had a sliver of truth in them, but most were complete fabrications. Alastair Campbell urged us to fight back and to attack the police, but there was no way in which we could without seriously jeopardising the constitutional relationship between the police and the government. Our hands were tied. To take one example, *The Times* ran a story in November asserting that there was a 'killer email' from me saying, 'Michael Levy will be unhappy' and that the email would bring Number 10 down. The paper announced that I was to be interviewed under caution. But there was no such email and I had not been notified of any such request by the police. There was absolutely nothing we could do, and the constant drip, drip of poison helped weaken Tony politically in his last year. It was clear that Yates, for his part, also felt hard done by. He told the *Mail* that he was being got at by the New Labour spin machine.

For me there was a certain irony in being dragged into such a scandal. My uncle had written the definitive biography of Maundy Gregory, the villain for whom the 1920s legislation banning the sale of political honours had been drafted. I went out and bought a copy of the book from a second-hand bookshop, and it helped put the whole thing in perspective. When the campaign of leaks about the investigation would zero in on me from time to time, friends and relatives would call up expressing sympathy. It made me feel as though I was in an intensive care ward.

The police were pretty cavalier about their use of the power of arrest. Michael Levy was notified of his impending arrest the night before it happened and called Tony and me. I was at a dinner in the House of Lords and had just spent the first course complaining to Mark Thompson, the BBC's Director General, about their overly prominent coverage of the police investigation. I felt foolish over dessert having learned what was about to happen but being unable to refer to it. In the event, Michael's arrest lasted rather longer than expected the next day. The building next to the police station in which he was being questioned burst into flames and everyone had to be evacuated. Gerry Adams called me to sympathise about the police. He asked, jokingly, if Tony and I would seek political status as IRA prisoners had done and suggested that we refuse to recognise the court.

The arrest of Ruth Turner, who by this time had replaced Sally Morgan as head of government relations, was deliberately even more dramatic. She was given no warning. Four burly policemen turned up at her front door at six in the morning and held her in her flat. Eventually a policewoman arrived so she could shower and dress. They took her to a police station and held her there all day. Just before she was released, information that she had been arrested was passed to the media. Luckily we had an official car parked in a side street near the police station and managed to whisk her away before the cameras turned up.

The police were given to histrionic gestures like coming into Downing Street in the middle of a weekend to seize our computers in order to use sophisticated software to interrogate them for evidence. First, they searched for all references to 'ML' (Michael Levy) and got back every one of Number 10's emails going back over ten years because the machine read 'ml' as the standard computer code 'html'. They tried again with 'm l', as separate letters, and the search engine again returned tens of thousands of results. The computer thought they were asking for millilitres and had turned up recipes that staff had for some reason been saving on Number 10 computers.

For one brief moment the investigation came back to haunt Gordon when the police demanded to interview all the members of the Cabinet. Gordon was worried because he had recommended Ronnie Cohen, a Labour Party donor, for a peerage and his name was on the draft list. In the end, the police settled for writing to members of the Cabinet rather than interviewing them and Gordon put out a Jesuitical statement saying that he had not made any 'written recommendations'.

I was interviewed three times altogether. In January 2007, yet another story appeared in the press about me being questioned and I emerged from my front door to find a rather upmarket photographer outside my house in a BMW four-wheel drive. He kindly allowed me to pose with my bicycle outside on the street so that the number of my house didn't appear in the photo. The photographers in Downing Street were rather less kind, snapping me on my bicycle with my Number 10 pass clenched between my teeth. In briefing myself for the third interview, I wrote in my diary that I felt like someone preparing for an appearance on *Mastermind* with my special subject as 'Ruth Turner's emails from 2005'. The interview lasted four and a half hours in Tony's den. The police kept showing me new documents, which I had to go into the Cabinet Room next door to read. They had only one copy, so my lawyers and I each had to read it in turn. In the middle of it all, Ollie Robbins, the PPS, popped his head round the door to say that the Northern Ireland peace process was collapsing, and could I be released for a few moments. The police agreed, and I had to go and work the phones to sort out a crisis between Ian Paisley and Gerry Adams before going back to complete my interview.

The problem at the core of the whole fiasco was that the police had got themselves in too deep to be able to retreat with dignity. The more they dug themselves a hole, the more they were determined to turn something up. Unfortunately for them there was nothing to turn up, and in the end the Crown Prosecution Service and the independent lawyers appointed to review the case put them out of their misery by dropping the case just before we left government. No one lost face but we had expended a huge amount of time and emotional energy on the police instead of on policy and politics in our last year in government.

As the controversy took off in 2006, I suggested a package of reforms: that honours be put at arm's length from the prime minister and that nominations be sent directly from the Cabinet Secretary to the Queen; state funding for political parties, something I had first urged after the Ecclestone scandal; House of Lords reform, so that at least all new 'working peers' were chosen by vote rather than by the party leaders; the appointment of an independent standards commissioner, who could investigate allegations and report on the facts to the prime minister, who would then decide if a minister should be sacked or not; and the establishment of a statutory Press Complaints Commission. We never had a chance to put this package of reforms into practice although we did renounce the prime minister's role in putting forward the honours list.

The problem is the one identified by Machiavelli and set out at the beginning of the chapter: that is, the need for some agreed mechanism to investigate such 'indictments'. The police are not a suitable mechanism for this sort of political matter, and we should try as far as possible to keep the police out of politics. Of course no one should be above the law, and if a crime has been committed then certainly the offenders, whatever their status, should be investigated and prosecuted in the normal way. But since being dragged into the loans for peerages investigation, the police have been called in to a whole series of other largely trivial and wholly political disputes, including a dramatic raid on an Opposition spokesman's office in Parliament. Given police operational independence, this creeping role can only be prevented by a strong Metropolitan Police commissioner who can see the folly of being dragged into such diversions or by new legislation.

As an alternative, we do not, however, want to find ourselves being forced down the American road of politically motivated special prosecutors. The Clintons found themselves under investigation in the Whitewater probe for seven years. When the probe eventually closed down, it had found not a scintilla of wrongdoing but had cost a fortune and distracted the president from his day job. It seems that nowadays all US presidents spend their second term in court, from Reagan with Iran Contra, Clinton with Whitewater and Monica Lewinsky, and Bush with the leak investigations about the identity of a CIA agent. This is folly. Politicians should be held to account at the ballot box. You do not want to distract them from what they are paid to do by investigations that are essentially frivolous.

The best mechanism is probably the one I suggested to Tony in 2006, that of an independent standards commissioner who can investigate the facts of any allegation made against ministers and report to the prime minister. They would only investigate issues that the prime minister tasked them with, but their report would be made public. The action to be taken on the basis of their findings should be for the prime minister to decide. It is not sensible to have the composition of the government decided by an independent commissioner proposing the sacking of this or that minister: only the prime minister can do that.

When I was seventeen, I worked as the second undergardener at the British Embassy in Washington and lived with my brother in Georgetown. He was private secretary to the ambassador. It was 1973, and every evening the White House correspondent of *Time* magazine brought round copies of the transcripts of the Watergate tapes as they were released. I was enthralled and read every one of them down to the last 'expletive deleted'. The lesson ingrained in my mind from that period was the folly and impossibility in politics of trying to cover something up. Right at the beginning of the 'loans for peerages' inquiry, I made it clear to everyone that we must do everything to avoid even the appearance of a cover-up, but ironically, in the dying phase of their investigation, the police tried to suggest that we had concocted one. They were particularly mystified by a Number 10 Q&A brief that we had drawn up at the beginning of the scandal in order to try to gather together the facts and provide answers to questions that would be raised by the press. Q&As are a staple of political work, and I was surprised that it was a mystery to the police. I was even more surprised when, at about this time, they faxed us a letter that had appended to it, by mistake, an internal police Q&A about the investigation, which certainly suggested that they were familiar with the format. Whenever a scandal breaks, a prudent leader should be on the lookout for anything that might later be interpreted as a cover-up and stamp on it straight away.

The other lesson to be drawn from the 'loans for peerages' scandal – and most of the previous crises that had engulfed the government – is the need to do something to reform party funding. Party leaders do not enjoy raising funds. They find it demeaning and time-consuming. It puts them in an ambiguous position. With the assistance of Michael Levy, whose background was as a charity fund-raiser, we had managed to diversify the Labour Party away from complete dependence on the trade unions by bringing in private sector supporters, and we changed the law to require parties to publish the names of their donors. But the new transparency solved nothing. If anything, it made matters worse. The media now knew who the donors were and were able to question their motives in making donations, with the result that there were more scandals rather than fewer. From 1997 onwards, I thought the only solution was state funding so that politicians do not have to compromise themselves by having to solicit donations. But state funding is unpopular. Understandably, taxpayers do not want to pay for politicians. There is in fact no issue of principle, since the state already funds all sorts of activities undertaken by political parties, and the additional costs would be minimal in the absence of expensive political TV advertising in this country. Of course even state funding in itself is not a silver bullet. Countries that have it already but that allow supplementary funds to be raised still have funding scandals such as the one that felled Chancellor Kohl in Germany.

The only way to solve the problem is through a bipartisan understanding and we had a chance to achieve that in Tony's final years, but it slipped through our fingers. Tony met David Cameron a number of times to discuss a possible deal between the parties. Even though it was clear that in our third term, as we became unpopular, the Tories would outstrip us in the ability to raise funds, Cameron was sensible enough to see that an agreement would help him in the long term because the Tories are just as susceptible to funding scandals as Labour. However, we made the mistake of inviting Ian McCartney, as the Labour Party chair, to come along to one of the meetings, and he did all the talking. As the meeting went on and Ian piled demand on demand, I could see Cameron thinking that we were just not serious.

We couldn't close a bilateral deal, so we moved on to asking Hayden Phillips, a distinguished retired civil servant, to chair an independent study. Hayden was ready to offer a compromise that protected the key interests of both sides, including trade union funding for the Labour Party, but it was killed off by Gordon. The notion was put around that Tony was only seeking a deal on party funding to escape the sleaze in which he was mired and that he was doing it at the expense of the party and particularly of the party/union link. Gordon offered a pain-free alternative of legislating unilaterally to get what the Labour Party wanted, although he didn't explain how he was going to get his legislation through the Lords where the government had no majority. As a result, our initiative bit the dust. A prudent prime minister would strive to reach a bipartisan agreement on the reform of party funding. It will never be possible to solve the problem completely, but reform would reduce the chance of funding scandals tripping up governments – and the whole political class – quite so often in future.

British politics is notably uncorrupt, at least at the national level, even by comparison with other Western countries. Politicians rarely or never choose their career for venal reasons but because they are committed to public service or, at worst, because they want to be seen to be important. But you wouldn't know that from the press coverage. The danger is that, if the papers say often enough that many or most politicians are corrupt, they will find that they themselves have created a new reality. No one decent will want to go into politics and it will be increasingly attractive to rogues.

In my experience, in the US and the UK, there are very rarely real crimes at the heart of any political scandal. In Britain, in particular, the explanation is nearly always cock-up rather than conspiracy. Government is just too complicated and too unwieldy a machine to be able to organise a real conspiracy. If it is ever attempted, it goes wrong. Machiavelli says correctly, 'For the difficulties that attend conspirators are infinite, and we know from experience that while there have been many conspiracies, few of them have succeeded.' There does, however, need to be agreed machinery to investigate allegations, machinery that satisfies both accuser and accused and settles matters finally, so that people can see which has been cock-up and which conspiracy.

CHAPTER TEN

'How Unity May be Restored to a Divided City'

Europe

In the last chapter of *The Prince*, Machiavelli whips himself up into an uncharacteristic passion on the subject of the unification of Italy. He urges Lorenzo de' Medici to fulfil his destiny by being the man to bring it about:

> This opportunity then, for Italy at last to look on her deliverer, ought not to be allowed to pass away. With what love would he be received in all those Provinces which have suffered from foreign inundation, with what thirst for vengeance, with what fixed fidelity, with what devotion, and what tears, no words of mine can declare. What gates would be closed against him? What people would refuse him obedience? What jealousy would stand in his way? What Italian but would yield him homage? This barbarian tyranny stinks in all nostrils. Let your illustrious House therefore take upon itself this enterprise with all the courage and all the hopes with which a just cause is undertaken.

The same injunction could be addressed to a British prime minister if the enterprise were the unification of Europe rather than that of Italy. In government, Tony Blair achieved one half of his 'just cause' by giving Britain back a leading role in Europe, but he failed in his aim of persuading the British people to love Europe.

When Tony came to power in 1997, Britain was marginalised in Europe. We had been embroiled in the 'beef war' where the government had made itself look ridiculous and achieved none of its aims. Britain was effectively powerless. The other European leaders saw the new government's arrival as a chance for a new beginning for Britain in Europe. Mrs Thatcher had been respected but not liked.

John Major had been liked but not respected. Finally, here was a leader who was both liked and respected.

Mrs Thatcher started off her political career a pro-European but became increasingly Eurosceptic in her later years, particularly after she delivered the 1988 Bruges speech, in part drafted by my brother. She never got on well with Chancellor Kohl, the leading figure in Europe during her time. They had met in Salzburg, where Mrs Thatcher used to go on her brief summer holidays. Kohl had quickly tired of her company and broke off their encounter prematurely, saying that he had to leave to go to an important meeting. Mrs Thatcher was left with time on her hands and spent it wandering around the streets. She was horrified when she turned a corner and saw Kohl sitting at a pavement cafe stuffing his face with a huge cream cake. Their relationship never recovered.

As an avowed pro-European, Tony managed to get off to a better start with Kohl, and we went to meet him in Bonn while we were still in Opposition. Kohl shook me warmly by the hand in the receiving line and said he was glad to see the 'good Powell rather than the bad Powell'. In their meeting, Kohl spoke for forty-five minutes with simultaneous interpretation without drawing breath, let alone allowing Tony to speak – a sure sign of affection.

Britain was back at the top table. Tony was welcomed with relief at his first summit in May 1997 in Noordwijk, and we were able to take a more constructive attitude towards the Amsterdam Treaty, then in the final stages of negotiation, than the Major government had been, hamstrung as it was by Eurosceptic rebels. At the following Amsterdam summit, Alastair and I spotted an opportunity to make a visual point about Britain's return to a leading role in Europe. When the leaders went into the morning session, we noticed that the Dutch had provided bicycles for all the leaders to get from the conference centre to the lunch a short distance away. We snaffled one of the best bikes and got it ready for Tony so that he could head the procession of leaders over a canal, producing the desired photo for the press. Kohl sulkily refused to ride on a bike at all and walked, and the bulky Maarti Ahtisaari, the president of Finland, had to be held on his bike by two aides. Not that we got everything right straight away. At one of the early summits, Tony was asked two trick questions by European journalists to test his knowledge. A Romanian asked him if he knew who the Romanian prime minister was, and he replied 'Of course', but failed to provide the name. A Maltese journalist followed up by asking him about our position on Malta and Europe, and Tony replied that 'Our position remains unchanged', a politician's standby response to any question to which the answer is not known. He had no idea what our position was – or even if we had one.

Our key objective was to get Britain to play a leadership role again in Europe so that we could exercise some influence on the direction the EU would take. When President Yeltsin announced a joint initiative in 1997, but only with Chirac and Kohl, Tony was concerned even though it didn't lead anywhere; and we were equally worried when the three-way Russian/French/German alliance reappeared at the time of the Iraq War this time with Putin, Chirac and Schroeder. The Russian aim was clear in both cases: to split Europe off from the United States. We wanted to keep Europe together and above all to avoid the development of a two-speed Europe from which the UK was excluded. As the best way of avoiding such exclusion, we tried to insert ourselves into the Franco-German partnership without thereby disrupting it. We did not aspire to replicate the bureaucratic machinery of the Elysée Treaty, with joint Franco-German Cabinet meetings, but we did want to be involved when key decisions were being made.

While Kohl was in place we did not stand much chance of breaking into the two countries' exclusive partnership, but we made a point of cultivating Gerhard Schroeder even before he was elected Chancellor. Our cultivation paid off. On taking office, Schroeder visited the UK immediately after France and even talked about visiting London first. I was being a bit premature when I wrote in my diary in January 1999 that, when we looked back, the shift in the German position towards the UK under Schroeder would be seen as historic. It didn't work out quite like that in the end, but at the beginning Schroeder was far more willing to treat the UK on an equal footing than Kohl had been. Even as late as 2002 we were working closely with him. I persuaded Tony to call him after his second election victory to congratulate him, and the call paid off. Schroeder said Tony was the only one to call, and he would remember it. The next day he called back and proposed that he come for dinner in Downing Street the following day, a deliberate snub to Chirac for backing Schroeder's conservative opponent.

Deal-making lies at the heart of the Franco-German relationship. They will support each other on issues that are of real significance to one side or the other, even if in doing so they are going against their narrow self-interest on the issue concerned. The Chancellor's chief of staff will call the Elysée to propose a deal and a possible trade-off, and they will rapidly agree between themselves. As a sign of his willingness to put the Anglo-German relationship on the same footing, Schroeder offered us exactly such a deal. Tony was very concerned about draft EU legislation on the *droit de suite,* requiring royalties to be paid on the sale of an artist's work, which would have endangered the future of auction houses in the UK. He cared about it so much that he had threatened to invoke the 'Luxembourg compromise', an EU device invented by de Gaulle to allow the French to get their way by declaring a supreme national interest. Schroeder knew how important the issue was to Tony and offered to trade support for the UK on it in return for supporting him on the used-car directive that posed a threat to the German car industry. We did the deal, but the British machine failed to develop the mindset that would make such bilateral trade-offs a regular part of our approach to the EU, perhaps because it seemed too Machiavellian, and we never managed to emulate the Franco-German relationship. Instead, we relied on trying to build coalitions of smaller EU countries issue by issue, in part because we couldn't bring ourselves to make sacrifices on less important matters in order to secure bigger goals. As Machiavelli correctly says, 'Prudence . . . consists in knowing how to distinguish degrees of disadvantage, and in accepting a less evil as a good,' but we just couldn't acquire the habit of trading issues.

We angled for years for a trilateral meeting with the French and Germans, and we finally got one in the aftermath of 9/11. Chirac convened it in the margins of the Ghent European summit in 2001 in a cramped and airless room. It was hard to hear anything against the background of the simultaneous three-way translation, but a joint European approach to Afghanistan was agreed. When we tried to repeat the meeting three weeks later in London, it all went horribly wrong. Tony stopped in Genoa on the way back from Pakistan to see Berlusconi but as soon as we sat down to dinner Berlusconi said emotionally that Tony's visit made up for the humiliation of the Ghent summit from which he had been excluded. Not surprisingly,

Tony couldn't then bring himself to tell him what we had planned for the next weekend, and we were treated instead to a monologue by Berlusconi on the halitosis of Italian ambassadors and how to keep a young wife.

When we got back to London we announced the three-way dinner for Sunday 4 November, and all hell at once broke loose. First Berlusconi rang absolutely insisting he had to come. Tony agreed. Then Aznar of Spain phoned saying he must come too. Tony agreed. Then the Belgian prime minister, Guy Verhofstadt, as holder of the EU presidency, invited himself, together with Javier Solana, the EU foreign policy chief. And finally, a few hours before the dinner, the prime minister of the Netherlands, Wim Kok, announced that he was also coming. He arrived late, and we had run out of food so we had to give him the vegetarian plate. Schroeder and Chirac did not find the gatecrashing, and our failure to prevent it, at all amusing. The European leaders who weren't invited were even crosser.

That debacle put the idea of a *directoire* for Europe back in the deep freeze for the next two years, but the Germans called a trilateral meeting again in Berlin in September 2003. They and the French wanted to use it to repair our relations post-Iraq and to discuss the upcoming Inter Governmental Conference (IGC) and the top jobs in the EU. The meeting was fine, but we weren't able to reach agreement on any of the key points on the IGC. We had one final attempt with Chirac and Schroeder in 2004. Tony sent both of them a note in advance, of the sort he used to send to President Bush, setting out a substantive political programme for Europe to move us on from negotiating endlessly on process. But it was perfectly clear when Tony got there that neither of the others had read the note and that neither wanted to discuss the top jobs in the EU in front of their foreign ministers. In Europe there is a wide gap between presidents and Chancellors and their foreign ministers. In some cases, it is because they are members of coalition governments and come from different parties. In others, it is because the president is too grand to concern himself with a mere foreign minister. In 2004 Berlusconi was very upset at being excluded once again, and the next time we saw him he was like a jilted lover in a terrible sulk, full of dark looks, and Tony had to woo him all over again. That was the end of the experiment. Neither Angela Merkel nor Nicolas Sarkozy wanted to risk stirring up the small countries by bringing the three of us together again. Sarkozy did offer to hold a dinner for Tony and Gordon with Merkel in June 2007, just as Tony was leaving. Gordon at first accepted but then, presumably under the influence of his advisers who didn't want him to be seen with Tony, changed his mind and declined.

An enlarged EU does, however, need a *directoire* in order to operate effectively. Twenty-seven leaders and their foreign ministers sitting around the table are far too many for focused discussion. If each of them speaks, you have already used up an entire day. There needs to be some sort of steering group for the EU, probably including Spain, Italy and Poland as well as the UK, France and Germany; but persuading those left out to acquiesce in such an arrangement will require luck and real leadership skills.

A good deal of politics at the European level depends on whether the leaders get on with each other. It was to our advantage that the personal relationship between Schroeder and Chirac was so poor, at least to start with. Schroeder called in December 2000 furious about Chirac's behaviour following the French president's visit to his home. He wanted a new alliance with Britain and proposed a joint Cabinet meeting in London before that year's Labour Party conference to discuss economic reform, but it never came off.

Unfortunately, Tony's relationship with Schroeder eventually soured. This was partly a result of small acts of unintentional disrespect on our part. Tony had a habit of asking us to get other leaders on the phone and then getting tied in up in something else, leaving them hanging on while he finished whatever he was doing. He did that once too often in December 2003. I listened to Schroeder gradually getting crosser and crosser as he waited, having been pulled out of a Cabinet meeting. Finally he got fed up and rang off. In June 2005, we committed an even worse sin during the run-up to the German election. On arriving in Berlin, Tony first met Angela Merkel, the opposition candidate, and the meeting overran so that we were late for Schroeder, who was left hanging around on the red carpet outside the front door of the Chancellery in full view of the TV cameras waiting to welcome Tony. Schroeder was furious. His interpreter told us later that he had said that Tony was not a beginner, he knew what he was doing, and he was treating him like dead meat and should know better than to humiliate a colleague. He took his revenge by being very unhelpful to Tony in the subsequent press conference over the British rebate. Schroeder's opposition to the Iraq War as part of his re-election campaign in Germany was of course the crucial breaking point. That forced him back into the arms of Chirac and Putin and the resuscitated Russian/German/French troika.

Tony made repeated efforts at winning over Chirac, but the old man was always suspicious of him. On one occasion, at an Anglo-French summit under 'cohabitation' just before the presidential election, we had a terrible time juggling meetings with both Chirac and his socialist prime minister, Lionel Jospin, who was running against him in the election. One had to leave Number 10 before the other could come through the front door, and Chirac was furious at having to wait. I discovered later that Jospin had been upset because Chirac had been allowed to see Tony's infant son Leo and he had not. At the dinner itself, Chirac was sat on Tony's right and Jospin on his left. I was next to Jospin. They both competed to attract Tony's attention. Chirac won hands down by talking to Tony without drawing breath so that Tony didn't have any opportunity to turn to his left. Jospin was increasingly forlorn, stuck talking with me, but there was nothing we could do. We had discovered that it was Chirac's sixty-ninth birthday, and we arranged to have a cake with candles brought into the dinner. He didn't seem unduly grateful. We only discovered later that his age had become an issue in the presidential campaign and that he thought we were deliberately rubbing it in.

Tony had learned French working in Paris as a barman when a student and was rightly proud of it, but he faced a real test of his skill when he was invited to speak to the French Assembly in 1998. We got the Foreign Office to provide two French teachers to practise with him. He was calm enough when we got to the Assembly building, but as the meeting with Laurent Fabius, the Speaker, went on he became increasingly distracted till it was clear he wasn't paying attention to what was being said at all. The walk to the chamber itself felt like the march to the guillotine. He had to proceed down a long gloomy corridor by himself, with French dragoons in their traditional uniforms on either side beating huge drums in what sounded like a funeral march. He delivered the speech well, in good French, starting with a few jokes. (They clearly weren't used to jokes in the Assembly.) The right had decided to use his speech to make a point. Every time Tony said something New Labour they applauded loudly while the socialists sat on their hands looking glum, and every time he said something faintly left-wing the socialists clapped wildly while the right sat in silence. The right got the better part of it.

Tony's relationship with Jospin was not much better than his relationship with Chirac. Jospin had promised to help get the beef ban lifted in France when he was prime minister in 1999, but in November he suddenly stopped returning our calls. We discovered that he was scared of Martine Aubry, Jacques Delors's daughter and Minister of Health, who was opposed to lifting the ban. We eventually succeeded in getting it removed but with little help from Jospin. In an attempt to build a closer friendship, Tony invited him to his Sedgefield constituency, a special mark of favour. After lunch at the Dun Cow pub they held a joint press conference on the doorstep of Tony's house in Trimdon. Tony decided to conduct it in French, but on this occasion his French was not quite as good as he thought it was. When asked how he planned to cooperate with Jospin, Tony thought that he said that he looked forward to working with him on many different issues. Jospin looked quizzical as Tony started his reply and had to suppress a fit of giggles as he got to the end. Afterwards Tony asked him what the problem was, and Jospin told him that what he had actually said was that he 'desired Lionel Jospin in many different positions'.

Chirac had a wonderful tendency to drive a coach and horses through political correctness. In 2005 we met him in the Elysée and were trying to find a new European policy which Britain and France could agree on and promote together, as we had earlier on European defence at St Malo. Chirac gave us a lecture on demography and the need for Europe to breed to keep up with immigration. He insisted France was doing its bit, but Germany and Italy were letting the side down. The staff on his side of the table looked increasingly uncomfortable as we started contemplating a common breeding policy for Europe – a CBP to compete with the CAP. At a summit in Sweden to discuss where European agencies should be based, always a tense issue, he turned to the Swedish prime minister, Göran Persson, and said that Sweden should have a European agency for beautiful women. This was only surpassed by an emotional speech from Berlusconi on why the European Food Agency couldn't possibly be in Finland, because they had such terrible food, but should be based in Bologna because of their tasty sausage, mortadella. No one told him it was a food safety agency.

Tony endured ridicule for visiting Berlusconi in Sardinia during his bandanna-wearing phase, followed down the street by his personal troubadour complete with guitar. Meetings with Berlusconi were certainly memorable, from the identical meals we had with him on each visit – green, red and white pasta, followed by chicken and red and green vegetables, and red, white and green ice cream – to his racy jokes. His most repeatable joke was about President Hu and Prime Minister Wen, which his interpreter obligingly rendered as President Qui and Prime Minister Quando. However strange a figure Berlusconi may appear to the British public, he was a man of his word and, if he said he would support us on an issue, he invariably would. A prudent leader is willing to swallow a good deal of humiliation to secure reliable support in the EU.

Once Chirac and Schroeder left, Tony had a better shot at forging good relations with Angela Merkel and Nicolas Sarkozy. Unfortunately, by then he did not have long left in power himself, or we might have been more successful at building a three-way alliance.

We started working with Merkel before she was elected Chancellor, with the aim of preventing Guy Verhofstadt becoming president of the EU Commission. When Tony met her in person for the first time on 13 June 2005, she was extraordinarily direct. We met her in the spanking new British Embassy in Berlin, and she started straight off with 'I have the following problems: no charisma; I am a woman; I am no good at communicating' and so on. Despite these self-deprecating comments, she was confident she would win and said that once elected she would side with us on Common Agricultural Policy reform and deregulation.

In the autumn, just before the election, Tony sent me over to see her again by myself just before the election. I managed to arrive late thanks to British Airways, but she was very understanding and made time for me by rearranging her other meetings. I said we doubted she would be able to achieve radical domestic reform given the likelihood of a coalition with the SPD and suggested that therefore, in order to demonstrate political momentum, she should focus on what she could achieve in Europe. She could be the change-maker in Europe, and I suggested we work together to agree a deal on the budget and reform of the European social model at the summit in December. She said there were limits to what she could do. In particular, she was worried about regional funds for the old East Germany, but she liked the overall idea of demonstrating political momentum through Europe. She said Verhofstadt had called her asking her to attack the British and to visit Brussels first, which she thought was very funny. She would visit London right after Paris.

Tony certainly found it easier to get on with Chirac's successor than he had with Chirac. Following a bilateral meeting in 2005, Chirac asked Tony not to meet Nicolas Sarkozy who had requested a meeting with him on his forthcoming visit to London. Chirac suggested that Tony tell him that he had a more important meeting. Sarkozy was furious when he discovered what had happened and phoned Tony, accusing him of a lack of courage. Chirac was a bully – something we already knew – and it was important to stand up to him. Sarkozy asked if they could meet somewhere other than in Downing Street, and we agreed that Tony would see him at the old Greater London Council building, now a hotel, but with no press. When we did meet, Sarkozy was very friendly and said he wanted a new relationship with Britain. At the end of the meeting, he insisted on escorting Tony down to the lobby. To our not very great surprise, we were met by the French press corps as we came out of the lift. Tony was criticised for going so far out on a limb for Sarkozy, so far indeed that Ségolène Royal, Sarkozy's socialist rival, decided not to come to London as part of her pre-election tour. But Tony was firmly of the view that there is no point in being half-pregnant. If you side with another leader, you should go the whole way rather than hedging your bets. He admired Sarkozy's irrepressible nature. Had Tony remained in office longer, he would have made an excellent go-between in the sometimes stormy relationship between Sarkozy and Merkel.

Europe is no longer part of foreign policy for any British prime minister but a central part of domestic policy and politics, and the Foreign Office has a perennial worry that Europe will be removed from its purview. When he was Foreign Secretary, Robin Cook complained to me in May 1998 that Peter Mandelson, at that time Minister without Portfolio, was trying to turn the Cabinet Office into the Ministry of Europe. I reassured him, and Peter soon moved on. The worry lingered, though. Robin's successor, Jack Straw, asked in 2004 if he could run the referendum campaign on the European Constitution from the Foreign Office. Tony said he could not and that it needed to be run from the Cabinet Office. Jack was not happy, but there was no campaign in the end so it didn't matter. In fact, because the vast majority of European business nowadays is directly related to domestic matters, leaving Europe in the Foreign Office is an anachronism. A prudent prime minister would move it to the Cabinet Office headed by a Cabinet-level Minister of Europe.

A good deal of the high-level policymaking and politicking in Europe is conducted among the network of European-affairs advisers to the presidents and prime ministers of the EU countries, and it is essential for the British prime minister to have someone who can fulfil this role in Downing Street. For prime ministers themselves, however, Europe is experienced through the summits, usually four a year and now all held in the godforsaken Justus Lipsius building in Brussels and finally winding up only at three or four in the morning. European leaders don't really feel they have had a serious negotiation unless it runs right through the night.

Summits are particularly stressful if you find you are in the chair as the temporary president of Europe, because you are then responsibile for shepherding the other leaders into an agreement. Tony's first substantive summit under the British presidency was charged with appointing the first president of the European Central Bank for the launch of the euro in 1998. When Tony arrived in Brussels to chair the summit, we were informed that Chirac and Kohl had reached agreement: Wim Duisenberg from the Netherlands would be president of the bank for the first half of the term, and Jean-Claude Trichet, the governor of the French central bank, would take over for the second half. Tony saw Kohl first and we put Chirac in a holding room, but Chirac was soon fed up with being made to wait and stormed off. Tony persuaded him to come back, and together with Kohl and Wim Kok tried to pin down an understanding, which Kok said should to be acceptable to Duisenberg. We then went into the lunch that kicked off the summit and told the other leaders what the agreement was. Tony asked for permission to slip out and phone Duisenberg to tell him the good news. It turned out to be one of the longest lunches in history.

I accompanied Tony across the corridor to a big empty conference room, and Stephen Wall, our EU ambassador, gave Tony a mobile phone with Duisenberg at the other end. Tony told him the news, paused, and his face fell. I could tell from the length of the answer at the other end that all was not going well. Tony's face was a picture of horror, and he started reasoning with Duisenberg. He rang off. No one had told Duisenberg about the deal, and he wasn't going to accept it. He felt that to accept an early date for his departure would make him a lame duck from day one. Tony was in despair. We saw Kohl and then Chirac. Chirac said Duisenberg must be told to accept the deal and summoned Wim Kok, who said it was not that easy.

We persuaded Duisenberg to come in to the conference centre and got Kok to talk to him but he was very stubborn. We finally ground Duisenberg down, and he was poised to accept the compromise when Hans Tietmeyer, the head of the German Bundesbank, came in, very angry, and persuaded him to reject the proposed deal. We suggested that Kohl go and talk to Tietmeyer, but when he did Tietmeyer threatened to resign. Kohl had a rebellion on his hands led by Theo Waigel, the German finance minister, and terrible TV coverage back in Germany saying that the euro treaty had been undermined and would be challenged in the constitutional court. Kohl returned an hour later and reopened the whole issue. In fact, it was the beginning of the end for Kohl as Chancellor. He visibly deflated in the course of the day, as if someone had stuck a pin in him. Chirac kept threatening to veto the proposed deal and said we should look for a third candidate; but eventually he backed down. Towards midnight we finally arrived at an understanding, and Duisenberg came to talk to the heads of government and said he would want to retire after about five years. The other leaders were furious at having been kept waiting for twelve hours without knowing what was going on. We had reached a deal thanks to Tony's considerable powers of persuasion, but of course he got no credit for it and the proceedings were seen as a shambles. The real event had been the disintegration of Kohl, but no one outside the Council building had yet noticed.

The lesson is never to take anyone's word that a deal is really in place unless you have heard it for yourself from all the participants. As we had the presidency, we had tried to contact the various leaders in the weeks before the summit, but the French and Germans had told us to back off since we weren't actually joining the euro. Ten days before the summit they told us that they had a deal between themselves and just needed to sell it to the Dutch. They failed to do so, however, or at least to sell it to Duisenberg, and Kohl hadn't told his colleagues that he had conceded what the French wanted. The French, by overbidding and being unreasonable, had let a good deal that had been within their grasp slip away and had to settle on Duisenberg's terms instead.

The Franco-German relationship, when it works, is the motor that drives the EU and once the two countries' leaders have decided on something it feels impossible to halt the juggernaut. Tony managed to do so, however, at the European summit in 2004 over the choice of a new president of the Commission. Chirac and Schroeder had spent 2003 trying to bully Tony and the rest of Europe into accepting Guy Verhofstadt. Verhofstadt himself phoned Tony asking for his support and was taken aback when he said we could not support him because we were already supporting another candidate, Antonio Vitorino of Portugal. Tony spoke to Angela Merkel, then leader of the opposition in Germany but also chair of the European People's Party. She said she was committed to blocking Verhofstadt. A day later Anders Fogh Rasmussen, prime minister of Denmark, a liberal, called up also urging us to block him. We gradually built up a blocking minority of the smaller countries, which together could prevent the French and Germans getting their way. In the face of their concerted opposition, Schroeder called Tony to ask if he could accept Jean-Claude Juncker, the prime minister of Luxembourg, instead of Verhofstadt. That threw us into a spin. We had visions of a repeat of what had happened to John Major, who had blocked an able but federalist Belgian prime minister and ended up with a less able and federalist Luxembourger, Jacques Santer, as president of the Commission.

When we arrived in Brussels for the summit in June, feelings were running high. Schroeder was at his most overbearing. He and Chirac had decided to try to ram their choice through the Council despite the opposition. Over dinner, José Manuel Barroso and Costas Simitis, the Portuguese and Greek prime ministers, joined Tony in speaking out against Chirac's and Schroeder's bullying.

After dinner we assembled the centre-right leaders at a caucus in Berlusconi's office, including the leaders of Estonia, Malta, Spain,

Portugal, Slovakia, Austria and Greece. It was like a revival meeting. We agreed that we could not beat someone with no one and looked round the table for a potential candidate. Chancellor Schussel of Austria would have been possible, but he was anathema to the French for having formed a coalition with the neo-Nazi Jorg Haider. So instead we opted for Barroso and he became the candidate of the anti-Franco-German block. We were worried that Schroeder and Chirac would block Barroso and insist on a third candidate, but they in turn thought that we were planning, perfidiously, to slip Chris Patten through the middle. They were in any case exhausted and gave in. The emperor had been shown to have no clothes. Neither man ever recovered his power in Europe.

The real skill is to reach an agreement when you are in the chair and at the same time have a vital national interest to protect. That is what Tony had to do in our presidency in 2005. We had managed to defend the British rebate at the European summit in Berlin in 1999, when Tony and Gordon had worked together. Schroeder had been angry at our obstruction but figured he owed Tony a break politically and let him maintain the rebate untouched. This time it was different. Enlargement had taken place, and the other Europeans were determined that the UK should pay its share since we had been such enthusiastic supporters of the Central and Eastern Europeans joining the EU. After the defeat of the referendum on the European Constitution in France and the SPD's electoral setback in Germany's biggest state, North Rhine Westphalia, Chirac and Schroeder wanted to talk about something else. Reducing the British rebate was a perfect crusade on which they could unite the rest of Europe.

Tony suspected that Gordon, who refused to contemplate any compromise whatsoever, intended to use any concession that Tony made on the rebate as a stick with which to beat him at home. We were in a very uncomfortable position.

The Luxembourgers held the presidency in the first half of the year, and acting with the French and Germans they cobbled together an agreement on the budget among all the other EU member states, leaving us isolated. The one thing everyone else could agree on was that the Brits should give up their rebate. Juncker asked Tony to come and see him in Luxembourg to confront us with a fait accompli. Given the Treasury's refusal to share information with us, we had real trouble working out what the financial implications for Britain of the Luxembourg proposal would be. In desperation, we kidnapped the Treasury's expert at the UK mission in Brussels and took him with us to Luxembourg so that he could explain to us what the offer really meant. He was enormously relieved when we finally let him go. He didn't mind that he was being dumped in Paris, the next stop on our trip, without a passport or any money. He just wanted our assurance that we wouldn't tell the Treasury that he had been travelling with us: that would blight his career for ever.

At the subsequent summit, Juncker tried to bounce us into accepting his proposal. Luckily, he made it easy for us to say no by miscalculating the numbers and putting forward a cut in the British rebate that was plainly unacceptable. Jack Straw was an excellent note-taker and kept a full record of the meeting as it progressed behind closed doors. The notes were smuggled out to us every twenty minutes or so by his protection officer, putting us in a position to brief the European media as the argument progressed before any of the other governments could thereby helping us keep the initiative in the way the story was covered.

We took over the presidency in June determined to try and reach agreement on the budget on our watch. If we left it to the next presidency, we would find all the others ganging up on us again. Gordon refused to let us have the Treasury financial model for the budget, which made life difficult, and in November he threatened to publish a paper calling for a £5 billion cut in the CAP in an attempt to disrupt any chance of our reaching an agreement. Even without the computer model, we realised that to save the rebate and still make the numbers add up we were going to have to take money off the Central and Eastern Europeans, though it was galling to have to do so having long been their champions. We started with the Baltics, who were understandably grumpy but went along with our proposals, and then on to Budapest to meet the Visograd Four (the prime ministers of Poland, the Czech and Slovak Republics, and Hungary).

The meeting was held in the Gothic splendour of the Hungarian Parliament building by the Danube. I was sitting outside the conference room reading the British press cuttings. For the first and only time in my experience, the *Daily Mail* played a useful role in the British national interest. I was staring at the screaming front-page headline 'BETRAYAL' about Tony's negotiations on the rebate when the Hungarian prime minister's aide looked over my shoulder and saw it. She had copies made and took it into the prime ministers' meeting. The other leaders finally had a sense of what Tony was up against and agreed to help.

By the time we got to the summit in December it looked as if we were within shouting distance of an agreement. We started with the French and Germans and I had a sense of déjà vu back to the beginning of the 1998 summit when Duisenberg was the problem. Chirac said the French had a position of principle: the British would have to pay one hundred per cent of something. It didn't matter of what or when we paid, as long as it was one hundred per cent. Merkel was businesslike and happy to help. We knew the Poles were going to be unpredictable under the new leadership of the Kaczynski twins, but it was almost impossible to negotiate with their silent prime minister, Kazimierz Marcinkiewicz. He would speak entirely in riddles, very quietly and with a faint smile that conveyed a sense that he was being ironic. If we put specific sums to him, he would simply start talking about 'solidarity'. He reminded me of the footballer Eric Cantona in his famous TV advert talking apparent gibberish about seagulls following the trawler but giving the impression that it was sophisticated stuff that you just weren't understanding. It was either a very clever negotiating tactic so that we would keep offering him more and more money, or he simply wasn't all there. We were never sure which, and we dubbed him the first postmodern prime minister.

Eventually, after talking to all the leaders, we worked out that we had about 13 billion euros in hand to settle all the various demands made on us and sat down to dish them out. Once we had done so and told the Dutch, the Finns, the Poles and the others what they were going to get, the officials came back to Tony shamefaced to say that they had miscalculated. We had given away about 2.25 billion euros too much. We were in a desperate position. We could not reopen the negotiations now. No country would accept less than it had just been offered. One official suggested extracting some money from the EU's external action budget which never gets spent in any case, but Barroso said that that could not be done without the agreement of the European Parliament. Finally, the officials came up with the idea of reducing the deflators built into the budget model, and doing that made the numbers add up again. In the meantime, we witnessed an extraordinary negotiation between Chirac and Merkel. Before the summit, Chirac had promised publicly to get French restaurants zero-rated for VAT. He pressed Merkel and tried to persuade her to agree as part of the end game of the budget negotiations. She was polite and smiling but remained absolutely firm and refused. Chirac said in that case he was finished. He would face a general strike of restaurants.

We went back into the Council chamber and tabled the budget at one in the morning. Tony asked Chirac and Merkel to speak first, supporting the deal to make it difficult for others to shoot it down. We knew that Verhofstadt would wreak his revenge by trying to block the deal, but by the time he spoke the momentum was too much for him, although he carried on heckling for some time. Even then we weren't quite there. The Pole said he would welcome a final gesture. Tony sent me round the table to see Angela Merkel to ask if we could have some of the money promised to the eastern provinces of Germany to satisfy the Pole. She agreed and walked round to the Pole and made him an offer. We finally had a deal. I prevented the Council staff bringing in champagne for the leaders. I did not think it would sit well with a tough budget settlement.

Jack Straw told me that he thought Gordon's ally Douglas Alexander had been following him around throughout the summit, noting down anything compromising he said and sending it back to Gordon. Douglas told Jack the outcome would have been different if Gordon had been handling the negotiations. He would have been far tougher. Jon Cunliffe, the senior Treasury official, had been keeping Gordon abreast of developments by mobile phone as the negotiations continued. At the last moment Gordon demanded to speak to Tony, and Jon stood at the edge of the delegation room waving his mobile at Tony. Tony couldn't face it, turned a Nelsonian blind eye to the request and concluded the deal anyway. Gordon briefed the papers the next day that he was opposed to the outcome. When we got back to London, Tony asked him what he would have done instead. He said he would have insisted on a much smaller budget with a ceiling of only 1 per cent of EU spending. Tony asked him who would have supported that kind of position, and he replied the German finance ministry. Tony pointed out that that would not have been of much use when the German Chancellor herself had proposed a higher ceiling in the course of the negotiations.

A wise prime minister understands the need to reach agreements in the EU that leave everyone feeling like a winner, or at least able to go home and make a reasonable case for what they have accepted. As Machiavelli urges in such situations, 'Prudent men always and in all their actions make a favour of doing things even though they would of necessity be constrained to do them anyway.' A prime minister has to negotiate with fellow European leaders again and again and is certain to need their goodwill in due course. Gordon's bulldozer approach to negotiations might be successful once, as it was over the Witholding Tax (the hotly contested tax on savings in Europe designed to stop people avoiding tax by holding their savings in another country), but only at great cost on other issues. Almost as soon as we came into government, we received complaints from other European leaders about his rude and bullying behaviour in the Euro-X group of eurozone finance ministers. Antonio Guterres, the former Portuguese prime minister, told Tony in 2000 that he couldn't understand why Gordon couldn't be satisfied with winning on the issue rather than insisting on humiliating the other side. Gordon took great pride in his success and summed up his approach in a later conversation, in which he accused Tony of being a weak negotiator, saying: 'If you were as tough as me, you would tell them they are getting nothing, and they would be grateful for the crumbs we let them get away with.' But the cost of his victory on the Witholding Tax was bruised feelings all over Europe. If you adopt a completely unreasonable position in one negotiation, you will pay a price in another.

Gordon wanted to accompany Tony to his final summit in June 2007, but I didn't think it was appropriate. When we were there, we had a taste of a new generation of French bullying. Sarkozy had told Tony when he met him in January that it was his aim to put a mini European constitution to the summit in the summer to get it (the constitution) out of the way, and he asked for Tony's help in persuading Merkel. The summit in June was poised to ratify the new treaty. At the last minute, Sarkozy tried to bounce through an additional clause on the limits to the role of competition as a gesture to demonstrate that the Anglo-Saxon model was not carrying all before it. Peter Sutherland, a former commissioner, called to warn us of what was being stitched up. The Germans told us that they had gone along with the insertion because it was much better than Sarkozy's alternative proposal of requiring the European Central Bank to take economic growth as well as monetary stability into account as an objective. We made our opposition clear to the presidency. Sarkozy summoned us to his office and sat Tony opposite him, with Nigel Sheinwald and me to one side of the table. Instead of addressing Tony, he turned towards us and gave us a piece of his mind. He said he had helped us achieve all we wanted on the treaty and adopted all our changes, and now he was asking for just one '*petit truc*' and we were opposing it. Unlike Chirac in his bulldozer mode, it was hard to take Sarkozy's rage too seriously, and we accepted the clause when assured by the Commission lawyers that it made no substantive difference. That didn't prevent Sarkozy trumpeting his triumph at home.

The prime minister of the UK suffers one major disadvantage by comparison with all other European leaders, one that massively complicates his negotiating hand at European Councils, and that is the British press. They set up every summit as a make-or-break crisis for the British leader and insist that he will have failed unless he wins on some particular issue. Then, when he gets to the summit, they report that Britain is isolated. If the prime minister achieves anything less than a complete triumph, Britain has been humiliated. Even worse, British journalists go to all the press conferences, not just the one given by the British prime minister, and they contrast the French and German and even Belgian claims of what was agreed with those made by our prime minister. None of the other leaders suffers from this doubting of their description of their national triumphs; their press patriotically attend only their own leader's press conference and loyally record what he claims has been achieved on behalf of the nation.

We did, despite this, succeed in restoring Britain to a leading position in Europe, but we failed to persuade Britain to love Europe. Our biggest and earliest failure was over the euro. The problem began in October 1997 when Gordon rang Tony saying he wanted to kill off press stories that suggested there were differences between the two of them over economic and monetary union (EMU). He said he had an interview in *The Times* which he could use to stabilise the situation. Tony was preoccupied elsewhere and distractedly said that would be fine as long as Gordon cleared his line with Alastair. Having listened to the phone call, I urged Alastair to stop the briefing but he, who was in any case personally pretty ambivalent on Europe, called Philip Webster of *The Times* and told him Gordon would be calling with an agreed line on EMU. The intention had been to rule out entry to EMU for 1998 and 1999, but not beyond that. By the time we realised that Charlie Whelan had briefed *The Times* on behalf of Gordon that we would not be going into EMU in the course of the entire first Parliament, it was already too late. Tony was furious with Gordon and Charlie and vowed to change their way of working. Charlie went around for the next few weeks looking like a quivering jelly. There followed days of negotiations over what the formal position of the government should be, and I found myself fielding calls between Tony at the Commonwealth Heads of Government Meeting at Gleneagles and Gordon in London while attending the birth of my first daughter in hospital. The pass had been sold by then, however, and there was nothing more we could do on EMU before the next election. All too often in government the really important decisions slip past you without you even realising it, and the true significance of what you have done only dawns on you when it is too late.

Tony returned to the issue with Gordon just before the 2001 election. We were thinking about the possibility of a referendum on the euro in autumn 2002 or summer 2003 but we didn't think we could go in at an exchange rate of 2.80 DM to the pound as the economic cost would be too high. We hoped the exchange rate would change. Gordon had other plans. He was furious when he discovered that John Kerr, the Foreign Office Permanent Secretary, had inserted a passage on the euro in the Queen's Speech and had it taken out. He saw the euro as a political lever and told Tony in June that he would consent to entry only if Tony stood down as leader.

In 2002 and 2003, we were subject to a series of technical seminars on each of the five tests of whether we should join which were led by Treasury experts almost literally wearing white coats. They all took the matter desperately seriously, but it was perfectly apparent that Gordon had already made his decision for political reasons. On 25 June, just as Tony was heading to the airport to fly to Canada, Gordon gave Tony a copy of a speech that he was to make that evening. I got Tony to call him from the car and propose amendments, but as always it wasn't what the speech said but what the associated briefing said that mattered, and Gordon got Ed Balls to brief Andy Marr, the BBC's political editor, that Britain would fail to meet the five tests and would not join the euro.

Despite that setback, Tony still kept a candle burning for the euro. He had been trying to lure Gus O'Donnell into moving to Number 10 from the Treasury, but decided it was better to leave him in place to keep an eye on the way the economic tests were being assessed by Treasury officials. In November 2001 Tony thought Gus was gearing up to show that the tests were being met, but by October 2002 Gus told us that we would either have to accept a no to the euro or else change Chancellor.

At the final seminar in the series in March 2003, when Tony was at his weakest, Gordon announced that we had met four of the tests but not the fifth, the exchange rate. Gordon wanted to announce his decision in the Budget. Tony agreed so long as Gordon would say that we would run the tests again in the following year, but Gordon wanted to rule out any further assessment till after the election. Once again, the Treasury tried to create a fait accompli by briefing Andy Marr that we would not be going into the euro. Tony had one last card to play. We knew the Cabinet would be largely sympathetic on the euro, and he said he would take the issue there. Gordon tried to insist that it could only be discussed in the economic subcommittee of the Cabinet which he chaired. They then had a spectacular row with Gordon accusing Tony of being 'morally corrupt', but in the end Gordon accepted the issue should be discussed bilaterally with Cabinet members. The Treasury sent out eighteen huge and unintelligible papers on the euro to ministers in advance. Discussions went well for us, with the overwhelming majority of Cabinet ministers on our side, although David Blunkett, one of our natural allies, was opposed on the merits.

In the end the exchange rate did not change and we had to concede. Jeremy Heywood managed to negotiate some improvement to the texts of the papers to be published on the five tests, to ensure that the euro was not ruled out altogether, and Tony inserted some changes in Gordon's statement, but we had finally lost the battle. Our European adviser, Stephen Wall, was in despair, arguing that we should have stood up to the bully. In a final blow, Gordon refused to leave open in his statement the possibility of a referendum in the following year; and, although Tony still hoped he could have a referendum jointly on the European Constitution and the euro, the issue was effectively dead for the rest of his government. During the current economic crisis, many will be glad that we did not join, although that may turn out to be a false comfort if and when we face a sterling crisis.

To have succeeded on the euro, we would need to have done so in the first term, but we allowed ourselves to be deflected in the autumn of 1997. Once we agreed to put off the issue till after the 2001 election, and handed the keys to the Treasury through the economic tests, it was very unlikely that we would succeed. As Machiavelli observes, 'You ought never to suffer your design to be crossed in order to avoid war, since war is not to be avoided, but it is only to be deferred to your disadvantage.'

In terms of domestic politics the European Constitution was always going to be a nightmare for us. It is true that Europe needed to reform its institutions to manage its increased size after enlargement, but any discussion of the institutional minutiae of the EU loses British public opinion from the outset. We put on a brave face and managed to persuade Giscard d'Estaing, the former French president and chair of the Convention to draw up a European constitution, to be sympathetic to British problems. We invited him to dinner in Tony's flat in Number 11 in February 2002 and asked the Government Hospitality Fund to provide the very best wines from their cellars. They did, and it worked spectacularly. In a mellow mood after dinner, he commented on the quality of the claret and the Château d'Yquem and told us that the Elysée did not have a wine cellar of its own. Each new president has to bring his own wine with him.

At first, we intended to handle the constitution in the same way as any normal European treaty, but Jack Straw gave me a personal note for Tony on 1 April 2004 proposing a referendum. I left it on my desk and to my alarm it disappeared in the course of the afternoon. I had become sufficiently paranoid to suspect that it had been stolen by one of the Brownites and was convinced it would be leaked. I got another copy from Jack and gave it to Tony. Gradually Tony became convinced that we should have a referendum to prevent the constitution becoming a killer issue in the 2005 election. With the promise of a referendum, Eurosceptics could still support Labour confident that they would be able to vote against the constitution afterwards.

On the whole, referenda are not a good way to decide complicated issues. They act more often as a measure of the unpopularity of the incumbent government than as a test of the popularity of the issue on the ballot paper. If we had ever had to fight a referendum on either the euro or the constitution, we would have had to fight it on the question of whether the UK should stay in the EU or leave. Only that sort of broad question can really be decided by plebiscite.

During the negotiations we succeeded in inserting the idea of a president of the Council into the constitutional treaty. Our aim was to strengthen the intergovernmental part of the EU at the expense of the supranational. In federalist theology, the Commission is the kernel of a new European government and the Council is the precursor of a senate, whereas in the view of countries like Britain and France, the Commission is the Civil Service of the EU and the Council is the government, because it is the Council that represents the democratic wishes of the people of Europe. We wanted a leader of the Council for five years who could take the initiative in setting the agenda for the EU and keep the wilder ambitions of the Commission in check, and not have the existing weak and disjointed rotating six-month national presidencies. I had been banging on about creating a president of the Council for years, and in December 2001 Tony finally adopted the idea. It was only agreed reluctantly by the more federalist governments at the end of the negotiation, because for the Germans it was counter to their euro-theology, and the small countries feared it was a ruse to stitch up Europe in favour of the big countries.

Tony made it clear that he was not running for any of the top European jobs on offer so that no one could accuse him of having an interest in the result of a referendum when and if we came to have one on the outcome of the Convention. He had, however, flirted with the idea of European jobs in the past, including as President of the Commission. It was Sarkozy who first publicly raised the idea of Tony becoming the president of the Council and told Tony at their meeting in January 2007 that he would fix it. He continued to promote the idea from then on but unfortunately it never happened.

Continental European politics is quite different from British politics. Tony campaigned for socialist colleagues a number of times in their national elections, but those campaigns were quite unlike what we were used to. In May 1998, Tony campaigned for Victor Klima in Vienna. There was huge interest in Tony's visit in the Austrian media, but the actual campaign event turned out to take the form of a rather low-key and earnest discussion in a small Viennese coffee house. It was far from the cut and thrust that we expect in Britain or the razzmatazz of American elections. Later, Tony went to campaign for the Labour prime minister, Wim Kok, in the Netherlands. Again we expected a large rally but found instead that Tony was invited to make a short speech in a closed disco in Rotterdam. The required standards of public speaking in European politics are far below those demanded in Britain, and this discrepancy leads British politicians to fail to take European politics sufficiently seriously. The conservative European People's Party and the Party of European Socialists may seem to us to be irrelevant, but to many European leaders they are genuinely important alliances where deals are made.

A British leader has natural advantages in the European Parliament. The Westminster system produces politicians good at debating and reacting to questions on their feet, unlike the more staid procedures of Continental politics. The difference between the two is rather like the difference between rugby, with its fluid play, and American football, with its set pieces and long gaps to think. Tony had to give his 2005 presidency speech to the European Parliament in a hostile atmosphere. Britain was in the doghouse for vetoing the budget deal under the Luxembourg presidency, and Juncker, a perennial if somewhat unlikely darling of the Parliament, had just made a speech, to general acclaim, attacking the British rebate and Tony's obduracy. The MEPs were sullen and the mood tense when Tony rose to his feet, with even a smattering of booing, but by making a House of Commons-type speech, complete with self-deprecating jokes and name-checking the leaders of the parliamentary groups, he managed to win them over. He stayed in the chamber throughout the debate, noting down what they all said, and he then rose again to reply, quoting the points they had made, offering little bits of flattery and answering their questions. They loved it. British prime ministers should make more of the inbuilt advantage their Westminster training gives them.

The Europhiles criticised Tony for not making the case for Europe strongly enough at home. That is unfair. It is true that Euroscepticism is wide but shallow in Britain and that the argument could be won, but it will take more than assertion alone to win it. In his Nobel Prize acceptance speech, the Unionist leader David Trimble described Northern Ireland as 'a cold house' for Catholics, with solid walls and roof but not welcoming. The same is true of Europe for Britons, in part because of our history of separateness and because we still look outwards to the rest of the world rather than inwards to the rest of Europe. Most of the resentment in the UK is caused, however, by our feeling that Europe is something that happens to us rather than something we can control. British people tend to feel that we are powerless and that Europe is driven by the French and Germans. If, for a sustained period, Britain were to be a leader in Europe and were able to make Europe seem a less cold house, we might feel more confident about it, as the French and Germans do.

We tried to assemble a cross-party pro-European movement, but it never really took off. In 1998, we launched 'Britain in Europe' with Michael Heseltine, Ken Clarke and Paddy Ashdown as well as numerous business leaders. The pro-European Tories tried to blame Tony and Gordon for the movement's failure by demonstrating a lack of bravery, but by then they were an endangered species themselves and could offer almost no political cover. They gradually lost hope over time. Ken Clarke told Tony in 2003 that his supporters said he could be leader of the Tory Party if he dropped his support for Europe, but he was not prepared to. Heseltine continued to be bold, for example defending the European Constitution in 2004, but Ken Clarke and his supporters were notable by their silence. I got Tony to call Ken and he produced a variety of excuses. We decided the real reason was probably a residual loyalty to Michael Howard, with whom Ken had been at university.

The one thing we were not prepared to do was choose between Europe and the US. Traditionally, British prime ministers have gone one way or the other: Heath was pro-Europe and anti-US; Thatcher was pro-US and anti-Europe. It is, in fact, madness for a British leader to choose. Tony's metaphor of Britain as a bridge between Europe and America was much mocked but does capture something of the position British leaders find themselves in. We wanted to use our relationship with those at each end of the bridge to strengthen their relationship with those at the other. Schroeder came to us in September 2002 asking us to help him with President Bush and we attempted to. Similarly Merkel asked for the same help in her efforts to rebuild US–German relations after her election victory in 2005. Tony pushed Bush to meet her and she asked Bush to establish regular videoconferences of the sort he had with Tony, but he didn't seem keen. At the other end of the bridge, we tried to persuade Bush to seek reconciliation with the Europeans after the Iraq invasion. Lord Ismay famously defined the purpose of NATO in the 1940s as 'to keep the Russians out, the Americans in and the Germans down'. After the Iraq War, Henry Kissinger adapted the quotation in his advice to Bush 'to punish the French, ignore the Germans and pick off the Russians'. We thought that approach a mistake and persuaded Bush to reach out to the Europeans, but he never had a chance to test any such approach as his popularity sank to such low levels that no one in Europe wanted to be reconciled to him.

The problem with a bridge comes when the two sides to which it is attached start to separate. Doing the splits can become very uncomfortable, as we discovered over the Iraq War. The division of Europe into New Europe and Old Europe at the time was not our idea, but it reflected how fed up the Central and Eastern Europeans, in particular, were with the French and Germans. But dividing Europe, either in this way or by France and Germany siding with Russia, is a mistake. As Machiavelli says, 'I do not believe that divisions purposely caused can ever lead to good; on the contrary, when an enemy approaches, divided cities are lost at once.'

Any British prime minister who allows themselves to be forced to choose between America and Europe is making a terrible mistake. Britain's continuing relevance rests largely on how it is able to leverage those two relationships, being able to be both a leader in Europe and at the same time listened to in America. To cut itself off from either side, or even worse from both, would be catastrophic for Britain. Our aim should always be to restore unity to the 'divided city'.

CHAPTER ELEVEN

'A Staunch Friend and a Thorough Foe'
War and Peace

Machiavelli argues that:

> A Prince is likewise esteemed who is a staunch friend and a thorough foe, that is to say, who, without reserve openly declares for one against another, that being always a more advantageous course than to stand neutral. For supposing two of your powerful neighbours come to blows, it must either be that you have, or have not, reason to fear the one who comes off victorious. In either case it will always be well for you to declare yourself, and join in frankly with one side or other. For should you fail to do so you are certain, in the former of the cases put, to become the prey of the victor to the satisfaction and delight of the vanquished, and no reason or circumstance that you may plead will avail to shield or shelter you; for the victor dislikes doubtful friends, and such as will not help him at a pinch; and the vanquished will have nothing to say to you, since you would not share his fortunes sword in hand.

This was the reasoning behind Tony Blair's approach to both the Clinton and the Bush administrations, and it is what led to the charges in the British media of 'poodlism'. Like Machiavelli, he believed there was no earthly point in taking an ambivalent position, as for example Harold Wilson or Ted Heath did to successive American administrations. It makes sense to distance yourself from what an American administration does if you disagree with it, and it makes sense to be strongly in support if you agree, but it makes no sense at all to hover in the middle ground neither agreeing nor disagreeing. Tony took the view that America was of central importance to Britain and that, as the only superpower, it was central to world security. He opted to 'hug them close'. As Machiavelli says, trying to have it both ways will get you the worst of both. It is illogical to remain a member of the European Union but to stand on the sidelines complaining and having no influence. The same is true of relations with the US president. If you are going to have any influence on him, you need to convince him you are on his side.

When Tony came to office, war was the last thing on his mind, and yet he ended up fighting five wars, more than any other modern British prime minister. It is worth considering how this happened.

Newly elected prime ministers usually have no intention of spending their time on foreign policy. Their aim is to resolve the pressing domestic problems that brought them into politics and got them elected. Yet all prime ministers, like all US presidents, find themselves dragged into foreign policy, usually in their first term, and over time they come to enjoy it more than domestic policy. The problems are difficult but easier to deal with than reforming the welfare system or reducing the budget deficit. Diplomacy moves more quickly than the glacial pace of public-service reform, and it is easier to make decisions because you have more room for manoeuvre than you do in most domestic policy areas.

Tony was not widely travelled before he became prime minister and not particularly well informed about foreign affairs. The few meetings we had with foreign leaders in Opposition were usually pretty thin on substance and sometimes embarrassing, as when Tony told Prime Minister Chernomyrdin of Russia that 'he looked forward to visiting his beautiful country'. When he became prime minister, however, Tony did begin to take an interest and to think about what he wanted to achieve. One of his first overseas engagements was the G7 summit in Denver in June 1997. We chartered a British Airways Concorde to fly there, accompanied by the press. The other leaders welcomed him and listened carefully to what he had to say. He got a big cheer when he entered the stadium for the rodeo. During one gap in the proceedings, he took Alastair and me for a stroll in a nearby park. It was at the time when the handover of Hong Kong to the Chinese was taking place, and he suddenly said to us, apropos of nothing in particular, that Britain was too small to play a major role in the modern world and we must not give away any more territory. Alastair and I burst into laughter and christened it the 'bigger Britain' policy. Actually, it was an expression of Tony's desire to make Britain count for something again. Douglas Hurd and others in the previous government had talked a lot of 'Britain boxing above its weight', but in fact Britain had been sidelined in Europe and had little influence on the Clinton administration, not least because of Tory attempts to assist the Bush campaign's efforts during the 1992 election campaign to discredit Clinton by digging through his records while a student at Oxford. With Tony as prime minister, we were once again of significance in Europe and with the US.

The essential dividing line in foreign policy is between open and closed. On the one side, there are the internationalists who believe their country should be engaged in the world, open to free trade and immigration, and concerned about what happens in other countries. On the other, there are those who favour protectionism, isolationism and nativism. Superimposed on that fundamental divide is another split between advocates of realpolitik and idealists. Kissinger is of course the patron saint of the first group, which believes that national interests are best protected by shifting alliances even with countries of whose regimes you disapprove. Values are neither here nor there. The latter group believes that values are worth fighting for. They share the spirit that imbued those who volunteered to fight against Franco in the International Brigade during the Spanish Civil War.

Tony was firmly in the internationalist and the idealist camps. Over his first two years in office, he refined his thinking, and he set out his position in its fullest form in the Chicago speech of April 1999.

His argument was that we could no longer ignore what happens in other countries but had an interest and a duty to intervene if peoples were being suppressed by their rulers. The Peace of Westphalia of 1648 had brought to an end the Thirty Years War between Catholic and Protestant armies that had ravaged the Continent as each side tried to impose its beliefs on the other. The rulers of Europe finally accepted that they ought to tolerate what the other side did within its own territory and not seek to interfere. This Westphalian consensus lasted for the following three and a half centuries and was used to justify the non-interference of the West during the Cold War and our failure to come to the aid of the Hungarian uprising in 1956 or the Prague Spring of 1968.

With the end of the Cold War, however, it no longer made sense to ignore what rulers did to their own populations, not least because their actions could have consequences for us at home. We ignored Milosevic's ethnic cleansing in Bosnia, which resulted in a wave of refugees and crime in Europe, and we ignored the Taliban seizure of Afghanistan, which created a failed state from which terrorist attacks could be launched on the rest of the world. To their eternal shame the previous Conservative government, along with the rest of the global community, stood limply by while Rwandan genocide and Bosnian ethnic cleansing took place.

I had asked Lawrence Freedman, the distinguished professor of war studies at King's College London, to suggest passages for the Chicago speech, and he provided the five key tests for determining when force should be deployed. The five, which remained pretty much unchanged throughout the speech-writing process, were: 1. Are we sure of our case? 2. Have we exhausted all diplomatic options? 3. Are there military operations that we can sensibly and prudently undertake? 4. Are we prepared for the long term? 5. Do we have national interests at stake? The tests seem to me to be as valid now as they were then. Of course, it is relatively easy for Western societies to agree on the principle of interventionism. The problem comes in how to decide on when and where it should take place. The make-up of the UN Security Council makes it all but impossible to build consensus on military action to deal with dictators. In the cases of both Kosovo and Iraq, it was clear that there would be at least one veto on military action. The argument Tony made in Chicago was that we therefore needed to reform the UN to make it more capable of intervening in such cases. The Secretary General subsequently appointed a high-level panel which deliberated for many years on how the right to intervene should work, and it came up with sensible proposals in 2004, but they were not accepted by the member states. The permanent members of the Security Council (P5) did not want to give up their existing rights, particularly the right of veto, and as a result the UN is still incapable of taking action to stop dictatorial regimes carrying out atrocities from Burma to Zimbabwe.

As Tony delivered the Chicago speech, I was sitting next to a grizzled American businessman. Before he started speaking, my neighbour asked me if the speech would have any policy content and looked sceptical when I said it would. At the end he leapt to his feet, applauding wildly and yelling, 'Run for president.' Interestingly, the opposition to the speech at the time came from a young American academic at Stanford who insisted that it was a mistake to expend American blood and treasure overseas in the pursuit of ideals. The young academic was Condoleezza Rice, and 9/11 changed her attitude. After 9/11 the Bush administration, which had originally tended towards isolationism, adopted a new doctrine of the pre-emptive strike: that the US should be permitted to take military action to prevent a terrorist attack and should be able to do so unilaterally.

The approaches of the neocons and the liberal interventionists overlapped briefly in Afghanistan and Iraq, but we and they started from very different points. We liberal interventionists believed that unpleasant dictators who murdered their own people and posed a threat to their neighbours should be removed, both because what they were doing was wrong and the international community had a duty to stop it, but also because in the long run failure to stand up to their behaviour would pose a threat to us at home. The neocons believed in a new doctrine of the muscular defence of American interests and values, if need be by unilateral pre-emptive military action.

For me, the issue at stake over interventionism was summed up by a conversation I had with the chief of staff to the Iraqi prime minister in Baghdad in 2006. He was a Shia and described to me life in his village in the south of the country and invited me to visit. He said he didn't understand why the Western press said life was better before the invasion for ordinary Iraqis. People were 'disappeared' under Saddam, they were tortured, they were not free to say what they liked, and they lived in fear the whole time. So who were the Western press to say that the Iraqis should not be liberated? Of course it is impossible to ignore the terrible cost in human life in Iraq that followed the 2003 invasion when an assessment is made, but the desire to put an end to human rights abuses and the rule of terror is what motivates liberal interventionists.

The Chicago speech was made in the context of Kosovo, but Kosovo was not our first experience of war. That too involved Iraq after Saddam Hussein had thrown out the UN arms inspectors.

On 10 November 1998, the hotline phone on Tony's desk rang for the first time since we had arrived in government. It was Bill Clinton calling to tell Tony the date on which the bombing of Iraq would start. Predictably the hotline didn't work and we had to call Clinton back on another line. Four days later we got a call from the National Security Adviser, Sandy Berger, to say that, even though the B52s were already in the air, the attack had been called off. A letter had been received from Saddam indicating that he might allow the weapons inspectors to return. Cancelling an attack in mid-air is never a good idea because it is so hard to launch it again. The next day I listened in as Tony spoke by phone to President Clinton, Vice President Gore, Defence Secretary Bill Cohen and Sandy Berger, arguing with all of them. We were having a transatlantic National Security Council meeting by phone. Finally, in mid-December, Sandy called to say the attack was on again. It started on the evening of 16 December and I listened to it on the radio as I drove back to Belfast airport from a negotiation in Northern Ireland. The criticism in the media was that the bombing was ineffective. Life was continuing as normal in Baghdad. As we were concentrating on military targets, that criticism seemed a little misplaced.

The discussions with Clinton on what to do about Saddam's defiance had begun in January. We were worried the issue would separate us from the French and Germans, and I noted that we would be accused in the media of being poodles. Cynics would say that Clinton was undertaking the military action to distract attention from the Lewinsky controversy. Chirac told us he would denounce any attack on Iraq. Tony, however, decided it was important to stand with the US administration in launching military action, even without a UN Security Council resolution, to try to force Saddam to accept the weapons inspectors back into Iraq. The bombing campaign, however, did not succeed, and we had to come back to the issue again later.

Kosovo was an easier decision, even though again we could not get a UN Security Council resolution to authorise force. Milosevic simply could not be allowed to get away repeatedly with the sort of ethnic cleansing that he had practised in Bosnia. We started with an exclusively air campaign. On the British side, we had problems because our bombers could not operate in cloud and our new seaborne cruise missiles all ended up in the mountains instead of reaching their targets. Charles Guthrie, the Chief of the Defence Staff, was furious at the public criticism being offered by his retired predecessors. He said he would never participate in the game of being an armchair general once he retired. The trouble with air campaigns is that after you have hit the obvious targets, then what? The targets you choose are more and more marginal and the bombs are bound to hit civilians. As Tony said at the time, the other side become the victims. In any case, you can't take and hold territory by air and the other side can just sit it out, as Saddam had done.

Tony raised the idea of using ground troops when we went to the White House in April 1999. Clinton allowed Sandy Berger to make the argument against and heard it out. But the air campaign was not working. Once NATO forces had by mistake bombed a convoy of civilians and the Chinese Embassy, the situation began to look grim as we lost popular support for the campaign. Tony was worried that we were way out on a limb and it might be cut off behind us at any time. We discovered that there was a division within the White House on the subject. Hillary Clinton, Secretary of State Madeleine Albright and General Shelton, the Chairman of the Joint Chiefs, were all in favour of deploying ground troops, but Berger and the National Security Council were against. The spectre of Vietnam was very real for them, as well as the more recent debacle of the intervention in Somalia, made famous by *Black Hawk Down*.

Despite that weight of history, Clinton made the brave decision on using ground troops by 24 May 1999, giving us just time, we thought, to conclude the necessary campaign by winter. Chirac said we would need 500,000 troops to carry out the operation, and we were told that we would find Serbian troops very tough. Again this is a regular pattern. Before an invasion, you are always told that the opposing soldiers, whether Iraqi Republican Guard or Serbian army, are ten foot fall, but when operations start they prove better at running away than fighting, unlike guerrilla movements like the Taliban. At this time, Tony visited a refugee camp in Macedonia. He spoke to an old Kosovar there, who had told him that when the

Serbian troops arrived in his village they separated the men and women. The young women were taken off and raped, and the young men were taken off and never seen again. He himself had been beaten up and had a ruptured spleen. He had fled across the border into Macedonia with his wife and had ended up in the camp. The visit reinforced Tony's determination to succeed in Kosovo. Shortly after his visit, the War Crimes Tribunal in The Hague indicted Milosevic. This was cause for rejoicing, but it also raised a problem that you often run into during conflicts: if leaders are indicted, it makes them more inclined to fight to the bitter end. You can't offer them a deal whereby they are given safe passage to exile in return for surrendering. That can result in conflicts lasting longer and being bloodier with increased suffering. In this case, however, happily, it helped bring about Milosevic's eventual fall when the Serbian people overthrew him.

I had my first experience of the fog of war when I saw on CNN that Milosevic was finally surrendering in late May. I called the Foreign Office to find out what was going on. In a scene reminiscent of *Yes Minister*, they told me that I was the one with CNN so that I knew more than they did. There was one more drama even after Milosevic had surrendered. On 12 June John Sawers, the foreign affairs private secretary, came rushing into a meeting in the Cabinet Room to say that Russian forces had left Bosnia for Priština airport in Kosovo, and Wes Clark, the NATO Supreme Commander in Europe, had called to say that six Russian military planes were seeking overflight rights over Hungary. We wondered who, if anyone, was in charge in Moscow. Clinton had called Yeltsin, who appeared to be on another planet and who had suggested that the two of them meet on a submarine. Charles Guthrie and the Defence Secretary George Robertson came over to Number 10 from the MoD and revealed that Wes Clark was ordering General Mike Jackson, in charge of British forces at Priština, to hold the airport and to fire at the Russian troops if necessary. Mike was not keen on starting the Third World War and threatened to resign. In the event, it turned out that the Russian planes had not taken off and that the Russian troops from Bosnia had stopped in Belgrade. The Russians, it emerged, were just keen to be seen to be asserting their influence and relevance. When they eventually did arrive, we let them stay.

Machiavelli wrote: 'I do not mean to say that armed forces should not be used, but that they should be used only as a last resort, when the other means prove inadequate.' Wars are terrible things in all circumstances, but sometimes, rarely, wars can be better than the alternative. It is for that reason that Britain, up to now, has maintained strong volunteer armed forces prepared to risk their lives in battle. We do so not because we can fight wars by ourselves – we cannot – but because we think it important that we participate in wars with our allies when our interests and values are at stake. As Machiavelli says: 'Against [foreign powers] he will defend himself with good arms and good allies, and if he have good arms he will always have good allies.' That is why we went to such lengths to protect the Defence budget against the wilder depredations of Gordon Brown, although of course we were not able to secure increases as large as the MoD wanted or anything like as large as the increases in the Department for International Development's budget.

Politicians do not enter into wars lightly. It is usually the military themselves who are keener to become involved. In the case of Iraq in 2002, the Chief of the Defence Staff told us that the forces wanted to participate on the ground at division strength with their own command and that it would damage morale if they were restricted to a mere supporting role from sea and air while the Americans and others carried out the ground campaign. Indeed, the army had welcomed the original plan to invade Iraq from Turkey and to occupy Tikrit, Saddam's heartland, rather than the easier target of Basra. In Afghanistan later on, it was the military chiefs who argued for going into Helmand in strength once we lost the command in Kabul, although both Tony and John Reid, who was then Defence Secretary, were reluctant. In the end, it is the politicians, not the military, who have to make these difficult decisions and take responsibility for them.

General Dannatt's attack on the deployment of British forces in Iraq caught us completely unawares in 2006. Tony and I were engaged in delicate Northern Ireland negotiations in St Andrews. When we were told the news of the interview he had given to the *Mail*, saying that the presence of British forces in Iraq made things worse and they should get out soon, we couldn't get hold of anyone. Des Browne, who had succeeded John Reid as Defence Secretary, was in a plane on his way up to Scotland. The Chief of the Defence Staff was in Australia and unreachable; the Vice Chief was giving a lecture and couldn't be disturbed. And Dannatt himself was refusing to return calls. We thought for a moment about sacking him but concluded that that would just make him into a martyr. His comments certainly didn't help our troops in Basra; Muqtada al-Sadr's JAM militia leaders celebrated, claiming that his comments proved that their efforts were working and that they should redouble their attacks on British forces. We immediately received complaints from the NATO Secretary General, the Americans, Australians and other countries with forces serving in Iraq. Although some of the responses in the military Internet chat rooms were favourable, his fellow chiefs were furious with him. In the aftermath, we arranged for Tony to have a sandwich lunch with the service chiefs in Jock Stirrup's office at the MoD. Dannatt insisted on talking, and after a few minutes it was quite clear to me that he was unsuited to his job. Tony explained to those present that politicians would not support maintaining a first-division army if they were caused too much political pain by serving generals speaking out against their mission. It was always easier for politicians not to risk soldiers' lives. But I fear he was too subtle for Dannatt, who was divinely convinced of his own rightness.

The sort of surprise attack that Dannatt launched will make political leaders think twice if military action is proposed in future, certainly if the military engagement is likely to be sustained over a year or more. Our armed forces will no longer be deployed so regularly and will lose their cutting edge. We will gradually become more like Germany and other Continental countries, unable to put our armed forces in harm's way. That is a choice, but one we should make consciously and not just stumble into it. It would be another step towards losing the ability to control our destiny as a country, a far more important one than sharing our sovereignty in NATO or the EU. Already we have lost the capacity to fight major operations by ourselves. We could no longer muster a taskforce like the one Britain sent to the Falklands in 1982, and I was told by a general who participated in the invasion of Sierra Leone in 2000 that British forces would now even find it difficult to manage another operation like that.

There seems to be a sense in the British media that prime ministers enjoy going to war. They do not. The decision to send British soldiers into battle is the worst and most stomach-churning senior politicians have to take. It makes them wake up in the middle of the night in a cold sweat worrying if they have done the right thing. For prime ministers it is a lonely moment. They can't really confide in their fellow ministers or aides; it is a decision they have to make by themselves. In the run-up to Kosovo, Tony spoke to Mrs Thatcher on the phone and then a few days later asked me to invite her in to talk to him about deploying troops. She too had been in the lonely position of having to decide on war. I took her to the flat. She told me on the way up that my job must be very exciting. Her advice to Tony was not to try to fight a war through a committee.

It is the call in the middle of the night about military casualties that a prime minister dreads most. I remember being woken from a deep sleep by a call about a Chinook helicopter brought down by a tragic accident on the first day of the Iraq War, with the loss of eight British marines and four American soldiers. Switch said there was a military officer on the line for me, and my mind adjusted, wondering what it could be about. The clipped tones told me very matter-of-factly what had happened and I was shocked. Sarah woke up, saw the look on my face and cried out, 'Oh God, what's happened?' I arranged for the news to be passed to the Prime Minister.

But sometimes war is necessary. After 9/11 it was clear that military action was essential, but we were all a bit hazy about Afghanistan and the Taliban neither of which had been high on our radar screen till then. The day after the attack I walked up Whitehall to Waterstone's on Trafalgar Square and bought all the books I could find on the Taliban. By far the best was Ahmed Rashid's *Taliban: The Story of Afghan Warlords*, and I sat at my desk and read it right through. Tony and Alastair were keen to borrow it once I had finished. I thought the sensible thing to do was to send the Taliban an ultimatum. We should give them the chance to avoid an invasion if they would part company with al-Qaeda, but, if they did not, we should be absolutely clear that they would be toppled. The purpose of an ultimatum is twofold. First, it gives the other side an opportunity to comply, as we did with Saddam in mid-March 2003, setting certain specific conditions from Hans Blix's 'Clusters document', which if he met them would lead to the invasion being called off. The second purpose is to provide the *casus belli* if the conditions of the ultimatum are not met. And if they are not met, you need to be ready to act swiftly. But the most important thing of all, of course, is to mean it. If you make a threat, you must have every intention of carrying it out and the means for doing so. Machiavelli observes: 'To threaten to shed blood is, in fact, extremely dangerous: whereas to shed it is attended with no danger at all, for a dead man cannot contemplate vengeance.'

When we were trying to secure the return of British marines kidnapped by the Iranian Republican Guard in 2007, Tony wanted to up the rhetoric and to threaten Iran. After the Iranians started parading the captives on TV, he said we had forty-eight hours before we got heavy. I asked him what that would mean. What would the 'or else' be in this case? And that is still the West's problem: no one believes we will invade Iran, so that threatening to do so undermines our credibility rather than making the Iranians fret. In the end, we got the marines out by patient diplomacy. Our go-between was Ali Larijani, the former nuclear negotiator. He said that if we could say something conciliatory, then they could get Ahmadinejad to do the right thing at his press conference the next day. He said we would have to listen to the whole of the press conference right up to the last sentence before we reacted. Unfortunately, Margaret Beckett had just issued an aggressive press statement, but we were able to draw attention away from it with more conciliatory words from Tony. I watched Ahmadinejad's play-acting all the way through and almost missed his last sentence, in which he agreed to release the prisoners. I then went out to tell Tony who was sitting in a meeting in the garden. We got the marines back, but the problem of how to deal with Iran remains.

President Bush accepted Tony's idea of an ultimatum requiring the Taliban to break with al-Qaeda four days after we had proposed it, but when it was put to the Taliban they turned it down. There were reports that Mullah Omar, the Taliban leader, might have been prepared to surrender Osama bin Laden, but they came to nothing. We asked our military for a plan for an invasion, and Mike Boyce, the Chief of the Defence Staff, told us it would take 250,000 men to mount. We were taken aback. He suggested instead deploying aircraft carriers, submarine-launched missiles and marines, which puzzled me given that Afghanistan is landlocked. Then I remembered he was an admiral. In the event, the Taliban were driven out of Kabul by the Northern Alliance supported by US special forces and a bombing campaign. When we eventually tried to send our troops into Bagram airbase in Kabul in November, we kept our intentions so secret that most of the American military did not know we were coming. The American forces on the ground thought we were grandstanding and were about to turn our troops away. For their part the Northern Alliance forces objected to them coming in without permission and demanded that they leave straight away. We had to move very fast indeed to make sure they were allowed to stay.

Tony believed that, if we were to succeed militarily in Afghanistan, we had to build a wide multinational alliance in support, and so we embarked on a grand tour of the key countries shortly after 9/11. We went first to Berlin. Schroeder said he thought he could get his countrymen behind the deployment of German forces in Afghanistan. We went on to New York. After attending a memorial service for victims of the attack, we got stuck in the most terrible traffic in Manhattan and it was soon clear that we were going to be hours late arriving in Washington to see the president. On the plane I had the duty of telling Christopher Meyer, the British ambassador, that he was no longer coming to dinner in the White House. Christopher did not take being stood down well and threatened to resign on the spot.

We had thought about taking a helicopter into Washington from Andrews Air Force Base, but the motorcade was unbelievably speedy. Motorcycle outriders are one of the best symbols of the differences between national characteristics. American outriders are sedate on their Harley-Davidsons but ride en masse with many more bikers than in other countries, as befits a superpower. In France you only get two – but they are highly individualistic and ride the whole way at high speed on the wrong side of the road, steering their bikes with their thighs and using their hands to wave little wooden batons. Occasionally they actually kick cars to get them to move out of the way. The Germans ride in a very orderly V formation down the middle of the autobahn in front of the visiting dignitary, observing the road signs and traffic lights. The British motorcycle cops specialise in teamwork, forming a tag team with one of them screaming ahead to the next traffic light and then waiting there till the visitor passes through. Of course, if you are in a motorcade in your own country, you try to sink down in your seat so no one can see you. Everyone you hold up is a vote lost.

When we got to the White House, Bush was relaxed about postponing our meeting. He said he had already rehearsed the speech he was to give to Congress after dinner and was ready to deliver it. Tony told Bush that he had called President Khatami of Iran from the plane to try and secure his support for action. Even though the CIA had asked us to make the call, Bush asked 'Why talk to terrorists?' After dinner he took Tony up to the private quarters of the White House for a chat and then drove up the hill to Congress. The remarkable thing was that, despite his relaxed demeanour, he delivered a brilliant speech brilliantly. There were repeated bipartisan standing ovations.

Immediately after the Party Conference three weeks later, we left on the second leg of our world tour, starting in Moscow. Putin was resentful and told Tony he had warned the West about the threat from Islamic extremists. He complained about being excluded from the world's top table and not being treated properly by the Americans. He and Tony played snooker in his dacha and took a joint call from Bush. Putin agreed to support action against Afghanistan and at the last minute tried to persuade Tony to visit Tajikistan with him on our way to Pakistan. He said that Tajikistan would be the perfect base for action in Afghanistan, but we knew the Americans were negotiating with Uzbekistan to provide a forward base, and Putin's aim was to show who was in charge in the 'Stans' and not to have the Americans building alliances in the region. We declined.

Our flight to Islamabad was the last in the old VC10 of the Royal Flight that was about to be retired. It couldn't fly high enough to get over K2 so we had to go round it with a beautiful view of the mountain. As we approached Pakistan the crew became very tense. The plane had to come in to land by a series of corkscrews to avoid any danger of being shot down by a Stinger missile; and as we landed, the crew rather disconcertingly burst into applause (usually the passengers do that). The airport was surrounded by troops and so were all the roads to the presidential palace. Musharraf's office was stuffed with soldiers in old-fashioned uniforms with plumes on their turbans. When Tony and he went into his office for their one-on-one meeting, the bodyguards left the door ajar and kept a careful watch as the servants went in to serve tea. I asked Musharraf's aide why, and he told me they had to keep an eye on them so they didn't try to assassinate the president. Musharraf described Mullah Omar as being from another planet, more concerned about the next life than about the present one. He offered Pakistan's support.

When we returned to London, the idea of setting up a war room in No 10 was broached. I was against. The Americans, not us, were in charge. And while it is tempting for prime ministers to become armchair generals when campaigns appear bogged down, they then own any military disasters that follow. Political leaders should maintain a firm control of the strategic decisions but avoid the temptation to be drawn into making tactical military ones. They are best left to the generals on the ground. By this stage, Mike Boyce had reduced the requirements for a military operation in Afghanistan to 40,000 men with six months' advance planning.

We then embarked on the last leg of our tour, to Syria, Saudi Arabia and Israel. President Assad, who had only recently taken over from his father, was welcoming. His wife had grown up in Britain, and his father-in-law had been chairman of the Acton Conservative Party. He had a long and frank session with Tony while we were left sparring with Syria's old-school Soviet-style foreign minister. Assad then drove Tony and the rest of us down through the souk to the mosque where St Paul had worshipped when it had been a church; and, in the car, where he couldn't be listened to, he was even more honest about his difficulties in reforming Syria. But when Tony and he strode into the press conference an hour later a change came over him. I noticed Tony looking apprehensive as Assad launched into a long diatribe against Israel and in praise of various terrorist groups. The British press loved it: a complete embarrassment for the prime minister. Assad, however, did not oppose the war in Afghanistan, and the Saudis supported it too. We had succeeded in building a truly global alliance.

Tony's trip may have looked to cynics like window dressing, but it was important. If you embark on a military campaign like the one in Afghanistan, it is essential to build a wide international

coalition of support so that when you run into unforeseen consequences, as you inevitably will, you have others with you. And other
leaders will not support you unless you go and ask them face to face.
They are required to commit their countries and, although they may
feel sympathy after a terrible tragedy like 9/11, they may not feel
the need to incur the political and financial costs of action. We tried
to convince President Bush to garner an equally wide coalition of
support before embarking on the invasion of Iraq and made similar
efforts to build one. It was clear that the invasion would bring un-
intended consequences, and that the US and UK alone would be left
with the responsibility if things went wrong. But we were unable to
persuade the Americans of the importance of this a second time,
nor were we able to persuade many significant countries to join a
coalition in the different circumstances of Iraq. A prudent leader
would be careful to build a wide alliance before embarking on a
war, especially if there is the possibility of it being drawn out, not
swift.

Afghanistan and Iraq raise the issue of how to handle long and
unpopular wars. Small wars, like the invasion of Sierra Leone, or
wars that succeed rapidly, like the one in Kosovo, are popular once
they have succeeded, although it is worth remembering how many
commentators were opposed to Kosovo at the time. But the West no
longer seems to have the appetite for wars that do not have the
prospect of an early or total victory. This is partly a problem of an
attention deficit disorder that affects Western society more generally, born of twenty-four-hour news and celebrity culture. People
appear to expect instant gratification. The constant and sad spectacle of returning coffins make people despair, and the inability of
political leaders to articulate either why the cause is worth fighting
for and dying for, or to set out what 'victory' would look like, make
it hard for the public to see a successful end to the fighting or any
purpose to it.

It may also be that the assumption made by al-Qaeda and the
Taliban that Western society is post-decadent and no longer willing
to fight – and that, if they out-wait us, we will just go away – is
correct. But, even if it is, a prudent leader would not allow our
enemies to believe it, because to do so would be fatal. Isaiah Berlin
says Machiavelli 'is convinced that states which have lost the appetite

for power are doomed to decadence and are likely to be destroyed by their more vigorous and better armed neighbours'.

The 1990 Gulf War was the first major US deployment since Vietnam, and Colin Powell, who had been deeply scarred by his experience as a young officer there, was determined that the Americans should go in in such strength that they would overwhelm any opposition immediately. The Vietnam experience also persuaded him to resist any temptation to continue to Baghdad to topple Saddam. As a result, the Americans and their allies left the Shiites and Marsh Arabs, who had risen against Saddam at the time of that war, to fend for themselves and to be brutally massacred. Obviously it is right to learn the lessons of Vietnam and not to be dragged into a pointless quagmire again, but it is equally wrong to enter a war thinking about nothing but the exit strategy. That was what worried us about Defense Secretary Donald Rumsfeld when he said after the invasion of Afghanistan that 'we don't do nation-building'. That's what we were afraid of: all he and neocons were really interested in was chasing down Osama bin Laden. We thought the task was to prevent Afghanistan from becoming a failed state once again so that the life of the people would be better and we wouldn't go on being attacked from their soil.

If, after Iraq and Afghanistan, the US were to enter another lengthy period of isolationism, Britain and countries like us would be the principal losers. No other power in the world can intervene with the force and technological advantages of the US. The rising powers like China and India will fill some of the vacuum left by the US in their regions, but Europe will be expected to deal with its own neighbourhood, including Eastern Europe and the former Soviet Union and North Africa. That will require us to become serious about European defence and to develop real EU fighting capacity on a scale beyond anything seen so far.

To turn Karl von Clausewitz's dictum on its head, diplomacy is nothing but the continuation of war by other means, and we spent most of our time in government not fighting wars but trying to prevent them. We tried to apply the same dogged approach to negotiations that we had pursued in Northern Ireland,to disputes elsewhere between India and Pakistan, in Africa, but particularly in the Middle East.

Not that the Israelis always welcomed British offers of help. On their first visits to Jerusalem, both Robin Cook and Jack Straw received the traditional hazing that the Israelis administer to British foreign secretaries by organising an incident during a walkabout in a settlement, or some other embarrassment, to ensure that the new foreign minister is extremely reluctant to do anything that can cause offence in future. They are, of course, more careful with heads of government, but Ariel Sharon was always wonderfully patronising when Tony went to see him in Jerusalem. On every visit he would say to Tony: 'Thank you so much for coming and spending time on our problem when you have so many problems of your own at home.' Tony would persevere in trying to persuade the old bulldozer to do the right thing, but whether we had much or indeed any impact is hard to say. For our part, we now seem to have reached the situation where Israeli leaders cannot visit London without fear of prosecution. Jack Straw at one point told us he was thinking of attaching Sharon to the staff of the Israeli Embassy so that he would not be arrested during his visit.

Most of our pressure on the Middle East was applied through the Americans rather than directly on the Israelis or Palestinians. Having failed to gain any leverage on Clinton and the Camp David process, Tony tried hard to persuade Bush that addressing the Middle East peace process was the most important thing he could do. It was uphill work. Bush was convinced that Clinton had wasted his time and political capital on the Middle East, and he was not going to repeat his mistake. He did not believe that Arafat was acting in good faith or would ever conclude a deal and decided to wait till he was removed from the scene before making a real effort. He was probably correct in his assessment of Arafat, who was a perpetual negotiator. On the other hand, he was a charismatic leader who could have sold a deal to his people and to the Arabs more generally if he had wanted to, in the way that Ian Paisley was able to do in Northern Ireland, partly because of his personal history and partly because, as in the case of Paisley, no one ever believed he would agree to a deal. What came after Arafat was worse. A split on the Palestinian side meant that Fatah's leadership could never come to an agreement because they feared being outflanked by Hamas if they did. The Palestinian leadership was so weakened that it did not have the confidence that it could sell a peace agreement that would inevitably involve compromise. When Hamas won the elections in Palestine in 2006, we tried to persuade the Americans of a more modulated approach that would enable us to offer a carrot as well as a stick and to be able to deal with a coalition government of both Fatah and Hamas, but we failed.

Although Bush could never work out why Tony thought the Middle East conflict was quite so important, he did make commitments to us in the context of our support over Iraq. We pushed and cajoled him into releasing the Road Map just before the invasion, and we got him to endorse publicly a two-state solution. On 26 March 2003, he told Tony he would give the Middle East a real push and spend his post-Iraq invasion political capital trying to resolve the conflict. He said that he thought the Road Map was too timid. He wanted instead a new Madrid Conference and promised to halt Israeli settlements. When he came to Hillsborough in Northern Ireland for a summit immediately after the invasion – a site we had chosen because it was the only place we could think of in the British Isles where he would be safe from a massive anti-war demonstration – he committed himself to making the Middle East a priority. In the press conference after the meeting, he said he would devote as much time and as much effort to resolving the issue as Tony had to bringing peace to Northern Ireland. Privately, he said he would appoint a special envoy for the Middle East and convene a Madrid-style conference in London. We kept pushing him to appoint the envoy he had promised, but he never did.

My Democrat friends in the US told me I was being naive in believing that Bush would ever agree to make progress on the Middle East. My own belief is that he honestly intended to but was unable to in practice.

As he approached the end of his time in office, we suggested ever more insistently that Tony should have a role in the Middle East. Bush liked the idea and asked rhetorically if Tony could talk direct to Hamas in a way the Americans could not. I pushed the idea of Tony taking on a role with Josh Bolten, Bush's chief of staff, in the margins of the St Petersburg G8 summit in 2006. The famous 'Yo, Blair' TV clip from the summit was in fact a conversation in which Tony was trying to persuade Bush that he should visit the region in the midst of the Lebanon war, which had begun while we were at the summit, to try and broker a peace. Unfortunately it never happened.

Tony got badly caught in no-man's-land over Lebanon. He played a crucial role in negotiating a text at the G8 summit that could be agreed by the French, the Russians and the Americans. Thereafter he was reluctant to call publicly for a ceasefire, not because he didn't want the fighting and bloodshed to stop, but because he was more interested in bringing it to an end in practice than in saying the popular thing in public. The two didn't necessarily go together if he wanted to maintain any influence on the Israelis. As a consequence, he was severely criticised in Britain and lost support precipitously in the Labour Party. Since the Americans didn't give him a mandate to visit the region, he also failed to play the role that he could have in bringing the conflict more rapidly to an end. A wise prime minister would always eschew a declaratory foreign policy for a role in bringing about peace in practice, but it is difficult to balance the need to demonstrate to the people at home and in the wider world that you have moral principles with the need not to put yourself in a position where one party to the conflict will not talk to you because of what you have said publicly.

Towards the end of 2006, Condi Rice returned to the idea of Tony playing a role in the Middle East. She rang me to ask if Tony would still be interested in taking on such a role once he left Number 10 and, if so, would that be a problem with his successor, Gordon Brown. John Alderdice, the speaker of the Northern Ireland Assembly, presciently asked me if Tony might become the George Mitchell of the Middle East peace process, referring to George's role as the international chairman of the peace talks in Northern Ireland, little realising that George himself would take on the role of Middle East peace envoy under the Obama administration. It took quite a few months of negotiation to pin down Tony's job as the Quartet's representative, but we finally got it agreed just days before he left office.

It is all too easy to slip into thinking that there are easy answers to a conflict like Israel/Palestine. Gordon told Tony that the real answer was economic and if only Palestine could be built up economically then a political solution would follow. He sent Ed Balls out to the region, to pursue that economic solution. While it is perfectly true that Palestine is in desperate need of economic assistance, it is not the answer to the problem. The difficult political and security issues cannot be avoided. Those who search for painless solutions are just avoiding the hard questions.

The world is full of leaders, such as Mugabe, whom a British prime minister does not want to be seen meeting. When Tony attended the Pope's funeral in April 2005, he was horrified to discover that Vatican protocol had seated him and Cherie in the front row next to Mugabe, alphabetical order putting Zimbabwe next to the United Kingdom. Luckily, Mugabe had not yet arrived and Tony wandered to the back row and planted himself there despite attempts by the flunkies to shoo him back to his designated place. Later that year, when we arrived at UN headquarters in New York, we had another close encounter with Mugabe just after Jack Straw had been trapped into shaking his hand at a UN reception. As our motorcade pulled up at the entrance, Tony spotted the Bahraini prime minister at the front door and strode up to greet him. The official from the embassy travelling with us saw Mugabe standing behind the Bahraini, and Nigel Sheinwald and I rushed to position ourselves strategically behind Tony and with our backs to Mugabe. When Tony had finished talking to the Bahraini and turned round to enter the building, Nigel and I pushed him in the opposite direction and told him not to turn round. Mugabe lost another opportunity for an embarrassing photocall.

It is not sensible to leave pariah countries like Libya out in the cold over the long term. We made a major effort during our years in office to bring Gaddafi back into the international fold by negotiation rather than force. Our first approach came through Prince Bandar of Saudi Arabia in 1998, which kicked off a gradual process leading in the end to Libya agreeing to pay compensation for the Lockerbie bombing, extraditing the man suspected of carrying it out and settling the WPC Fletcher case. Our interest in making progress was intensified by the intelligence we received about Gaddafi's plans to acquire weapons of mass destruction. The final negotiations were undertaken by a dashing Lawrence of Arabia figure from SIS, and Gaddafi agreed to settle immediately after the invasion of Iraq. The eventual, humiliating capture of Saddam helped rub in the message of 'settle or else'. I heard first about Saddam's capture on a Sunday morning from a British colonel at Centcom who told me he had been authorised to tell us about it. I phoned Tony when he returned from church at Chequers to tell him and drafted a short statement to make when the capture became public. I sent the statement to David Hill. To my horror, he put it out straight away to the press, and we announced the capture before Washington had even learned of it. Bush was very understanding and had no problem with Tony doing the first TV statement to set the tone.

Tony's first contact with Gaddafi came in the form of a phone call in which Gaddafi said he was glad to be talking to 'a leader of oppressed peoples', which was presumably his way of describing a Labour prime minister. We eventually visited Tripoli in March 2004 and landed at an old US airbase that was littered with broken-down MiGs but otherwise looked much as it must have done when the Americans left in 1969. The Libyans deliberately took us to the compound that the Americans had bombed, killing Gaddafi's adopted daughter, even though we had made it clear we did not want to go there. They then took us out into the desert where we saw a smattering of rather unassuming tents and trucks beside a secondary road. There were twenty white camels milling around among the waiting journalists. Tony asked Gaddafi what the camels were doing there, and he said he didn't know. They weren't normally there, but our press people had asked for some local colour, so the Libyans had installed some traditional hangings and rugs in the tent and imported the camels. Gaddafi took us into the tent and asked his private secretary to bring in a chart of the Jamahiriya, the system of government set up after the revolution. He set up the chart on an easel in front of us. It was circular and extraordinarily complicated

Libya had been the last stop on a macabre terrorism tour. We had started in Northern Ireland, where we were in the final stages of trying to conclude peace, and then flew to Madrid for a memorial service for the victims of the al-Qaeda train bombings before ending up in Libya whence many of the weapons used in attacks in Northern Ireland had come.

Terrorism is a recurring problem for a modern prime minister. The bombings of 7/7 took place when we were at the G8 summit at Gleneagles in Scotland just after the triumph of winning the

Olympics for London. Tony was meeting President Hu of China. I was sitting next to Hu's chief aide who was turning the pages of his briefing cards as Hu spoke. I was marvelling at his ability to follow a prepared script that he had evidently succeeded in memorising word for word. A message was passed in to me saying that something had happened on the Tube, then another a few minutes later saying that there seemed to have been some sort of accident. I left the meeting and phoned the office in London, and it became clear that whatever it was it was serious.

I went back into the meeting and extracted Tony and we went upstairs to the UK delegation offices. I could get no sense out of the Metropolitan Police about what was happening but I did get a call from Tim O'Toole, an American who was head of London Transport. He knew exactly what had happened and was the lifeline that I held on to as I tried to keep briefed on events as they unfolded. The fog of war pervaded everything. At first, it wasn't at all clear that the attack was over, and there were suggestions of more explosions, so all Tubes and buses had to be stopped. I called my family to make sure they were safe. We decided Tony had to fly down to London but that the G8 summit should continue with Michael Jay, the head of the Diplomatic Service, in the chair. The other leaders held a joint press conference and expressed solidarity. The French ambassador asked if he could come with us because there were suggestions that French citizens had been caught up in the attacks. We took him on the RAF plane from Aberdeen to Northolt. When we asked for food, the RAF served up some two-day-old sandwiches. We were certain the ambassador thought this was a deliberate slight, given the unfortunate comments about British food that President Chirac had made a few days previously.

As we drove into London from Northolt, all public transport was shut down and the streets were lined with people trudging home by foot. It was eerily quiet and had a flavour of Blitz spirit to it. We went straight to COBR where the police, security services and ministers were gathered. They outlined the bare bones of what had happened and what was being done, but Eliza Manningham-Buller, the head of MI5, would not talk openly in front of so many people and we had to take her back to Number 10 to learn more. What shocked us was the realisation that the perpetrators were British-born, and, not only that, but also fairly comfortably off. We were worried both that there might be more bombers and that there might be a backlash against Muslims in Britain. Luckily the good sense of the British people prevailed and there was no retaliation. At first, there were suggestions of a fifth bomber, but there wasn't one. Michael Howard called to say that he would not play politics with the issue, but immediately afterwards went on TV to call for an inquiry.

In the aftermath, Eliza explained to us the great depths of the unknown around us. We had no idea how many networks might exist and how far they trailed back into Pakistan. She asked for more money and more staff for MI5 and we provided both immediately. The security service has since had a number of successes in frustrating plots, but it is still unclear how much of an indigenous threat there really is. It may be that we overreacted in piling so many resources into counterterrorism rather than into community relations, but if the security service asks for resources in those circumstances you have no choice but to provide them. If you do not, you will be held responsible for any disaster that follows.

A couple of weeks later Tony was entertaining John Howard of Australia to lunch in the small dining room on the first floor of Downing Street. I got a call saying that there had been an incident on the Tube. I spoke to Andy Hayman, head of counterterrorism, but he knew very little, so I called Tim O'Toole who had been so useful during the previous attack and he was able to describe to me what was happening minute by minute. Again the fog of war was thick, and it was unclear how many attackers there were and how many had got away. I went up to the lunch and dragged Tony out to go and attend COBR.

The most difficult decision for any leader is what to do if a terrorist attack is threatened. In 2003, we were told of a plot to shoot down a plane at Heathrow and were advised to deploy the army to protect the perimeter. The hope was that a visible presence would discourage any attack. We knew we would be criticised for using the army, but we also knew that, if we did not take the action and lives were lost, we would rightly be criticised even more. What we did not know until we saw it on TV was that the army would turn up in armoured cars. When we asked why, we were told that that was how they always deployed and that it was none of our business. As we had predicted, we were roundly criticised by the press for deliberately trying to scare people in the context of the war in Afghanistan, and the Tories piled in too, even though we had shared the relevant intelligence with them.

It is even trickier when you receive a threat and decide not to take action. On another occasion that year we received warning of a planned attack on the Tube. Tony chaired a COBR meeting and asked for advice. The police declined to advise whether or not the Tube network should be shut down, leaving the decision to Tony. He decided not to close it. To have done so would have caused displacement, and if there was going to be an attack, it would just happen somewhere else; and in any case you would be allowing the terrorists to cause the disruption they wanted. Instead he ordered an increased police presence and a raising of the state of alert. It was a brave and lonely decision. The Cabinet Secretary warned him afterwards that he had no cover. If it went wrong and there was an attack, he would have to pay a very high price. As we walked back to Number 10, Tony told me his daughter was arriving back from Paris at Waterloo the next day and I told him my son was leaving from Victoria at the same time.

The following day, when the IRA put out its historic statement ending its thirty-year campaign, I wrote in my diary, 'So one terrorist chapter closes just as another begins.' There is no easy answer to terrorism, whatever its origin. One component of the solution has to be talking to the terrorists in the way that we talked with Irish Republicans, and the same rule applies to new groups of terrorists as it did to the IRA. A prudent prime minister would be ready to talk to the Taliban and al-Qaeda, because in the end the only effective counter-insurgency strategy is one that combines tough security measures, so that the terrorists realise they cannot win, together with dialogue, demonstrating that there is a political and non-violent way forward to meet their grievance.

One of the things a leader needs to learn is how to use intelligence properly. It can be extremely useful but needs to be handled with great care. We had two advisers in Number 10, one madly for the euro and one madly opposed. I used to think that, if you were a foreign intelligence service and had the first of the two on your payroll, you would be certain Britain was about to join the euro and be equally sure we were not if you employed the other. So intelligence should be used to test your assumptions rather than to build a completely different picture of the world. It is also important to be careful with raw intelligence. No country has yet found the right way of dealing with it. In Britain, we have always prided ourselves in having the Joint Intelligence Committee, which assesses all the available intelligence and provides a homogenised product with an 'on the one hand and on the other' approach. The Americans have no such cross-departmental assessment system, and the different agencies evaluate their own intelligence product. The problem with the Joint Intelligence Committee, however, is that they produce lowest common denominator-type reports, hedging their bets and failing to give a clear steer in any direction. That approach makes their product less useful and makes it more likely that politicians will rely instead on raw intelligence.

There is always an institutional tension between Number 10 and the Foreign Office, particularly if there is a strong prime minister heavily engaged in foreign policy. When I was in the Foreign Office and my brother was Mrs Thatcher's foreign policy adviser, I attended the Permanent Secretary's morning meeting of senior staff. Every day part of the meeting was devoted to some new indignity that Number 10 had inflicted on the office, and those present would all turn and look at me in a meaningful way. When the then Foreign Secretary, Douglas Hurd, interviewed me for an assistant private secretary job, he mused aloud about having a Powell/Powell problem and decided, wisely, against hiring me.

We had the same sort of issues with Robin Cook and Jack Straw. They resented the fact that Tony was dominating foreign policy, leaving little space for them, and they disliked having to clear most of their decisions with us. Much of diplomacy these days is conducted between the offices of heads of government, particularly through the permanent conversation between the foreign policy adviser to the prime minister and the national security adviser in Washington. The same network of advisers operates in Europe. The German Chancellor and the French president each have separate foreign and European advisers, and they need to have someone in the British system to talk to. It is therefore essential to have a senior foreign policy adviser inside Number 10 who has the confidence of the prime minister and can build relationships with all their opposite numbers. Gordon Brown's experiment of removing the role from Number 10 backfired badly. We contemplated creating a National Security Adviser in Number 10 in 2007, but the post wouldn't in essence have been very different from the one filled by David Manning and then Nigel Sheinwald, and we decided creating it would have to wait for a successor government.

One of the most delicate parts of diplomacy is negotiating on international jobs. If another leader calls you and asks you to support a candidate, it is difficult to say no, but equally you don't want to commit yourself. In any case, you would normally expect something in return for your support. Gordon's interventions into the game were usually disastrous. He called Tony in March 2002 demanding that he phone Schroeder to tell him that the German candidate for the IMF, Horst Kohler, was unacceptable and should not get the job. When Tony called, Schroeder appealed personally to him in the strongest terms, promising all sorts of sweeteners in return and explaining that, because the nomination had become public, he would lose face if he failed. Tony agreed to support him but when Gordon got wind of the decision he attempted to forbid the Number 10 press office from announcing our support. Gordon tried the same approach when Paul Wolfowitz was proposed by Bush as the head of the World Bank in 2005. He demanded Tony veto Wolfowitz. In Number 10 we could see no point in opposing the appointment: it was an American job and President Bush had decided to give it to Wolfowitz. All we would achieve by opposing the appointment would be to create an enemy for life. One American candidate we would have strongly supported was Bill Clinton. President Bush surprised us by suggesting him as a candidate for the UN Secretary Generalship in 2005. He would have been a strong secretary general, which is exactly what is needed, but unfortunately the conventions prevent a P5 national taking the job.

The main problem with the UN is that the membership of the Security Council no longer reflects the true balance of power in the world. But there is no way any existing member will agree to drop off, nor is it possible to agree who the new members should be. Nigeria won't agree that South Africa should be the African representative, nor will Mexico accept that Brazil should join without them, nor will China accept that India can join. So as well as becoming increasingly powerless, the UN is in danger of becoming increasingly irrelevant. Given our inability to change the Security Council, we tried instead to build a new, representative, global body out of the G7. First, we cut the G7 back to heads of government only and abolished the huge travelling circus of foreign and finance ministers that used to accompany it, and we then, in 1998, formally added Russia to make it the G8. The G8 summit retreat that year was held at Weston Park, a stately home just outside Birmingham, and the highlight for me was the visible panic in the US secret service when they realised that they had lost President Clinton, who had strolled off across the parkland with Jean Chrétien for some fresh air. I pointed out to them where the president had gone and they launched a manhunt. The next time we held the presidency of the G8 we invited the other key countries of the world, including China, India, South Africa and Brazil, to attend as well. Mexico made a huge fuss so we allowed them to come too. This is essentially the same membership as that of the G20, which has become the main forum for coordinating economic policy and is likely to take over political and foreign policy responsibility from the G8 and from the UN Security Council. It alone has the right membership to reach global decisions that will stick.

Russia has ceased to be a superpower, and it was probably a mistake to add it to the G8 given the size of its economy, but it is important to show the Russians respect if we want them to behave responsibly. They feel very bitter if they are excluded from the global top table, and we did what we could to make them feel loved. Tony went out on a limb to support Vladimir Putin even before he became president. We decided in December 1999 that he looked like a reformer, and Tony went to meet him in St Petersburg in the middle of the presidential campaign. He decided to cut Putin some slack on Chechnya in a way other Western leaders had not, and he defended him to the Western press at their joint press conference. The meeting took place in the newly restored Peterhof Palace outside St Petersburg. On the way out of the city, Putin pointed out to Tony the shabby block of flats where he had grown up as a child. When we got to the palace, we had to put on special slippers to protect the floors. Rod Lyne, our ambassador, managed to break a priceless seventeenth-century chair when we sat down at the beginning of the session. Putin demanded compensation, only half jokingly.

Putin impressed us by conducting the entire meeting without briefing notes. Even leaders as bright as Al Gore used to depend on clutch cards to remind them of key questions. That evening Putin took us to the Kirov to see an opera about 1812 and the Russian defeat of Napoleon. It was glorious to cheer along with the Russians in the tsar's old box as the French flag was trampled underfoot. After that Putin became a friend, at least for a while, and even called in the middle of the 'hanging chads' saga in the American presidential election to ask if he should call Bush to congratulate him on his victory. We advised him to wait.

It was hard to maintain warm relations, however, after the Russians killed a dissident on our soil, especially doing so in a way that put so many other people's lives at risk. When we first discovered that a number of BA planes that plied the London to Moscow route had been irradiated, the BA crew deserted their plane at Moscow airport. The police discovered two trails of radiation criss-crossing London, one left by Alexander Litvinenko, the unfortunate victim, and the other by his killer, who had returned to Moscow. We considered ways of retaliating, like imposing visa restrictions, but Tony rejected all of them and said we would just put relations with Russia in the freezer. We received no support from the Americans or the Europeans in our dispute.

If you want to create a lasting friendship with another leader, it is important to reach out to them while they are down politically and at their most vulnerable, as Tony did with Bill Clinton at the height of the Monica Lewinsky scandal. As that crisis intensified, Tony had me send a message of support to Clinton via Sidney Blumenthal who told me that the White House staff was in panic but that Clinton was grateful for the message. When Tony called Clinton on 27 January 1998, Clinton made it clear that he did not want to talk about the issue on the phone. It is impossible for presidents to have a frank conversation on the telephone with tens of aides listening in, but he said they could discuss it when Tony came over. We flew to Washington a week later for Tony's first official visit as Prime Minister on a chartered Concorde. We landed at Andrews Air Force Base in a thunderstorm, and the scheduled nineteen-gun salute had to be cancelled. Tony stayed in Blair House, the presidential guest house opposite the White House, which Clinton said jokingly in his welcoming speech 'will for evermore be named after you'. They went on a visit to Blair High School just outside Washington. Tony had prepared a serious speech about education but threw it away when he saw the school's gym full to the rafters with pupils wearing Blair sweatshirts and in a raucous mood. Every time he or Clinton mentioned 'Blair' the place erupted in cheers. The event helped to energise Clinton who was preoccupied with the Lewinsky affair.

The main event, though, was the press conference on the second day. Clinton came down to Tony's holding room before they went in, clearly nervous. His aide Rahm Emanuel was whispering in his ear about developments in the Lewinsky case. Tony had made a conscious decision to give him his full support, and he stood up for Clinton marvellously in the press conference itself, although he was criticised in the UK for doing so. Clinton was deeply grateful, and it laid the basis for a remarkably warm relationship throughout their time in office and thereafter. A prudent prime minister in these circumstances will always stand by his man.

In 2001, Tony managed to make the difficult transition from Clinton to Bush. Tony thought it important to have a close relationship with the US president, whether he was an ideological soulmate or not. Clinton, on a farewell tour, was staying at Chequers when Al Gore finally conceded defeat. Tony helped Clinton with his remarks on Gore's defeat, and Clinton advised Tony on how to handle Bush. They went together to Warwick University for a farewell event. John Prescott had asked to come and was rather overwhelmed by the panoply surrounding the president. He had a letter he wanted to give Clinton, but he told me he was afraid he would be shot by the secret service if he did so and he gave it to me to deliver. I got him to shake Clinton's hand. After the tearful farewells to the American delegation and as Marine One rose over the university, Tony went into the vice chancellor's office to phone Bush and congratulate him. Tony said that he had been a good friend to Bill Clinton and would continue to be so now that he had left office. Bush said he understood and would have thought less of Tony if that had not been so. Luckily, the two men had a mutual friend in Bill Gemmell, who had been at school with Tony at Fettes, and whose father had been in the oil business with Bush Sr and at whose house in Scotland Bush Jr had holidayed as a boy. Bill was able to assure each of them that they would like the other.

Tony sent me and John Sawers, our foreign policy private secretary, to see the Bush team before the inauguration. The transition office was quite different from the Clinton one I had known in 1992. That had been noisy and full of young people rushing around and eating pizza, like a student dorm. This one was hushed, sedate and with ultra-thick carpets, like a corporate office. I met Dick Cheney, who was remarkably monosyllabic. I charged through all the messages I had been told to deliver and, after gabbling away at a breakneck pace for ten minutes, subsided into silence. Cheney looked at me for a few moments and then asked, 'How's Charles?' He had known my brother in Mrs Thatcher's time and in the corporate world. I felt suitably put down. I preferred Josh Bolten, a young ex-banker who was then Bush's deputy chief of staff, but whom I marked down for greater things. He later became head of the Office of Management and Budget and eventually took over from Andy Card as chief of staff.

It was during Tony's visit to Camp David in February 2001 that he and George Bush cemented their relationship. Most of the press comments were about Tony's overtight trousers and Bush's comments on toothpaste. They overlooked Tony's wooing of Bush. Bush liked leaders he could trust. He held against Schroeder the fact that he had promised to be with him on Iraq when they met in the White House but a few months later turned against him. Bush gave us a warm family welcome at Camp David, and in the evening both delegations watched *Meet the Parents* in the private cinema. Condi Rice had the good sense to go to sleep and had to be woken when the lights came up. We had been told that Bush greatly admired Churchill, and so we had brought with us as a gift a cheap imitation bust of the great man. But we took one look at it and realised it wouldn't do. Instead, we arranged for a famous Epstein bust to be loaned to the White House, and Bush kept it in the Oval Office during his entire time in office. The meeting came to an unexpectedly early end the next morning and as a result, we left Cherie's hairdresser André and the Garden Room girl behind at Camp David. We had to send Marine One back to collect them once we had arrived at Andrews Air Force Base. André was a quivering wreck, afraid he would never see England again.

Bush had an endearing ability to laugh at himself and did not mind being laughed at by others. In our fortnightly videoconferences from 2003 onwards, he would be at one end of the table in the Situation Room in the White House with Condi and Andy Card. Dick Cheney would join from another location, appearing at the top of the screen in a separate picture looking ominous and wearing headphones. We would be in the basement of Number 10, where we had built a secure videoconferencing suite. Bush had a habit during the videoconferences of being upbeat about everything, even the dire situation in Iraq. In October 2006, he was in a terrible position politically, in the depths of his unpopularity, but he told us with a straight face that everything was going swimmingly in the forthcoming midterm elections and that the Republicans were going to do really well. Nigel Sheinwald and I thought he was joking and both collapsed in helpless laughter. Luckily, Tony realised he wasn't joking and kept a straight face so that Bush didn't take offence.

There are two approaches to trying to influence the Americans. The first is the French way, pioneered by General de Gaulle, which is to be as cussed as possible in the hope that the Americans will seek after you and pay a big price to bring you back on board. The other is the traditional British way, which is to try and stay as close as possible to the Americans in the hope of being included in their counsels.

We opted for the latter, but there is a trade-off. If you want to exercise such influence, you have to keep quiet about it. We learned this lesson rather abruptly over Kosovo. When an article appeared in the *New York Times* about Tony's courage in pushing for the deployment of ground troops and about Clinton's dithering, Clinton called Tony from Air Force One absolutely incandescent. He knew what was going on. We were positioning Tony as the macho one and him as the weak one. It had to stop. I had never heard him so angry. Sandy Berger threw in for good measure that we could invade Kosovo with British ground troops without the Americans if we wanted to. Tony managed to talk Clinton down, explaining that we had had nothing to do with the article, and friendly relations were resumed,

but it was a salutary lesson about how to handle the Americans. If
you want to have influence, you have to give your advice in private.
If you boast about your successes, or brief the media on your role,
you immediately negate any influence you have and deal yourself
out of internal American discussions. The bind for a British prime
minister is that you therefore cannot tell your own public about
the arguments you have won and the influence you have had, so you
are accused of having no influence at all and of being nothing more
than a poodle following American instructions. That is what happened
to us over Afghanistan and Iraq with President Bush. We kept our
advice private, we shifted the American position – for example on
going to the UN on Iraq over Dick Cheney's nearly dead body – but
we could not tell people that that is what we had achieved. A wise
prime minister would accept this trade-off and shrug off the charges
of 'poodlism' in return for real influence over the policy of the world's
only superpower. He should support his fellow leader when things
get tough because they will remember it, but be careful in following
them down a particular path unless he knows a way out. Otherwise
he may find it hard to retrace his steps.

Britain always has an alternative. It could adopt a declaratory foreign
policy, as the French do, and win support around the world by saying
things people want to hear. But that would result in our having less
influence in Washington and less ability to change anything in the
real world. It is for that reason that, so far at least, Britain has always
stuck to doing rather than saying, and a prudent British prime minister
will always prefer influence on real events to merely cutting a *bella
figura*.

Britain is teetering on the edge of becoming irrelevant in foreign
policy terms. If we have neither the strong transatlantic relationship
nor a central role in Europe, we will fall back to our natural weight
in the world, measured by population and wealth, somewhere around
Italy. To allow this to happen would be a betrayal of our heritage.
The only way in which a slide into irrelevance can be countered is
by a strong leader who can build firm personal alliances, win the
confidence of the US president, be a central player alongside France
and Germany in the EU, and have the courage to take a leading role
in world events. We must be a firm friend or a thorough foe if we
want to prosper.

CHAPTER TWELVE

'The Arrogance of One Who Rises to Power in a Republic'

Hubris and Leaving Office

Machiavelli writes that 'Those who governed the state of Florence from 1434 to 1494 used to say it was necessary to reconstitute the government every five years; otherwise it was difficult to maintain it.' Some countries, like the US, have term limits built into their constitutions, so that a leader can only remain in office for two terms; but even in countries that do not have a formal constitutional require-ment of this sort there are now, in my opinion, effective informal term limits. If leaders want to leave power on their own terms, they cannot stay in office for more than ten years. People's attention span is shorter now than in the past, the media are in the market for a new narrative, everyone is bored, and for the same reason that the shelf life of celebrities has become shorter and shorter, so has that of politicians.

Mrs Thatcher was bundled out of office by her party after outstaying her welcome, and Jim Callaghan, John Major and Gordon Brown were dispatched by the electorate. Even leaders who know that they should really depart can always find a reason to stay just another six months or one more year to sort out some problem or other. They miscalculate the length of their welcome and find them-selves chased from office. In some cases, leaders declare they will serve for only two terms, as José María Aznar did when he was first elected in Spain, and then stick to it. It is not possible for a leader in a modern democracy to last longer than two full terms without people wanting to be shot of them, and it is sensible to leave before the voters or your colleagues show you the door.

Tony wanted to leave at a moment of his own choosing, but it is always difficult to identify that moment. As early as March 2002, I told Alastair Campbell that I felt we had arrived at the beginning of the end. He looked nonplussed and said he didn't understand how the end happened. I said it was not a case I could make logically, just something I felt through the hairs on the back of my neck. From then on the end was constantly in my thoughts. In June 2002, Tony told us he might stand down at the next election and perhaps even announce his departure in advance. A month later he said he felt more comfortable now that he had decided to resign before the next election. He was still toying with how to make the announcement. During the lead-up to the Commons vote on the Iraq War in 2003, Andrew Turnbull, the Cabinet Secretary, kept popping into my office demanding to be shown the Labour Party's rules for selecting a successor if a leader resigned in office. He was trying to plan the succession if Tony lost the vote in the Commons. And in May 2003, Tony was again agonising about whether to run for a third term or not. He told Gordon he might suddenly announce that he wasn't running for a third term and Gordon panicked, saying, 'But then you would lose all your power of patronage.' He was clearly worried that announcing a sudden but not immediate departure would give others time to organise leadership campaigns against him. The problem I raised every time that Tony said that he wanted to go was that, if he announced his departure in advance, he would from then on be a lame duck. His power would flow away in an instant. And that near certainty, among other things, made him hesitate.

The pressure for Tony to go started to build up in earnest in 2004. When Tony asked me for my opinion, I said that he should not go just yet but he should stay in office for ten years and not try to stay for twelve years to match Mrs Thatcher. Tony said he felt that, if at the next election he said he was standing for a full third term, then he had to mean it and actually to remain for the whole of the term. We discussed the matter again a few weeks later. Alastair advised him to go, but Peter Mandelson felt strongly that he should stay. Peter thought we had to put on a new display of energy instead of looking as if the air had gone out of us. Using the analogy of the Thatcher period, I said that we were in 1986 and that that had not been the end for Thatcher but a moment of recovery. Now should not be the end of Tony. I wasn't certain, however, that Tony himself had the spirit to fight on. He was in the midst of his now well-chronicled wobble.

Finally, towards the end of May, Tony began to fight back. He took a leaf from Harold Wilson's book. When asked in 1969 about plots against him and suggestions that he might be leaving, Wilson announced, 'I know what's going on. I'm going on.' Tony told Sally Morgan and me in June that he had decided to stay on after the election. Andrew Turnbull came to us with a plan for Tony to move out of Number 10, so that a £45 million refurbishment of the building could take place. Number 10 was badly in need of emergency work; the electric riser into the building was running red hot. We said no, partly because we were worried about the symbolism of his leaving Number 10 combined with his heart condition which had been diagnosed the previous year. We decided the refurbishment could not be started before the election.

After the 2004 summer holidays, Tony said he had decided to serve a third term but that he would not seek a fourth. He then astonished us by rather coyly telling us that he had bought a £3.6 million house in Bayswater while he was contemplating resignation earlier in the year. Peter Mandelson saw no problem, but I was worried that the price would leak and horrify most people. Tony dropped another bombshell on us after his conference speech in September. In his Brighton hotel suite, he told David Hill, Sally and me that he had to go back into hospital for another heart operation. Perhaps, he said, he should give up after all, if the people of Britain no longer wanted him. Even I started to wonder if eight years weren't actually enough. We concluded that we had to get all three bits of news out together: house, heart and the decision to run for a third term. The announcement that he was staying on would cancel out the two other pieces of news, which suggested that he might be about to depart. To my surprise we managed to keep all three parts of the package secret until the announcement on 30 September.

That day, we divided up the members of the Cabinet, and each of us rang a number of them, just as Tony was going into hospital, to tell them the news. When I spoke to Gordon's ally, Alistair Darling, he said, 'So that means he will retire in the middle of the next term.' I said, 'No, he is serving a full term.' He said, 'Well, people will think he will retire early.' I said, 'No, we are explicit. He will serve a full third term. His successor will serve a fourth term.' He laughed and said he got the message. Gordon was in Washington in a meeting with the US Treasury Secretary. We called him, but he wouldn't come out of the meeting so I had a note giving him the news passed in to the meeting to his private secretary. The aide left the meeting and phoned back saying that he had been passed a garbled message. Once we had repeated it and Gordon had grasped it, he was furious. He accused us, through the papers, of conducting an 'African coup' while he was abroad. Funnily enough though, he was the one who first publicly announced that Tony was going into hospital. Colonel Gaddafi and Ayad Allawi, the prime minister of Iraq, sent flowers, and Prince Charles sent a get-well card along with a box of Duchy of Cornwall fudge from 'Dr Wales'. Unfortunately, the box fell foul of the Number 10 security screening process for outside mail and, as a suspicious parcel, the box and the fudge were duly blown up. They sent me the remains afterwards, since the card was handwritten, asking who it was from.

The 2005 election was an ordeal, even leaving aside Tony's inflamed disc. Gordon and Tony were campaigning together, and all the time Gordon was pushing him to set a date for his departure and to endorse him as his successor. Alastair and Philip held meetings with Gordon Brown's team on a transition. Alastair emailed me to say that, if I wanted to, I could be Ed Balls's driver in the new regime. After the election Cherie wanted Tony to go straight into hospital for an MRI scan on his back. I said that if he went into hospital he would come out politically dead, so the appointment was put off till later. We were beginning to lose control of the party. A public row had broken out between Cabinet members on a proposed ban on smoking, with Patricia Hewitt siding with the doctors and John Reid with the working men's clubs. When we tried to rein both of them in, they each blamed the other. It also looked as though we would lose the vote on legislation allowing terrorist suspects to be imprisoned for ninety days without charge; if that happened, it would be seen as another example of power deserting Tony. He said he would rather be defeated than back down, but it all felt very *fin de régime*.

When Tony and Gordon met at Chequers in December 2005, Tony told him that he was not going in 2006. Gordon threatened all sorts of consequences and said if that were so, he would make his own dispositions. Tony got up and said the meeting was over. They would just have to fight it out. In March 2006, I went down to Chequers and got a bit of a shock because all the furniture had been removed from the Great Hall. I thought perhaps it was a sign that Tony, unknown to me, was planning to leave, but it turned out just to be in preparation for Kathryn's eighteenth birthday party. A few days later, Gordon gave an interview to the *Sun* suggesting that Tony should quit now or face the fate of Mrs Thatcher in being forcibly ejected. Tony concluded that Gordon's aim was to make his life so miserable that he would plead to go, but he wasn't going to give in. When Tony met Labour MPs threatening to rebel on the education bill later that week, they told him that they wanted him to run again at the next election in order to protect their own seats but that, if he was going to go, then he should go as soon as possible.

In April 2006, John Prescott held another of his peacemaking dinners in Admiralty House. I walked out of the back gate from the Number 10 garden with Tony and across Horse Guards Parade. Tony was in a fighting mood. John proposed that Tony should leave the following July, but Gordon demanded an earlier date. When Tony and Gordon went to launch the local election campaign together the next day, they didn't say a word to each other in the car. Tony told me that even the detectives had found it excruciatingly embarrassing. Things were so bad that the BBC fielded a body-language expert to comment on the event rather than a political correspondent, and Tony deliberately put his arm round Gordon to try to deal with the problem. Two days later, Tony finally decided that he would leave in July 2007 and that during his last fourteen months in office he would ignore Gordon and put in place those reforms that he really cared about.

Gordon's first attempted coup took place after the local elections that spring. We knew the results would be bad, and we stacked the post-election television and radio programmes with loyalists as far as we could. I stayed in London, while Tony went on an overseas trip, to stymie the worst of Gordon's efforts. Luckily the results were not quite as bad as we feared, but Gordon's hit-and-run tactics were taking their toll.

Gordon gave a broadcast interview in which he said that he had no idea when Tony would go and that he had not discussed the issue with him. To try and reduce the pressure, Tony used his monthly press conference to make it clear that he planned to leave about halfway through the Parliament. Gordon came round to see him immediately afterwards and said menacingly that he 'had his answer now'. The media assumed from what Tony had said that he would be leaving in the summer or autumn of 2007, so we hoped we had managed to buy an extra year without conceding anything – a tactical retreat to ensure strategic success, or so we thought. Tony started planning his valedictory speech for conference. The next day an opinion poll showed us eight points behind. Tony said to me, 'So that's it then.' The media were bored with him and were desperate for a new story. Perhaps the public were, too.

Gordon, emboldened, went on *GMTV* and expressly denied three times that he had ever discussed a departure date with Tony. It was biblical: three denials before the cock crowed. John Denham went on *Newsnight* to call for a leadership election. The quandary Tony now found himself in was that he no longer thought that he ought to hand over to Gordon. He thought Gordon had given the Labour Party licence to 'be unserious again'. We consciously decided to adopt a Micawber strategy of hanging on and hoping that something would turn up. There didn't seem to be any alternative. The Number 10 staff grew nervous and some of them wanted to leave. Michael Wills, a Gordon loyalist, went on television to say that Labour would lose the next election unless Gordon could take over straight away. Sally told us that MPs were enervated and thought it inevitable that Gordon would become the next leader and also inevitable that we would lose the subsequent election. They just wanted the pain to end, even though the opinion polls continued to show the Labour Party further behind the Tories with Gordon at the helm than with Tony.

John Prescott during this period was in a miserable state following a row over his non-payment of council tax and the publicity surrounding his affair with his diary secretary. From time to time, we would hear rumours from the party's General Secretary that John had asked for the Labour Party rules on elections and was about to resign, precipitating both leadership and deputy leadership elections. When Gordon learned in July that Tony was addressing the annual Newscorp conference in LA, he demanded to know what he was going to say. Tony said light-heartedly, 'Oh, I guess I will talk about the need to jump a generation in the Labour Party so you don't become leader.' Gordon didn't appear to see the funny side. We had made the theme for the party conference, at my suggestion, 'New Labour, New Generation'. Before the summer, I concluded in my diary that 'the situation is grave but not hopeless'.

When we came back from the summer holidays, the whole situation became a lot more grave. So far, Gordon's tactics had been to feint and withdraw, but this time he had clearly decided to make a serious attempt at a coup. Our unpopularity in the country made us vulnerable. As Machiavelli says, 'a Prince has little to fear from conspiracies when his subjects are well disposed towards him; but when they are hostile and hold him in detestation, he has then reason to fear everything and everyone'.

On 31 August, Tony gave an interview to *The Times,* and was surprised when the headline turned out to be that he had refused to give a date for his departure. That was the signal for Gordon to mobilise his troops, even though Tony had told him that he would go the following year and that this would be his last conference. Sally and Alastair thought that Tony might have to stand down at the conference itself. He was haemorrhaging support. On 4 September, Tony's new PPS, Keith Hill, got hold of a letter circulating among Labour MPs from the 2001 intake calling on Tony to go. Two of the letter's signatories were former Blairites who had not been given jobs in the most recent reshuffle, Siôn Simon and Chris Bryant. Another was Tom Watson, a junior minister in the MoD. They thought they had waited long enough for promotion, and now they appeared to have an offer from the next leader. As Machiavelli wisely says, you 'cannot keep the friendship of those who helped you gain [power]; since you can neither reward them as they expect, nor yet, being under an obligation to them, use violent remedies against them'. It was a case of the equation of the appointed versus the disappointed coming back to haunt us. There were two more letters circulating among the 1997 and 2005 intakes. I called Tom Watson, and he eventually called back and we had a rather frosty conversation. I asked him if he was planning to resign since he had signed a letter calling on the prime minister to go. He said no and asked if I was telling him to resign. I asked him how the letter was compatible with his remaining a minister, and he had no answer.

Tony took a fatalistic view. If the PLP did not want him to stay, he would go. His staff, however, were determined to fight. The next day Gordon threatened a second wave of letters so we organised a rival letter from Tony's supporters in the PLP and got David Miliband to go on television to say that Tony would go by July in the following year. I got a call from Josh Bolten, now Bush's chief of staff, asking how Tony could be replaced as prime minister without an election. I tried to explain the parliamentary system. On 6 September, Gordon came to see Tony for a meeting that lasted two hours. He had three demands: that Tony endorse him as leader, that they have a co-premiership till Tony left and that Tony suppress Alan Milburn, Steve Byers and any other critics. Gordon said he could get Tom Watson to recant, but only if Tony met all his conditions. Tony refused and said he was going to sack Watson. Gordon contacted Watson immediately after the meeting and persuaded him to resign before we could sack him, at the same time sending the most damaging resignation letter he could concoct. That launched a rolling programme of suicide bombers as junior members of the government began resigning one after another. Gordon had insisted on arriving and leaving through the side door of Number 10 for the meeting, but as he left he was photographed through the window of his car with a sinister smirk on his face. The whips had been negotiating with one PPS, Ian Wright, about his concerns over his local hospital. Wright said he did not want to resign but that he shared a flat with Tom Watson and felt he had to. In this febrile atmosphere, everything gets over-interpreted. Hilary Benn, Alan Johnson and Jack Straw came to a meeting in Number 10. They were all supportive of Tony, but the media who had seen them arrive declared that they were 'the men in grey suits' who had come to tell him to go. We discovered that Gordon, rather ominously, had chosen that moment to finally move into the Number 10 flat.

The next day John Prescott weighed into the debate, demanding that the timetable for Tony's departure should be agreed with the NEC and not just announced in the *Sun*. Tony had to put up with ten minutes of finger-jabbing and shouting. By that stage, though, Tony had reached a Zen-like state. Gordon phoned to talk to him but I declined to put the call through. Tony had decided what he wanted to do. He went to a city academy accompanied by Alan Johnson and made his announcement, complete with self-deprecating jokes. He said what he had been planning to say at conference in a few weeks' time: that this would be his last conference and that he would go in the middle of next year.

The terms of trade changed overnight. The Labour Party's phone banks were jammed with calls from party members fed up with the way Tony had been treated. As Machiavelli says, 'Not to be hated or despised by the body of his subjects is one of the surest safeguards that a Prince can have against conspiracy. For he who conspires always reckons on pleasing the people by putting the Prince to death; but when he sees that instead of pleasing he will offend them, he cannot summon courage to carry out his design.'

At first, Gordon put up Doug Henderson to say that they were not satisfied with Tony's statement, but then he thought better of it and briefed the papers that he had won and claimed that Tony had agreed to all his conditions. We immediately made it clear that he had not. Gordon called to demand that Tony endorse him at conference. Tony said that his support would have to grow organically. Gordon also demanded that Tony denounce Charles Clarke, who had dared to criticise him. He refused to do so. Alastair and Sally wanted to persuade a rival candidate to compete with Gordon for the leadership but I was worried that such a move would only expedite Tony's departure. Bit by bit Gordon's involvement in the coup became public. First it was revealed that Tom Watson had visited him in his house in Scotland just before the coup. They acknowledged that they had met but implausibly claimed that they had only talked about babies. Then it was reported that Ian Austin, Gordon's spokesman, had been involved in the Balti House meeting in Birmingham when the MPs had met to draw up the letter calling on Tony to go. Tony's supporters wanted to go after Gordon full pelt, but we restrained them.

Contrary to conventional wisdom, the coup did Gordon no good. He didn't secure any of the terms he had demanded and Tony had been going to announce the timing of his departure a few weeks later at conference anyway. As for the disappointed Blairites who had joined the coup, Machiavelli says, 'Men, thinking to better their

condition, are always ready to change masters, and in this expect-
ation will take up arms against any ruler; wherein they deceive
themselves, and find afterwards by experience they are worse off
than before.'

Following the coup, Gordon unleashed his 'inevitability strategy'
so that it was assumed that he would take over and that no one could
possibly challenge him. Nick Brown and some of his henchmen
started threatening junior ministers; if they didn't sign up to 'Blairites
for Brown', they would not be getting a job under the new dispens-
ation. Gordon came to see Tony and told him he had never insisted
that he go or set a date for his departure. Gordon had a curious
need to adjust reality to what he had said on television rather than
the other way round. The Treasury Permanent Secretary told the
Number 10 Principal Private Secretary that we would be gone by
the time of the spending round in the autumn, so there was no need
for the Treasury to consult us about it. Gordon demanded that Tony
put a stop to the psychological studies of him that were appearing
in the papers. Tony observed mildly that he could hardly stop people
studying him. Gordon finally took his revenge for someone's earlier
comment about his being 'psychologically flawed' when the *Mail on
Sunday* wrote that Tony was 'psychologically unprepared to give up
the leadership'.

Tony's attitude throughout the coup attempt was literally 'que
sera sera'. He would start singing the Doris Day song at the slightest
provocation. That is the appropriate attitude for a wise leader in
these circumstances. To hold on to power successfully, a leader must
not mind losing it. Some politicians have what Denis Healey called
a hinterland. Others don't. Tony started talking about what he might
do after leaving office as early as 2001. He had other things that he
wanted to do with his life. Mrs Thatcher and Gordon Brown had
nothing but politics in their lives, and they wanted to stay in office
indefinitely. The only way to oust such leaders is by means of
defenestration. Politicians, when they leave office, divide into two
types. There are those who stay on, as Ted Heath did, sitting on the
aisle bench in the House of Commons exacting revenge on their
successor or, as in the case of Teddy Roosevelt, who are determined
to rip their party apart. And there are those who depart and do
something different. There is also a cycle in the reputations of former

leaders which ebbs and flows over time. Jimmy Carter's reputation boomed after he left office while Ronald Reagan's dwindled. Some politicians, when you deprive them of the heroin rush of office, curl up and die. Others flourish.

Tony's insouciance continued into his last conference in Manchester. I attended Gordon's speech. He tried to shed his driller-killer personality and to play with some light and shade; but, as a result, his speech was unusually flat and boring. Events were livened up by a journalist claiming to have overheard a cheeky aside from Cherie while touring the conference centre during Gordon's speech, suggesting that he was lying when he said how much he liked and admired Tony. We thought it rather amusing, but Gordon didn't and we had to deny it. The speech-writing process was easier than usual that year and, while we were waiting, Phil Collins told me the old Les Dawson joke about the man who comes home and discovers that his wife has run off with the man next door. A friend commiserates, and the bloke says, 'Yes, I'll really miss him.' We thought we should work this into the speech, and David Bradshaw, the ghost author of so many of Tony's newspaper articles, started to play around with the idea. Eventually, in light of Cherie's reported comment, he came up with a very funny line for the speech : at least Tony could be sure that his own wife wouldn't run away with the bloke next door. Tony wasn't sure he should use it, but I urged him to. He had Liz Lloyd check with Sue Nye whether Gordon minded. His staff came back just as Tony got to his feet, demanding that he take it out. It was too late. When Tony delivered it, it brought the house down. Ed Miliband later complained to Liz that we had set up the entire conference so that Tony would look good and Gordon would look bad.

On the evening after Tony's speech, gangs of young Gordon supporters roamed around the hotels in a 'new owners of the place' manner. At three in the morning, one group of fifteen of them occupied the bar of the hotel where we were staying, singing 'Hey Jude' and demanding that everyone join in. That evening I went to a dinner hosted by Les Hinton of News International. When I got there a few minutes early, I looked at the place names and discovered that the other guests were all Brownites – Ed Balls, Yvette Cooper, Ed Miliband, Harriet Harman and Douglas Alexander.

I concluded that News International's political intelligence unit must not be up to much. The conversation over dinner was rather stilted.

In an ideal world, it would probably have been better if Tony had been able to avoid announcing that he was going. But, had he adopted Mrs Thatcher's approach of saying that he was going on and on, the PLP might well have ejected him. As it was, as soon as he made the announcement, ministers and civil servants anticipated Gordon's accession, power seeped away and all the flowers turned their faces towards another sun. A prudent prime minister would try to ensure that their departure came as a total surprise, as Harold Wilson's did. But, even if this could be managed in the modern media world, the commentators would still speculate about 'the real reasons'. No one ever believes that leaders will willingly relinquish power, and so they search for conspiracy theories. Even in the case of Tony's departure, people doubted the real motivation. Romano Prodi, the prime minister of Italy, was convinced that it was all a bluff and part of a cunning plan to stay in office. Others thought there was a hidden reason. Gaddafi called Tony to press him on why he was standing down. When Tony tried to explain, Gaddafi said, 'So you won't tell me the real reason then.'

Tony, however, didn't really have a choice. The problem he faced was having had a dauphin in place for all of his ten years in office. Mrs Thatcher didn't suffer in the same way. She had no obvious successor once Michael Heseltine had resigned in 1986. If Tony had not had Gordon Brown snapping at his heels from 2001 onwards, he could have managed his departure more gracefully. But that was not to be. A prudent prime minister would try to ensure that he has more than one potential successor waiting in the wings.

Speculation mounted in February 2007 that David Miliband would challenge Gordon for the leadership, and we feared a fresh onslaught from Gordon in response. Gordon came to see Tony, raging about Labour being four points further behind the Tories in the polls with him as leader than with Tony still in place. Somehow it was our fault. He accused Tony of trying to get David to run, but Tony made it clear that he wasn't. Tony was convinced that, if David ran, he would win; but he felt he could not encourage him to do it.

In March, Tony thought about bringing forward the announcement of his date of departure to April, before the May elections, so that it wouldn't look like a reaction to a Labour defeat in the Scottish and local elections. He said he had lost the emotional energy to fight, even, for example, over the publication of Alastair's diary. I said he couldn't give up early. He should think of it as being like Pilgrim's Progress. It was a marathon and he should keep his eyes on the finishing line. Gordon tried to turn the doctrine of inevitability into a doctrine of irrelevance by behaving as though Tony had already gone. He said he wouldn't set out his stall until he was prime minister and, in an effort to head off a leadership challenge, he suggested that a debate on ideas in the party would be sectarian.

According to Machiavelli the key objective of a leader must be to avoid contempt. I was worried when Liz Lloyd described to me the contempt with which the two Eds (Miliband and Balls) were treating Tony at his meetings with Gordon. The battle moved on to whether and when Tony would publicly endorse Gordon. Douglas Alexander, who was running the Scottish elections, told Liz Lloyd that Tony would have to endorse him if we were to win those elections. He said Tony 'owed it to all of us'. On the tenth anniversary of his first election victory, Tony said in an interview on Scottish TV that 'in all probability the next PM will be Scottish'. Gordon called him immediately to complain that he had not endorsed him by name. Finally, on 11 May, Tony bit the bullet and started working on his endorsement of Gordon. He struggled to find the right words. He tried out on me a reference to his 'long-term friend and partner'. I said jokingly it sounded too gay. Tony wanted to make the endorsement from memory rather than reading it out, but the result was that he had to pause to remember the exact words, and the pauses made it look as though he didn't mean what he was saying and that the words had been forced out of him.

When departure looms, a wise leader needs to start thinking about how much they can achieve before they leave. In particular they will want to make as many of their reforms as possible totally irreversible, thereby to tie the hands of their successor. In his last two years, Tony launched a series of five-year plans in all the major domestic policy areas, and much of our best policy-making work was done then. Tony's reforms of the public services now look pretty safe despite Gordon Brown's attempts to water them down during his brief time in office. The Conservative/Lib Dem government have committed to taking them further rather than reversing them, and there now exists a new variant of 'Butskellism' that will give city academies and the reforms in the health service a chance to bed down for the long term.

Prime ministers worry about their legacies. Even in 1998 we were speculating about what Tony would be remembered for. I suggested at the time Northern Ireland, constitutional reform and shifting politics to the centre. As we got nearer to the time of his departure, the question became more pressing. Ben Wegg-Prosser wrote a long memo about a victory lap, leaving the public begging for more. Embarrassingly, the memo was leaked and caused much ribaldry. In fact, their legacy is something prudent leaders should think about on their first day, not their last. The principal element in Tony's political legacy is perhaps most obvious, and that is the changing nature of British politics. New Labour never lost an election; and when it is reborn with a different name and different generation of politicians, while remaining as a centrist progressive force, it will once again dominate British politics.

We did not have the same tearful departure from Number 10 that Mrs Thatcher had in 1990. Tony's last day had been anticipated for much longer, and we were well prepared for it. We had our last Cabinet meeting on Thursday 21 June. Jack Straw led an orchestrated trio of tributes with David Miliband and Gordon. They were all a bit laboured. They presented him with a picture of Chequers, and as Tony got to his feet and left the room they gave him a standing ovation. He was fairly flat and low-key and worried that his Middle East job wouldn't be announced in time. We were having trouble pinning down the details with the Quartet. The other envoys met in Jerusalem on Tuesday 26 June and agreed the remit and the announcement.

The final day was quite emotional. Gordon finally gave up trying to prevent Tony resigning as an MP, although Ed Balls continued to brief against his role as a Middle East envoy which he thought would interfere with his economic solution to the problem of conflict in that region. At PMQs, Ian Paisley graciously praised Tony for his work on Northern Ireland and wished him well in sorting out the Middle East. The Labour benches gave Tony a standing ovation, and the Tories joined in. I walked back with Tony through Portcullis

House, and he was clapped all the way. I said to him, 'At least we managed to get out of it on our own terms.' He had been the first modern prime minister to do so. For ten years, we had joked about being one step ahead of the sheriff, keeping just clear of the next terrible crisis snapping at our heels, and we had finally managed to escape without the sheriff ever catching up. We had a glass of champagne with the staff upstairs, and then he was clapped out the way he had come in ten years before and left for Buckingham Palace. I collected my papers, said goodbye to the staff and slipped out of the side door and off to Oslo. I watched Gordon on the television at the airport. His statement outside Number 10 was fine, but he didn't have 'it'; he wasn't a leader. I thought of Machaivelli: 'in untroubled times, men of first-class ability are ousted by the envy and ambitious scheming of others, men fall back on what by a common error is judged to be good, or else by those who are seeking popularity rather than the common good. Such mistakes are discovered afterwards when things go wrong.' And I said to myself, now all I have to do is let go.

What brings down all leaders in the end is hubris. There is no escaping it, whether in a dictatorship or a democracy. Once leaders are sucked into the embrace of the government machine, they are inevitably cut off from the real world. In the quietness of Number 10, more senior common room than buzzing office, they are isolated from the stresses and strains of normal life but exposed to a completely different set of pressures. The ever-present security means that they cannot easily go for a stroll in the park or even sit out in a garden if it is overlooked. If they want to go to the theatre or cinema, they have to wait till the lights go down before they slip into their seat to escape the fate of President Lincoln. They don't live a life of luxury, and unlike in Berlin, Paris or Washington they have to do their own cooking and cleaning and there is no official photographer to record their every move. But wherever they go there is someone to drive them, someone to open the door and someone to make the arrangements. They are never alone. It is not surprising, therefore, that after a while prime ministers lose touch and the isolation and the attention people pay them leads to hubris.

You see the examples of this hubris in almost every leader. Vladimir Putin when we first met him was modest and unassuming.

But each time Tony visited him in his dacha he had acquired more grooms for his horses and lived in greater luxury. Angela Merkel described a joint German–Russian Cabinet meeting in Siberia in 2006. She said she had found it difficult to convince Putin that Cabinet ministers should be treated with respect rather than contempt. For Putin the hubris resulted partly from the trappings of office but partly also from the price of oil. As someone wisely put it, hubris in Russia is oil at $60 a barrel, because the high price allows the president not to worry about the economy and to avoid making the necessary and difficult reforms. Before the G8 summit in St Petersburg, Tony had decided to visit the British Council offices which had been under attack by the Russian security and tax authorities. The city removed the building's fire permit the day before Tony got there, but he went ahead with the visit anyway. At the summit itself, Putin was asked by British journalists what he would say if he were asked by Tony Blair about democracy in Russia. He responded that he would ask him about Michael Levy, who had just been arrested in the context of loans for peerages. In the private session, Tony and Merkel pushed Putin on the subject of democracy, and he responded angrily. President Bush sat silent.

Hubris afflicted Harold Wilson in a different way. Bernard Donoughue once told me on a plane back from Dublin a hysterically funny story about late-vintage Wilson. Wilson summoned Bernard up to his study on the first floor of Number 10 and put his finger to his lips as Bernard came through the door. He beckoned him halfway across the room and pulled back a painting. Behind it was a small hole where a screw had gone in to hold up the painting. Wilson then got Bernard to follow him to the little bathroom off the far end of the room, shut the door and said, 'Did you see it?' 'What?' asked Bernard. 'The bug,' said Wilson. He was convinced that the security service was bugging him, and he had a private security company sweep the room the next day for listening devices.

The peril of hubris was really brought home to me in 1989. As a junior official, I attended the G7 summit in Paris. It was the two-hundredth anniversary of the French Declaration of the Rights of Man, and the French government had laid on official celebrations. Mrs Thatcher had made some disobliging remarks about the

Declaration being a hundred years younger than, and not nearly as good as, the British Bill of Rights of 1689. This had caused some aggravation in Paris. When we arrived, I was in the last car in the motorcade, and we passed through an angry demonstration near the Place de la Concorde, with protesters waving placards and their fists. The British Embassy on the Faubourg Saint-Honoré has a circular drive in the courtyard and, when I got out of the car, I found myself standing next to Mrs Thatcher and my brother as they dismounted from the armoured embassy Rolls-Royce, and I heard the prime minister say to Charles, 'Wasn't it nice to see all those people waving at us?' I swore to myself at the time that if I ever found myself in the position of being an adviser to a prime minister I would do my very best to stop them becoming cut off. Mrs Thatcher was back at the same embassy a few months later, and that is where she was informed of the result of the vote among Tory MPs that spelt her end.

All regimes have the seeds of their own destruction built in from the beginning, and hubris is the most pernicious of them. It is the job of a chief of staff to keep hubris at bay as long as he can, partly by constant mockery of his boss but, more importantly, by making sure that the prime minister is in touch with as wide a range of outside influences as possible. I had seen how Thatcher depended on a narrower and narrower circle as time went on. In the case of Tony, it was easier because he had small children. It is difficult to take yourself too seriously with young kids, and a rant from Ian Paisley on the phone somehow seems less serious if you are listening to it sitting on a couch with your children watching *The Simpsons*. Even better, Tony had his mother-in-law Gail staying with him for much of the time he was in government. As I said in Chapter 4, she and the children's nanny, Jackie, would often give him a forceful exposition of what most people thought of his policies. He also spoke regularly to John Burton, his election agent in Sedgefield, one of the most sensible and in-touch people in the world.

As Seneca advised, leaders should remind themselves every day of their political mortality. They should govern from the first day as if it were their last. In that way, it is possible to avoid leaving office with regrets because you will have achieved everything you could in the span allotted to you.

Of course, expressing regret is as difficult for modern politicians as it was for the Bourbons. We found ourselves apologising for many things that were not our direct responsibility, from the great Irish famine of the nineteenth century, to the 1919 Amritsar massacre in India, to the wrongful incarceration of the Maguire family. We frequently debated whether Tony should say sorry over some particular issue for which we had been responsible, starting with the Millennium Dome and the measly 75p rise in the retirement pension in 2000, but we concluded it was not possible. In modern media-driven 'gotcha' politics, it is hard for any politician to say sorry. Any apology is immediately leapt upon and used to condemn everything they have done rather than being accepted as a sign of natural human sympathy. Unless politics returns to a more civilised dialogue, it may not be possible to return to a situation in which politicians can risk saying they are sorry in public, whatever they may feel in private.

There have been few great political leaders, and you cannot tell whether or not someone will be great until he or she has taken office. Few if any of Tony's contemporaries at Oxford, for example, had him marked down as a potential prime minister, let alone a potentially great prime minister. Such leaders need to have ambition and the skills described in this book, and then anything is possible. Machiavelli writes towards the end of *The Prince* that 'where the disposition is strong the difficulty cannot be great, provided you follow the methods observed by those whom I have set before you as models'.

Leaders also have to have luck. Machiavelli writes at length about 'Fortuna', which in his lexicon was more than just luck. He believed it was crucial in the fate of a prince: 'Fortune is the mistress of one half of our actions, and yet leaves the control of the other half, or a little less, to ourselves.' Just as Napoleon wanted lucky generals, we want and need lucky leaders.

Although neither would regard themselves as lucky in this regard, Mrs Thatcher was fortunate to have the Falklands War as a springboard for her second election, because it was not at all clear she would have been re-elected on her economic record, and Tony Blair was fortunate to have left office before the world was engulfed by the global economic crisis. The record of a leader cannot, however, rest on luck alone. As Machiavelli says, 'a Prince who rests wholly on Fortune is ruined when she changes'. A great leader has to have the courage and the instincts to seize opportunities when they appear, as Moses, Cyrus, Theseus and Romulus had: 'But while it was their opportunities that made these men fortunate, it was their own merit that enabled them to recognise these opportunities and turn them to account, to the glory and prosperity of their country.'

As I said at the beginning, Machiavelli is misunderstood. So too is Tony Blair. Caricatures are very difficult things to reverse, and it is perhaps four hundred years too late to rehabilitate Machiavelli and perhaps twenty years too soon to persuade people to re-evaluate Tony Blair. The history of the Blair government won't be written for another decade or more. What has been written so far is mostly regurgitated journalism or unprocessed raw material for future histories. When the considered history is written, I would be surprised if Tony Blair were not seen as one of Machiavelli's great princes, one on whom 'Fortuna' smiled and who had the courage and intelligence to take advantage of it. Whatever his faults, Tony Blair will certainly be counted as one of the four or perhaps five great British prime ministers of the last hundred years.

Bibliography

The Texts

Machiavelli, Niccolò: *The Prince* (translated by N. H. Thomson, Quality Paperback Book Club, New York, 1992) and *The Discourses on the First Ten Books of Titus Livy* (translated by Leslie J. Walker, Pelican Books, London, 1970)

Machiavelli was a prolific writer and other works include: *The Art of War* (translated and edited by Christopher Lynch, University of Chicago Press, Chicago, 2003) *A Discourse on the Remodelling of the Government of Florence*, in *Machiavelli: The Chief Works and Others* (translated and edited by Allan Gilbert, Duke University Press, Durham, NC, 1989); and *Florentine Histories* (translated by Laura Banfield and Harvey C. Mansfield, Princeton University Press, Princeton, 1988)

Machiavelli's Thought

Benner, Erica, *Machiavelli's Ethics* (Princeton University Press, Princeton, 2009)

Berlin, Isaiah, *The Originality of Machiavelli* (in *Against the Current*, edited by Myron Gilmore, Editore Sansoni, Florence, 1972)

Plamenatz, John, *Man and Society: A Critical Examination of Some Important Social and Political Theories from Machiavelli to Marx* (Longmans, London, 1963)

Raab, Felix, *The English Face of Machiavelli: A Changing Interpretation 1500–1700* (Routledge, London, 1964)

Skinner, Quentin: *Machiavelli* (Oxford University Press, Oxford, 1981) and

The Foundations of Modern Political Thought, Vol. 1: The Renaissance (Cambridge Uuniversity Press, Cambridge, 1978)

Skinner, Quentin, Bock, Gisela and Viroli, Maurizio (eds), *Machiavelli and Republicanism* (Cambridge University Press, Cambridge, 1990)

Machiavelli's Life

Hale, J. R., *Machiavelli and Renaissance Italy* (English Universities Press, London, 1961)

Ridolfi, Roberto, *The Life of Niccolò Machiavelli* (translated by Cecil Grayson, University of Chicago Press, Chicago, 1963)

Viroli, Maurizio, *Niccolò's Smile: A Biography of Machiavelli* (translated by Anthony Shugar, Farrar, Straus & Giroux, New York, 2000; original Italian edition, 1998)

White, Michael, *Machiavelli: A Man Misunderstood* (Little, Brown, London, 2004)

The Genre

There exists a genre of books imitating Machiavelli. I cannot refer to them all, and most of them deserve to be forgotten. By far the best is the novel *The New Machiavelli* by H. G. Wells (Penguin, London, 2005; original edition, 1911). Others include:

Jay, Antony, *Management and Machiavelli* (Pfeiffer, New York, 1994; original edition, 1967)

Ledeen, Michael A., *Machiavelli on Modern Leadership: Why Machiavelli's Iron Rules Are As Timely and Important Today As Five Centuries Ago* (Truman Talley Books, New York, 1999)

Lord, Carnes, *The Modern Prince: What Leaders Need to Know Now* (Yale University Press, Yale, 2003)

McAlpine, Alistair, *The Servant* (Faber and Faber, London, 1993)

—*The New Machiavelli: The Art of Politics in Business* (John Wiley & Sons, New York, 2000)

Morris, Dick, *The New Prince: Machiavelli Updated for the Twenty-First Century* (Renaissance Books, Los Angeles, 1999)

Other

Campbell, Alastair: *The Blair Years* (Hutchinson, London, 2007) and *The Alastair Campbell Diaries, Vol. 1: Prelude to Power, 1994–1997* (Hutchinson, London, 2010)

Donoughue, Bernard: *Downing Street Diaries: With Harold Wilson in No. 10* (Jonathan Cape, London, 2005) and *Downing Street Diaries: With James Callaghan in No. 10* (Jonathan Cape, London, 2008)

Kaufman, Gerald, *How to be a Minister* (Sidgwick & Jackson, London, 1980)

Index